CW01150388

Loan Loss Provisions in Alternative Banking Landscapes

# Schriftenreihe des Kärntner Instituts für Höhere Studien

Herausgegeben von Robert Holzmann und Reinhard Neck

Volume 22

PETER LANG

Berlin · Bruxelles · Chennai · Lausanne · New York · Oxford

Ksenija Popović

# Loan Loss Provisions in Alternative Banking Landscapes

PETER LANG

Berlin · Bruxelles · Chennai · Lausanne · New York · Oxford

**Library of Congress Cataloging- in- Publication Data**
A CIP catalog record for this book has been applied for at the Library of Congress.

**Bibliographic Information published by the Deutsche Nationalbibliothek**
The Deutsche Nationalbibliothek lists this publication in the Deutsche Nationalbibliografie; detailed bibliographic data is available online at http://dnb.d-nb.de.

Cover Illustration : Author

ISSN 2944-3393
ISBN 978-3-631-91823-4 (Print)
E-ISBN 978-3-631-91824-1 (E-PDF)
E-ISBN 978-3-631-91825-8 (E-PUB)
DOI 10.3726/b21788

© 2024 Peter Lang Group AG, Lausanne
Published by Peter Lang GmbH, Berlin, Germany

info@peterlang.com - www.peterlang.com

All rights reserved.

All parts of this publication are protected by copyright. Any utilisation outside the strict limits of the copyright law, without the permission of the publisher, is forbidden and liable to prosecution. This applies in particular to reproductions, translations, microfilming, and storage and processing in electronic retrieval systems.

# Acknowledgements

The contents of this book originated from a doctoral thesis that has been revised and expanded. Throughout the writing process, I received invaluable assistance and support from numerous individuals and institutions. Among them, there are a few whom I would like to single out to express my special gratitude.

First and foremost, I am deeply grateful to Prof. Reinhard Neck for his support and guidance throughout my studies and research work. It is a great source of happiness and honor for me to have been mentored by such a respected and wonderful professor.

I would also like to extend my sincere gratitude to Prof. Alexander Brauneis for his invaluable suggestions and insights during my empirical research. I am equally appreciative of Prof. Dieter Bögenhold, Prof. Martin Wagner, and Prof. Norbert Wohlgemuth from the University of Klagenfurt, as well as Prof. Miomir Jakšić and Prof. Nikola Fabris from the Faculty of Economics at the University of Belgrade, and Predrag Ćatić, the legal advisor to the Association of Serbian Banks, for their support and encouragement.

I extend my heartfelt thanks to Prof. Jesús Crespo Cuaresma and Prof. Vincent Bouvatier for dedicating their time to reviewing my doctoral dissertation. Their constructive reviews and feedback significantly contributed to the enhancement and expansion of the original doctoral research. The empirical and theoretical research conducted by Prof. Bouvatier in the field of loan loss provisions served as the inspiration for my own doctoral research in the same area.

I am also deeply grateful to the Library of the European University Institute, and especially to Thomas Burke, for granting me access to library resources. I am also grateful to the staff at the University of Klagenfurt, and especially to Kornelia Kanyo and Christina Kopetzky, for providing me with all the necessary technical assistance.

Finally, I am grateful to my friends and colleagues, and especially to my husband and brother, who have been my most important sources of support and encouragement. I dedicate this project to the memory of my late parents and grandparents, who always believed in me and played an essential role in helping me realize my dreams.

# Contents

List of tables ............................................................................................... 9

List of figures ............................................................................................ 11

List of abbreviations ................................................................................ 13

Executive summary ................................................................................. 15

Abstract ..................................................................................................... 17

1. Introduction ........................................................................................ 19

2. Banking sectors in Southeast Europe ............................................. 23
   2.1 Bank reforms in transition economies ..................................... 23
       2.1.1 Advantages of the banking reform ................................ 26
       2.1.2 Disadvantages of the banking reform ........................... 27
   2.2 Bank reforms in Greece and Cyprus ......................................... 28
   2.3 Southeast Europe today ............................................................. 31

3. Loan loss provisions ........................................................................... 35
   3.1 Loan loss provisions as an indicator of credit risk ................. 35
   3.2 Components of loan loss provisions ......................................... 37
   3.3 Evolution of loan loss provisioning regulations ..................... 39
   3.4 Loan loss provisions in Southeast Europe ............................... 42
   3.5 Comparability of the data ........................................................... 46

4. Non-discretionary and discretionary components of loan loss provisions in Southeast Europe ...................................................... 53
   4.1 Theoretical framework ................................................................ 53

    4.1.1 Capital management .................................................................. 53
    4.1.2 Income smoothing ..................................................................... 55
    4.1.3 Signaling ...................................................................................... 58
    4.1.4 Pro-cyclicality ............................................................................. 59
  4.2 Empirical research ............................................................................. 60
    4.2.1 Data .............................................................................................. 60
        4.2.1.1 Variables ........................................................................ 62
        4.2.1.2 Analysis of outliers ...................................................... 65
        4.2.1.2 Descriptive statistics and correlations ..................... 69
    4.2.2 Method ........................................................................................ 73
        4.2.2.1 The two-step difference GMM estimation ............... 75
  4.3 Results .................................................................................................. 79
    4.3.1 Within regions ........................................................................... 79
    4.3.2 Between regions ........................................................................ 84

5. The effect of macroeconomic shocks on loan loss provisions in Southeast Europe ...................................................................................... 103
  5.1 Theoretical framework ...................................................................... 103
  5.2 Empirical research ............................................................................. 106
    5.2.1 Data .............................................................................................. 107
        5.2.1.1 Descriptive statistics .................................................... 109
        5.2.1.2 Analysis of outliers ...................................................... 113
    5.2.2 Method ........................................................................................ 114
  5.3 Results .................................................................................................. 119
    5.3.1 Within regions ........................................................................... 120
    5.3.2 Between regions ........................................................................ 124

6. Conclusions ............................................................................................ 165

Bibliography ................................................................................................ 171

# List of tables

| | | |
|---|---|---|
| Table 1. | Level of EU integration and year of reaching that level | 33 |
| Table 2. | EBRD banking sector transition scores in Southeast Europe in 2016 | 34 |
| Table 3. | The incurred loan loss approach (simplified) | 48 |
| Table 4. | The expected loan loss approach (simplified) | 48 |
| Table 5. | Dependent and independent variables | 88 |
| Table 6. | Expected sign of independent variables | 89 |
| Table 7. | SEE EU: Panel All commercial banks | 89 |
| Table 8. | SEE EU: Panel Selected commercial banks | 90 |
| Table 9. | SEE EU: Panel All commercial banks. Summary statistics | 90 |
| Table 10. | SEE EU: Panel All commercial banks. Correlation matrix | 91 |
| Table 11. | SEE EU: Panel All commercial banks. Variance inflation factor | 91 |
| Table 12. | SEE EU: Panel Selected commercial banks. Summary statistics | 92 |
| Table 13. | SEE EU Panels: Estimations | 94 |
| Table 14. | Western Balkans: Panel All commercial banks | 95 |
| Table 15. | Western Balkans: Panel Selected commercial banks | 96 |
| Table 16. | Western Balkans: Panel All commercial banks. Summary statistics | 96 |
| Table 17. | Western Balkans: Panel All commercial banks. Correlation matrix | 97 |
| Table 18. | Western Balkans: Panel All commercial banks. Variance inflation factor | 97 |
| Table 19. | Western Balkans: Panel Selected commercial banks. Summary statistics | 98 |
| Table 20. | Western Balkans Panels: Estimations | 100 |
| Table 21. | Variables in the SVAR model | 126 |
| Table 22. | Croatia: Unit root tests (2006Q2-2020Q1) (quarterly data) | 128 |
| Table 23. | Croatia: Summary statistics (2006Q2-2020Q1) | 128 |
| Table 24. | Croatia: Diagnostic checks of the SVAR (2) model (2006Q2-2020Q1) | 128 |
| Table 25. | Cyprus: Unit root tests (2008Q4-2020Q1) (quarterly data) | 131 |
| Table 26. | Cyprus: Summary statistics (2008Q4-2020Q1) | 131 |
| Table 27. | Cyprus: Diagnostic checks of the SVAR (2) model (2008Q4-2020Q1) | 131 |
| Table 28. | Greece: Unit root tests (2008Q3-2020Q1) (quarterly data) | 134 |
| Table 29. | Greece: Summary statistics (2008Q3-2020Q1) | 134 |

| | | |
|---|---|---|
| Table 30. | Greece: Diagnostic checks of the SVAR (3) model (2008Q3-2020Q1) | 134 |
| Table 31. | Romania: Unit root tests (2010Q1-2020Q1) (quarterly data) | 137 |
| Table 32. | Romania: Summary statistics (2010Q1-2020Q1) | 137 |
| Table 33. | Romania: Diagnostic checks of the SVAR (1) model (2010Q1-2020Q1) | 137 |
| Table 34. | Slovenia: Unit root tests (2009Q4-2019Q4) (quarterly data) | 140 |
| Table 35. | Slovenia: Summary statistics (2009Q4-2019Q4) | 140 |
| Table 36. | Slovenia: Diagnostic checks of the SVAR (1) model (2009Q4-2019Q4) | 140 |
| Table 37. | Albania: Unit root tests (2010Q4-2019Q4) (quarterly data) | 143 |
| Table 38. | Albania: Summary statistics (2010Q4-2019Q4) | 143 |
| Table 39. | Albania: Diagnostic checks of the SVAR (2) model (2010Q4-2019Q4) | 143 |
| Table 40. | Bosnia and Herzegovina: Unit root tests (2007Q1-2020Q2) (quarterly data) | 146 |
| Table 41. | Bosnia and Herzegovina: Summary statistics (2007Q1-2020Q2) | 146 |
| Table 42. | Bosnia and Herzegovina: Diagnostic checks of the SVAR (1) model (2007Q1-2020Q2) | 146 |
| Table 43. | North Macedonia: Unit root tests (2007Q1-2020Q1) (quarterly data) | 149 |
| Table 44. | North Macedonia: Summary statistics (2007Q1-2020Q1) | 149 |
| Table 45. | North Macedonia: Diagnostic checks of the SVAR (1) model (2007Q1-2020Q1) | 149 |
| Table 46. | Serbia: Unit root tests (2008Q3-2020Q1) (quarterly data) | 152 |
| Table 47. | Serbia: Summary statistics (2008Q3-2020Q1) | 152 |
| Table 48. | Serbia: Diagnostic checks of the SVAR (1) model (2008Q3-2020Q1) | 152 |
| Table 49. | Descriptive statistics for the panels | 154 |
| Table 50. | Optimal panel SVAR model selection | 154 |
| Table 51. | Granger causality tests for the panels | 155 |

# List of figures

| | | |
|---|---|---|
| Figure 1. | SEE economies ordered by GDP per capita (2017–2019) | 33 |
| Figure 2. | Loan loss provisions across SEE banking sectors | 49 |
| Figure 3. | NPL ratio and NPL coverage ratio in the SEE EU countries | 50 |
| Figure 4. | NPL ratio and NPL coverage ratio in the Western Balkans | 51 |
| Figure 5. | SEE EU: Panel All commercial banks. Average LLPs | 91 |
| Figure 6. | SEE EU: Panel Selected Commercial banks. Outliers | 92 |
| Figure 7. | Western Balkans: Panel All commercial banks. Average LLPs | 97 |
| Figure 8. | Western Balkans: Panel Selected Commercial banks. Outliers | 98 |
| Figure 9. | Croatia: Time series | 127 |
| Figure 10. | Croatia: Impulses and responses of $\Delta$ LLP | 129 |
| Figure 11. | Cyprus: Time series | 130 |
| Figure 12. | Cyprus: Impulses and responses of $\Delta$ LLP | 132 |
| Figure 13. | Greece: Time series | 133 |
| Figure 14. | Greece: Impulses and responses of $\Delta$ LLP | 135 |
| Figure 15. | Romania: Time series | 136 |
| Figure 16. | Romania: Impulses and responses of $\Delta$ LLP | 138 |
| Figure 17. | Slovenia: Time series | 139 |
| Figure 18. | Slovenia: Impulses and responses of $\Delta$ LLP | 141 |
| Figure 19. | Albania: Time series | 142 |
| Figure 20. | Albania: Impulses and responses of $\Delta$ LLP | 144 |
| Figure 21. | Bosnia and Herzegovina: Time series | 145 |
| Figure 22. | Bosnia and Herzegovina: Impulses and responses of $\Delta$ LLP | 147 |
| Figure 23. | North Macedonia: Time series | 148 |
| Figure 24. | North Macedonia: Impulses and responses of $\Delta$ LLP | 150 |
| Figure 25. | Serbia: Time series | 151 |
| Figure 26. | Serbia: Impulses and responses of $\Delta$ LLP | 153 |
| Figure 27. | Stability test for the panels | 154 |
| Figure 28. | Panel SVAR SEE EU: Impulses and responses of $\Delta$ LLP | 156 |
| Figure 29. | Panel SVAR, Western Balkans: Impulses and responses of $\Delta$ LLP | 158 |
| Figure 30. | Detected outliers in the SEE EU Panel | 160 |
| Figure 31. | Detected outliers in the Western Balkans Panel | 162 |
| Figure 32. | Annual growth rate of real GDP in EU members in Southeast Europe | 163 |
| Figure 33. | Annual growth rate of real GDP in Western Balkans | 164 |

# List of abbreviations

| | |
|---|---|
| ADF | Augmented Dickey-Fuller test |
| AIC | Akaike information criterion |
| CESEE | Central, Eastern and Southeastern Europe |
| DSGE | Dynamic Stochastic General Equilibrium |
| GDP | Gross domestic product |
| EBRD | European Bank for Reconstruction and Development |
| ECB | European Central Bank |
| EU | European Union |
| EUR | Euro |
| FSI | Financial Soundness Indicators |
| GFC | Global Financial Crisis |
| GMM | Generalized Method of Moments |
| HFSF | Hellenic Financial Stability Fund |
| IAS | International Accounting Standards |
| IASC | International Accounting Standards Committee |
| IFRS | International Financial Reporting Standards |
| IFS | International Financial Statistics |
| ILO | International Labor Organization |
| IMF | International Monetary Fund |
| LHS | Left hand scale |
| LLP | Loan loss provision |
| MA | Moving average |
| NPL | Non-performing loan |
| OECD | Organization for Economic Cooperation and Development |
| OLS | Ordinary Least Square |
| RHS | Right hand scale |
| RWA | Risk weighted assets |
| SEC | The United States Securities and Exchange Commission |
| SEE | Southeast Europe/Southeast European |
| SVAR | Structural vector auto-regression |
| USA | United States of America |
| USD | United States dollar |
| VAR | Vector auto-regression |

# Executive summary

Over the past few decades, in Southeast Europe (SEE), the banking sector has shifted from credit expansion to challenges driven by loan losses and contraction. The banking sectors in the observed transition economies underwent a transformation from state-planned to market-driven structures. This evolution involved transitioning from isolation to openness, marked by privatizations and significant capital inflows spurred by the entry of foreign banks. However, this was followed by organized bank consolidation processes and even the exit of some of the foreign banks due to the Global Financial Crisis (GFC). At the same time, the credit markets in Greece and Cyprus followed a similar trajectory, moving from market liberalization and credit growth to a phase of sharp contraction and bank consolidation triggered by both the GFC and the sovereign debt crisis.

**Amidst these transformations, regulatory oversight of bank operations and particularly the estimation of loan loss provisions (LLPs) has become vitally important.** Yet, the question of how to estimate LLPs inevitably sparks lively discussions, as viewpoints vary among accounting standard setters, banking regulators, bank supervisors, and security regulators. While regulations undergo continuous refinement, skepticism lingers regarding whether the issue of pro-cyclicality in LLPs has been adequately addressed.

**In the context of these shifts, my empirical study brings forth insights into the asymmetric impacts of the GFC and the sovereign debt crisis on SEE banks, particularly in their loan loss provisioning behavior.** Within SEE European Union (EU) states, a pro-cyclical leaning of loan loss provisioning towards the credit cycle over the economic cycle is evident. Conversely, in the Western Balkans, the pro-cyclical nature of loan loss provisioning is less pronounced. In addition, despite facing solvency challenges in their home countries during the crises, foreign banking groups bolstered the Western Balkans' financial stability through their well-capitalized subsidiaries. However, their subsequent consolidation and exit from these markets raises pertinent questions about the potential contributions of new market entrants to the region's financial stability.

**Moreover, macro stress testing in my research reveals different patterns: GDP shocks exhibit greater impact on LLPs in the SEE EU, while unemployment shocks have a stronger effect on LLPs in the Western Balkans, in both cases due to their persistence, thus highlighting the significance of shock persistence over size.** Individually, top-down macro-financial stress testing highlights the heightened vulnerability of the Greek and Cypriot banking sectors within the SEE EU region. The complementary analysis of non-performing loan (NPL) ratios and NPL coverage ratios further reinforces the conviction that their capacity to absorb potential new loan losses is limited. The banking models of Albania and North Macedonia have demonstrated greater resilience, particularly to GDP shocks, attributed to their historically subdued reactions to previous crises and notably high NPL coverage ratio. However, it is important to note that such resilience should also be interpreted in the light of their less developed economies, lower living standards, and limited integration into global financial markets.

**The research findings emphasize the importance of maintaining robust NPL coverage ratios** not only in some of the SEE EU banking sectors with their demonstrated vulnerability in macro stress testing but also across the Western Balkans economies due to the ongoing bank consolidation processes. As it is more feasible to increase loan loss provisioning during favorable economic conditions, vigilant monitoring of bank solvency becomes crucial during periods of macroeconomic uncertainties. Ultimately, timely NPL recognition and high NPL coverage ratios help to mitigate the pro-cyclicality of LLPs.

**In a world marked by increased uncertainty and rising fragilities, including the COVID-19 pandemic, the war in Ukraine, energy crises, and inflation pressures, the risk of policy miscalibration is increasing.** The banking sector is expected to undergo further consolidation, and this presents an opportunity to enhance financial stability by addressing issues like declining bank capital, rising non-interest income, delayed recognition of NPLs, and insufficient provisioning. Therefore, future research should prioritize strategies aimed at maximizing the positive impacts of banking sector consolidation.

**Abstract:** Using a dynamic panel dataset encompassing commercial banks and macroeconomic indicators in Southeast Europe from 2010 to 2017, along with the Generalized Method of Moments estimator, this study provides robust evidence that banks with lower capitalization tend to employ loan loss provisions for capital management. Moreover, weaker evidence suggests that banks with lower profitability utilize LLPs for income management, and banks with less strength are inclined to signal their stability by showing they can sustain higher provisions. Furthermore, in the SEE EU member countries, during credit contractions, banks exhibit tendencies towards increased loan loss provisions, while during credit expansions, they display tendencies towards decreasing provisions. These findings accentuate the importance of enhanced bank supervision to ensure counter-cyclical, prudent provisioning. Conversely, in the Western Balkans, banks increase provisioning during periods of falling GDP per capita growth and decrease provisioning during rising growth, demanding deeper insights into the underlying factors.

In a second phase, employing individual structural vector autoregression models (SVAR) for national economies and panel SVAR models for SEE EU states and the Western Balkans, this study examines the reaction of LLP changes to adverse GDP and unemployment shocks. At a regional level, the SEE EU banking sectors display sensitivity to negative GDP shocks, while the Western Balkans banking sectors react more to unemployment shocks. Individually, the Greek and Cypriot models exhibit the most pronounced negative impact on LLPs due to simulated macroeconomic shocks, underlined by elevated NPL ratios and lowered NPL coverage ratios. Conversely, individual macro stress tests reveal the resilience of the Albanian and North Macedonian models, evident in their responses to negative GDP shocks, yet vulnerable to unemployment shocks. Notably, North Macedonia's NPL coverage ratio exceeding 100 % implies a greater capacity to absorb potential loan losses. Despite the established resilience of certain banking sectors, the lower economic strength, sustained unemployment, and reduced living standards in the Western Balkan economies necessitate a cautious interpretation.

**Keywords:** Loan loss provisions, business cycle, income smoothing, capital management, signaling, macro-financial stress test

# 1. Introduction

Loan loss provisioning always provokes lively discussions, especially in the aftermath of economic downturn episodes. An envisaged or materialized post-contracting change in loan quality, which negatively affects loan repayment capacity, decreases the economic loan value from its nominal value. An estimation of this loan value gap, otherwise called loan loss provisions, is partly influenced by the macroeconomic situation and partly by management judgement. Discussions on non-adequate LLPs after the 1973–74 oil crisis, for example, motivated regulators in the United States of America (USA) to obligate banks to make supplemental disclosures of financial documents (Beaver, Eger, Ryan, & Wolfson, 1989). After the 1982 Latin-American debt crisis, one bank from the USA booked a significant amount of LLPs. This bank used its provisioning decisions to signal financial strength and distinguish itself from other banks on the market (Beaver & Engel, 1996). Growing criticism of management judgement in provisioning led to the introduction of a new international accounting standard, IAS 39, in 1998 (Gebhardt & Novotny-Farkas, 2011). However, following the GFC, discussions on the negative macroeconomic effects of pro-cyclical loan loss provisioning intensified (European Banking Authority, 2017). But, even the new international financial reporting standard, IFRS 9, which came into force in 2018, had to be suspended at the outbreak of the 2020 COVID-19 pandemic crisis for fear of pro-cyclicality.

This fear is understandable as the deterioration of banks' balance sheets due to loan losses, may lead to a spiral of negative events: credit contraction, a rise in the cost of borrowing, a decrease in the value of assets and in equity, and a further deterioration in banks' balance sheets (Gertler & Karadi, 2011). Bearing in mind that the credit market consists of intertwined networks of financial obligations, credit contraction during an economic downturn can produce financial gridlocks, credit defaults, and bankruptcy cascades (Brunnermeier, 2009). Loan losses as credit market imperfections contribute to the *financial accelerator effect* because "endogenous developments in credit markets work to propagate and amplify shocks to the macroeconomy" (Bernanke, Gertler, & Gilchrist, 1999, p. 1345).

A significant amount of literature has been written on LLPs.[1] One part of the literature provides useful findings from the empirical testing of hypotheses

---

1 Wall and Koch (2000) prepared a review of early theoretical and empirical literature on LLPs. Anandarajan, Hasan, and Lozano-Vivas (2005) reviewed studies that examine

related to the use of LLPs for income smoothing, capital management and signaling as well as the pro-cyclical behavior of LLPs (Bikker & Metzemakers, 2005; Bouvatier, Lepetit, & Strobel, 2014; Bouvatier & Lepetit, 2012a; Fonseca & González, 2008; Laeven & Majnoni, 2003). Bouvatier and Lepetit (2012b) also provide a theoretical explanation for inter-relations between LLPs and other financial and macroeconomic aggregates in the partial equilibrium model. Other authors have developed a theoretical analysis of shock transmission from the real economy to financial markets and inversely in a general equilibrium model (Agénor & Zilberman, 2015; Hristov & Hülsewig, 2017; Tayler & Zilberman, 2021). Macroeconometric stress tests comprising LLPs, or similar indicators of credit risk, are of equal interest to central banks and the academic community (Babouček & Jančar, 2005; Gambera, 2000; Keeton, 1999; Klein, 2013; Pool, de Haan, & Jacobs, 2015). LLPs are transmitters of macroeconomic shocks to banks' balance sheets and "if the business cycle does influence banks, financial surveillance may need to be strengthened during recessionary phases, when banks are more likely to become fragile" (Quagliariello, 2006, p. 7).

In most existing theoretical and empirical studies, the focus is on developed parts of the world (EU member states, the USA, Australia, members of the Organization for Economic Cooperation and Development (OECD), etc.). Research papers that are geographically related to SEE are infrequent and largely unknown. That is why I specifically mention Skala (2021) as well as Bonin and Košak (2013), who examine provisioning practices in emerging Europe,[2] as well as studies on provisioning practices in individual countries such as Greece (Makri & Papadatos, 2014) or Romania (Nikolaidou & Vogiazas, 2013). However, provisioning practice in the economies of the so-called Western Balkans, that is, economies which aspire to join the EU, are rarely the subject of research.

Using dynamic panel data on commercial banks and macroeconomic indicators during the period 2010–2017 and the Generalized Method of Moments (GMM) estimator, in the first study I tested pro-cyclicality, income smoothing, capital management, and signaling hypotheses to find (i) what loan loss provisioning is practiced in the commercial banks; (ii) whether there are any differences in the loan loss provisioning of commercial banks in the Western

---

the discretionary component of LLPs. Similarly, Ozili and Outa (2017) prepared a comprehensive review of recent literature related to LLPs. Finally Basel Committee on Banking Supervision (2021) compiled a review of significant theoretical and empirical studies on the pro-cyclical nature of LLPs.

2  *Emerging Europe* designates Central, East and Southeast European (CESEE) countries that became members of the EU in 2004 and 2013.

Balkans in comparison to EU members in Southeast Europe (or shortly SEE EU); and (iii) whether there are any differences in the loan loss provisioning of foreign-owned and domestically-owned commercial banks. Additional information on likely motives for management judgements when deciding on loan loss provisioning in the observed economies can be found in the segment of my study dedicated to outlier analysis.

In my second study, using time series and unbalanced panel data to model structural vector auto-regression (SVAR), I simulated GDP and unemployment shocks to determine the responses of LLPs (as an indicator of credit risk). The research aim was to find out whether there are differences in the response of credit risk to macroeconomic shocks between individual countries as well as between the Western Balkan economies and other economies in Southeast Europe that are EU member states. An analysis of outliers provides additional information on similarities between the observed economies with respect to measures authorities use to manage LLPs to maintain or attain financial stability.

My research contributes to the field by extending the empirical evidence not only on the discretionary and non-discretionary component of loan loss provisioning in this part of Europe but also on certain similarities and differences between provisioning in the SEE EU region in comparison to the Western Balkans region. Interesting findings also follow from the analysis of outlying observations, especially in terms of possible motives that influence decisions on LLPs. The importance of understanding the motives of management judgement is mentioned more often in recent literature (Bischof, Laux, & Leuz, 2021; Ozili & Outa, 2017), and it is reasonable to expect more research on this topic in the future.

The structure of this research is as follows. Chapter 2 covers a brief history of banking sector reforms in Southeast Europe. Chapter 3 then presents general information on LLPs, the development of international accounting standards and bank regulations concerning LLPs as well as credit risk characteristics in Southeast Europe. My first study examines the non-discretionary and discretionary components of LLPs in Southeast European commercial banks in Chapter 4. The second study forecasts responses of LLPs to a simulated negative GDP impulse and a positive unemployment impulse and is presented in Chapter 5. Chapter 6 concludes.

# 2. Banking sectors in Southeast Europe

In this chapter, as an introduction to the empirical research that follows, I briefly present the reforms that economies, and especially the banking sectors in Southeast Europe, have gone through in the last four decades. I believe that it is useful to understand the specifics of the economies and especially the banking sectors in this region in order to better understand and analyze the results of the empirical research. I will start with a brief overview of banking reforms in transition economies, and then in Greece and Cyprus. I conclude this chapter with the achieved transition scores of the observed banking sectors.

## 2.1 Bank reforms in transition economies

All of the Southeast European countries, except Greece and Cyprus, experienced years of transition from socialist state-centered to market-oriented economies. The transition started after the fall of the Iron Curtain in 1989 and is often perceived as a process of "catching up" with economically developed countries (Kutlača & Radošević, 2012). At the beginning of the transition, these economies had different starting positions.

Albania, Bulgaria, and Romania had a *planned* or *command socialist economic system* like in the Soviet Union. They were closed economies characterized by centralized state planning and state ownership. Their monobanking[3] systems were reformed during the late 1980s (Gregory & Stuart, 2014; Šević, 2000). In contrast, former Yugoslavia (which broke up into Bosnia and Herzegovina, Croatia, Montenegro, North Macedonia, Slovenia, Serbia, and Kosovo*[4]) had a *market socialist economic system* characterized by a combined market allocation and state intervention as well as collective worker ownership and management. As a relatively open small economy, Yugoslavia had a decentralized, two-tier banking system even from the mid-1960s (Gregory & Stuart, 2014; Šević, 2000).

---

3 In a monobanking system, a state bank has a monopoly on the supply side of the credit market. Credit decisions are based on plans and directives while the interest rate does not play a role in credit allocation. In a two-tier banking system, a central bank has monetary authority and supervision responsibilities (upper tier), while commercial banks take deposits and allocate credits (second tier).

4 This designation (Kosovo*) assumes a neutral stance towards its status and is in line with the United Nations Security Council's Resolution number 1244 from 1999.

In the first phase, the reform of the banking sector involved extensive preparations for privatization. In the countries with planned economies, the monobank system was split into a central bank and a network of commercial banks (Šević, 2000). In former Yugoslavia, the state first acquired majority ownership of banks by buying shares from large companies, which were at the same time owners of banks and their main debtors[5] (Ristić, 2006; Šević, 2000).

In some countries the first phase of banking reforms was conducted in an unfavorable macroeconomic environment marked by high inflation, low growth rates, high unemployment, devaluation of the national currency, etc. (Čaušević, 2003; Šević, 2000). In the early 1990s, a large number of banks had loans in their portfolios granted to state corporations, which themselves were going through reform processes. Borrowers had problems with the due settlement of their credit obligations, previously often on a roll-out regime, so that non-performing loans started to accumulate. As Šević (2000) points out, it was necessary to find a way to reduce NPLs as an important precondition for achieving higher selling prices for banks in the privatization process. NPL reduction solutions differed across countries: (i) through a bank restructuring agency, interest-bearing long-term bonds were issued to offer NPLs on the market; (ii) insolvent banks overburdened with NPLs were liquidated; (iii) high inflation lowered the real value of the loan portfolio, including NPLs; (iv) banks set up workout units to recover their problematic exposures; (v) bail-outs; and (vi) debt-to equity swaps, etc. (Barisitz, 2005; Borish, Long, & Noël, 1995; Cottarelli, Dell'Ariccia, & Vladkova-Hollar, 2003; Rostowski, 1995; Šević, 2000).

Other changes began to take place, such as improving the legal framework, strengthening banking regulations and supervision, aligning domestic accounting with international standards, improving bank governance, etc. (Borish et al., 1995). Authorities liberalized conditions in their credit markets, allowing free entry to domestic and foreign private capital. The general opinion was that state-owned banks were less efficient than private ones. In the second phase of the reform, therefore, the privatization of banks began in the late 1990s and early 2000s. Most investors entered credit markets by privatizing existing banks, either by voucher or share purchase, while green field investments were rare (Ristić, 2006).

---

5 In the late 1980s, commercial banks issued their own shares but had an agreement with their main clients that they could purchase these shares through favorable credit arrangements. As owners and debtors, however, large corporations were not interested in the business performance of their creditors (Šević, 2000).

Foreign banks from Western Europe entered the SEE market operating through their local subsidiaries rather than branches.[6] They benefited from the introduction of the euro because the conversion of pre-euro currencies into euros was done in banks. Since there was general confidence in foreign banks,[7] most of the converted euros remained in their deposits (Cottarelli et al., 2003). Compared to domestic banks, foreign banks did not have a problem with long-term sources of financing, which gave them a competitive advantage. They were able to offer new products, such as corporate long-term loans and housing loans (Ristić, 2006). Interest rates on loans were significantly higher than in the EU, providing high returns on capital. Favorable market opportunities were quickly recognized, leading to the dominance of Western European foreign banks on the SEE markets (Leko & Stojanović, 2006; Ristić, 2006).

Nevertheless, after entering some local markets, foreign banks were cautious, so at first they provided treasury and interbank transactions rather than retail and corporate lending (Čaušević, 2003). In general, the pace of banking reform was different across countries, distinguishing *early birds* from *late risers* (Cottarelli et al., 2003). Political stability was an important determinant of the speed of bank reforms. Countries that were part of Yugoslavia and declared independence, for example, could start/continue economic reforms only after the reintroduction of peace: Slovenia in 1991, Croatia in 1994, Bosnia and Herzegovina in 1995, Serbia and Montenegro in 2001, and North Macedonia in 1991 but with a pause during the 1999–2002[8] period (Nenovski & Smilkovski, 2012; Uvalić, 2003; Čaušević, 2003; Šević, 2000).

The banking sector is, of course, constantly changing, but when it comes to the transition to market-oriented banking, the reform process reached its limit in 2008 (Stojkov & Zalduendo, 2011). The negative effects of the GFC spilled

---

6   Subsidiaries are separate legal entities, licensed and supervised by local regulators. Branches, on the other hand, remain legally inseparable from the parent (Fiechter et al., 2011).
7   Lack of confidence in domestic banks can be explained by frozen savings on Yugoslavian bank accounts at the time of the dissolution of the country as well as the collapse of a few banks that operated on the basis of Ponzi schemes (Barisitz, 2008; Šević, 2000) or fraud (IMF Monetary and Capital Markets Department, 2017).
8   In 1999, Macedonia received about 360,000 refugees from Kosovo*. Although most of the refugees soon moved on, this was a major economic stress for a country of about two million inhabitants. Another even bigger stress occurred in 2001, when a short-lived war broke out in the country's north-west between Albanian rebels and Macedonian security forces (Nenovski & Smilkovski, 2012).

over, inter alia through the foreign banks channel, into the observed transition countries (Popov & Udell, 2012). In order to attenuate negative macroeconomic consequences, international financial institutions – the International Monetary Fund (IMF) and the World Bank – offered credit lines to affected SEE economies and organized the *Vienna Initiative* to mediate and ensure a gradual rather than abrupt exit of foreign owned banks from SEE markets (IMF European Department, 2013; Šoškić, 2015). However, since the GFC, some phenomena have become persistent, such as more stringent regulations, lower bank profitability, bank consolidation, and a retreat from non-core international markets.

### 2.1.1 Advantages of the banking reform

Reforms have fundamentally changed the banking sectors in transition economies. Šević believes that privatization, which has replaced less efficient state ownership and control, is the most important institutional and structural change that has happened to the banking sector (Šević, 2000). The implemented reforms created market-oriented two-tier banking sectors, in which bank decisions rather than state-central plans and directives determine credit allocation (Spendzharova, 2014, p. 35). Reforms have gradually strengthened contract, creditor and property rights, solidified banking regulation and supervision, strengthened deposit insurance funds, restored confidence in (foreign) banks, national accounting standards have converged towards international practice (Barisitz, 2008; Cottarelli et al., 2003). The chance to become members of the EU has motivated transition economies to adopt and implement reform processes.

The reforms have created favorable conditions for market entry and attracted foreign banks from Western Europe, which soon took a dominant share in the credit markets of the observed countries in transition. As Barisitz wrote: "around the turn of the millennium the environment stabilized and banking activities entered a path of sustained expansion, boosted by the resumption of robust economic growth and the anchor of EU integration or proximity" (Barisitz, 2008, p. 153). Foreign banks have brought credibility, know-how, improvements in operational work (such as risk management, information technology), and the capacity to borrow abroad (Barisitz, 2008; Spendzharova, 2014; Šoškić, 2015). They also brought fresh money into transition economies, through direct investments in privatized banks as well as through lending from sources borrowed either from parent banks or other international sources (Barisitz, 2008; Stojkov & Zalduendo, 2011). Thanks to their access to long-term sources of financing, foreign banks also diversified the supply of credit products on the SEE markets. They enriched the offer with long-term corporate loans, housing loans, and loans indexed in foreign currencies (Ristić, 2006). Foreign banks also attracted domestic savings that created additional resources for credit growth (Šoškić, 2015). In the period leading up to the GFC in all transition economies, the increased presence of foreign banks led to credit expansion, increased competition, and a gradual reduction in the cost of credit (Bonin, Hasan, & Wachtel, 2014). Credit expansion, competitiveness, and dominant private ownership in the banking sector are promotors of economic growth in an economy – but in general in such periods care should be taken not to lower credit standards, produce economy overheating or excessive leverage (Wachtel, 2001). Foreign banks became an attractive employer in transition economies not only because of employment growth (Barisitz, 2008) but also average wage growth – which is another positive macroeconomic impact.

### 2.1.2 Disadvantages of the banking reform

There were also some words of criticism of banking reforms in the Southeast European transition economies. Banking sector reforms were initially poorly managed. On the eve of the break-up of Yugoslavia in the early 1990s, for example, all commercial banks froze foreign currency savings, claiming that the funds remained trapped in the National Bank of Yugoslavia. Citizens were repaid only years later (Barisitz, 2008; Šević, 2000). In the mid-1990s, pyramid banks appeared in Bulgaria, Serbia, Montenegro, and Albania. They soon collapsed, leaving many depositors irretrievably without their savings (Barisitz, 2008; Čaušević, 2003; Šević, 2000). These events affected the general decline in confidence in domestic banks in favor of foreign banks. Even later, for example in Bulgaria, in 2014 a large domestic bank, Corporate Commercial Bank, was closed by the central bank due to massive fraud (IMF Monetary and Capital Markets Department, 2017).

Despite these reforms in the banking sector, they were not good enough to attract the world's largest banking groups to enter the market. With a few exceptions, the privatization of state-owned domestic banks attracted only regionally renowned banking groups from Europe. For the world's largest banks, these credit markets are most likely too small, insufficiently regulated, and risky (Ristić, 2006). Regionally renowned foreign banks were motivated to enter the markets of Southeast European transition economies by the prospect of gaining from interest rates that were much higher than the average in their home countries (Leko & Stojanović, 2006), thus increasing their competitive power (Ristić, 2006). In banks in transition economies from Southeast Europe, there was a general trend of a relative decline in corporate lending in favor of retail lending. For example, in 1997, Croatian banks had a higher share of loans granted to businesses than to households (69 % vs. 22 %), while in 2005 it was the other way around (40 % vs. 50 %): this trend is the result of a shift in the credit policy of foreign banks (Leko & Stojanović, 2006). From the perspective of foreign banks, retail loans are less risky, interest rates are higher than on corporate loans, the demand for loans is constant, and they also generate numerous services and non-interest income. But there are three downsides to this trend. First, it leads to over-indebtedness of the domestic population. Second, bank loans are the main source of financing investments and the working capital of domestic companies. Unlike companies from developed countries, local companies do not have access to other financial products such as equity financing, corporate bonds, venture capital, etc. to substitute for a lack of bank loans. Third, since the increase in retail lending was financed more from international sources than a growth in deposits (Barisitz, 2008), this negatively affected the country's external debt (Leko & Stojanović, 2006). In addition, foreign banks offered loans indexed in foreign currencies (mainly in euros, Swiss francs, and Japanese yen), which were very attractive due to interest rates being lower than on loans in domestic currency. However, due to the large proportion of loans indexed in foreign currencies, foreign exchange risk became significant (Marinković & Radović, 2017; Mihaljek, 2010), and it materialized in 2011 when the Swiss central bank capped the franc-euro parity. At the end of banking reform processes, the credit markets became overbanked and underbanked at the same time. They were overbanked because there were too many banks with a small individual market share and underbanked because of the somewhat lower bank penetration[9] (Barisitz, 2008, p. 159). Finally, due to the dominant participation of foreign banks in the observed transition economies, their exposure to external shocks increased. This type of shock materialized with the outbreak of the GFC, albeit in some SEE economies more than in others (Nenovski & Smilkovski, 2012; Sojli, 2009).

## 2.2 Bank reforms in Greece and Cyprus

In the mid-1980s, the Greek banking sector was dominated by the Bank of Greece and two large state-owned banks. During the 1990s, along with the establishment

---

9  Many banks in the SEE credit markets have unsustainable shares of 1–3 % or less. At the same time, with the exception of Croatia and Slovenia, all other credit markets have low bank penetration rates. It is highly likely, therefore, that the trend of consolidation will continue (Deloitte, 2019).

of the European Monetary Union, processes of deregulation and liberalization began in the EU banking sector, which included the Greek banking sector (Athanasoglou, Georgiou, & Staikouras, 2008). These processes were marked by two important trends in the Greek credit market: the first was a reduction in the share of state-controlled banks in favor of private banks, and the second was the trend of mergers and acquisitions[10] (Athanasoglou et al., 2008; Rezitis, 2010). In addition, Greek banks expanded their activities to credit markets in Turkey and other Southeast European economies (Athanasoglou et al., 2008; Makri & Papadatos, 2014). Liberal credit policies were followed by low interest rates and an under-appreciation of credit risks.

The Greek government was a significant borrower even before joining the Eurozone. Greece did not only have a high budget deficit relative to GDP but also problems with low growth rates and high inflation, which were only temporarily resolved by joining the Eurozone (Dellas & Tavlas, 2013). In the aftermath of the GFC, in 2008 and 2009, Greek public debt relative to GDP grew from 109.4 % to 126.7 % while the budget deficit relative to GDP increased from 10.2 % to 15.1 % (Eurostat, 2020). These trends signaled the increased risk of sovereign solvency. However, the risk did not become apparent immediately but in late 2009 because EU officials were primarily concentrating on stabilizing the GFC. When the Dubai government-owned conglomerate DubaiWorld called for a six-month moratorium on debt repayment in November 2009, attention shifted to sovereign debt risks and soon to the sustainability of the Greek government's debt (Dellas & Tavlas, 2013). That is how the sovereign debt crisis began in Greece, but all its negative consequences go beyond the scope of this work. It is sufficient to mention that the Greek banking sector was destabilized by both the GFC in 2007–2009 and by the government's debt crisis in 2010. Due to the deterioration in the macroeconomic situation, Greek banks were exposed to a combination of adverse effects, such as: a soaring volume of non-performing loans and plummeting bank capital; the writing off of 50 % of banks' exposure to the Greek government in 2012; the continuing deposit flight, especially after the emergency bank closure in 2015; being cut off from international markets, etc. (Bank of Greece, 2012; Economist Intelligence, 2015). In order to maintain financial stability, massive measures were undertaken (Bank of Greece, 2012; European Commission, 2012, 2015a, 2015b, 2015c), such as:

---

10  Rezitis (2010) argues that mergers and acquisitions rendered the banking sector less competitive because they were motivated by gaining a higher market share and profits, instead of greater efficiency and lower costs.

- To cover for banks' short-term liquidity needs, the European Central Bank (ECB), as a lender of last resort, granted Emergency Liquidity Assistance in several tranches worth tens of billions of euros.
- To restore banks' capital needs, tens of billions of euros were injected in Greek banks in several successive tranches. The Hellenic Financial Stability Fund (HFSF), set up by the Greek state in 2010 was an institution that managed the process of recapitalizing banks as part of Economic Adjustment Programs. The HFSF became the major shareholder in recapitalized banks. In 2014 and 2015, private investors paid for additional capital and thus re-privatized some of the banks.
- To ensure long-term viability, Greek banks entered into restructuring processes. Among others, restructuring involved the disposal of non-core assets outside of Greece. Several Greek banks sold their subsidiaries and left the SEE credit markets.

These measures were aimed at four systemically important Greek banks: Alpha bank, EFG Eurobank, National Bank of Greece, and Piraeus bank. Additionally, Attica bank, a bank under indirect state control, was also a beneficiary. All other "non-core" Greek banks were recapitalized by private investors, acquired by systemically important Greek banks, or ceased to exist. Over the course of several years, the number of banks dropped significantly. In 2018/2019 the support programs for Greece ended. Although the resilience of the Greek banking sector improved owing to the support programs, on the eve of the COVID-19 pandemic crisis, the profitability of the banking sector remained low, capital buffers were not strong, new loans were too expensive, and the stock of non-performing loans, although decreasing, was still high (Almunia, 2020).

The Cypriot banking sector was closed, stable, and well controlled before liberalization and EU and Eurozone accession. At the same time, however, various shortcomings were concealed which were not resolved in time, rather becoming increasingly pronounced. In the words of Clerides, "local institutions grew into inefficient banking behemoths with an abundance of staff and extensive branch networks but with little expertise in project appraisal and risk management" (Clerides, 2014, p. 4). During the financial liberalization and deregulation processes, Cyprus opened up to soon become an international business and financial center. Several advantageous features contributed to such a position: membership in the EU, the Eurozone, and the Commonwealth; its geographical placement between Europe, Asia, and Africa; and its tax haven status from the time the Iron Curtain fell until the sovereign debt crisis. There were huge capital inflows, leading to increased lending. The size of the banking sector grew constantly and exceeded its GDP by a factor of 7 by 2010 (Clerides, 2014; Stephanou, 2011). The Cypriot banking sector was dominated by a small number of large domestic banks, with numerous foreign banks operating alongside them. Around half of the deposit and lending activities were concentrated in three main domestic banks: Bank of Cyprus, Marfin Popular bank, and Hellenic bank. Benefiting from large capital inflows, these banks expanded their operations overseas, particularly in Greece (Clerides, 2014).

However the GFC and, more severely, the Greek government debt crisis hit the Cypriot banking sector hard. According to available estimations (Oehler-Şincai, 2013), the 50 % haircut on exposure to the Greek government debt produced (at the level of 2011) a loss of EUR 2.5 billion for Marfin Popular Bank and over EUR 1 billion for the Bank of Cyprus. The financial support program agreed with the Troika[11] in 2013 tackled the banking sector as well. The two Cypriot banks, Bank of Cyprus and Marfin Popular bank, had to disinvest their bank subsidiaries in Greece. Cypriot banks had to recapitalize in a bailing-in scheme, i.e. capital would be obtained by existent bondholders, shareholders, and uninsured depositors (referring to deposits greater than EUR 100,000 in value). In the end, Marfin Popular bank ceased to exist: the "good" part was transferred to the Bank of Cyprus while the "bad" part was wound down. In 2016, the support program for Cyprus ended. Clerides describes the period from the 1980s to the sovereign debt crisis as a period of "rise and fall of the Cypriot banking sector" (Clerides, 2014, p. 5).

## 2.3 Southeast Europe today

If the idea of transition was to "catch up" with the economically developed part of Europe, then it is worth measuring the success of banking reforms in the observed economies as well as integrating Cyprus and Greece in this analysis. It should be pointed out first that just like developed parts of Europe cannot form one homogeneous cluster, neither can the observed SEE economies. Depending on the level of political stability, the quality of the institutional framework, and the initial level of economic development, some economies converged faster than others towards the EU and became part of it (Filipovski, Trpeski, & Bogoev, 2018; Rozmahel, Kouba, Grochová, & Najman, 2013; Stojkov & Zalduendo,

---

11  The Troika designates the consortium of the European Commission, the ECB, and the IMF.

2011). Table 1 shows the status of the observed SEE economies according to their stage of integration in the EU.

There are opinions that some of the transition countries became EU members although they did not share typical characteristics of the European model (Gregory & Stuart, 2014) and despite the fact that they increased heterogeneity in the EU in almost all dimensions (Rozmahel et al., 2013). Nevertheless, the EU accession enabled new member states to develop faster economically thanks to the inflow of foreign direct investments. They managed to record economic growth, boost employment, and improve their living standards. In Figure 1, the SEE economies are ordered by the level of their living standards measured by their GDP per capita in the years 2017, 2018, and 2019. This order almost completely reflects the level of their integration in the EU.

Despite the heterogeneities between the observed transition economies, when it comes to their banking sectors, foreign banks gained a dominant competitive position in all of them. In the second phase of banking reforms, it was the dominant presence of foreign banks that accelerated structural catching up and convergence towards the EU (Barisitz, 2008; Crespo Cuaresma, Oberhofer, Smits, & Vincelette, 2012). Convergence advanced faster in Eurozone and EU members than in non-EU economies. However, in some aspects of banking reform, such as banking regulation, convergence is at a very high level in all observed economies (Barisitz, 2008). The European Bank for Reconstruction and Development (EBRD) calculates and publishes transition scores in the banking sector: Table 2 shows that in 2016 the transition economies of the so-called Western Balkans (the term comprises EU candidates and potential candidates) have a score ranging from 2+ to 3- while the observed EU member states have higher scores from 3 to 3+, a higher score indicating a higher level of transition within the banking sector.

Based on the transition score analysis, I decided to conduct my empirical research as a comparative analysis of the results for (i) the Western Balkans cluster and (ii) the cluster of Southeast European EU member states. The reason is that each cluster includes a relatively homogeneous group of banking sectors as measured by their EBRD scores.

**Table 1.** Level of EU integration and year of reaching that level

|  | Eurozone member | EU member | Candidate | Potential candidate |
|---|---|---|---|---|
| Greece | 2001 | 1981 | | |
| Slovenia | 2007 | 2004 | | |
| Cyprus (excluding North Cyprus) | 2008 | 2004 | | |
| Bulgaria | | 2007 | | |
| Romania | | 2007 | | |
| Croatia | | 2013 | | |
| North Macedonia | | | 2005 | |
| Montenegro | | | 2010 | |
| Serbia (excluding Kosovo*) | | | 2012 | |
| Albania | | | 2014 | |
| Bosnia and Herzegovina | | | | 2015 |
| Kosovo* | | | | 2016 |

Note: Although not inside the Eurozone, Montenegro and Kosovo* use euros in their payment systems.

**Figure 1.** SEE economies ordered by GDP per capita (2017–2019)

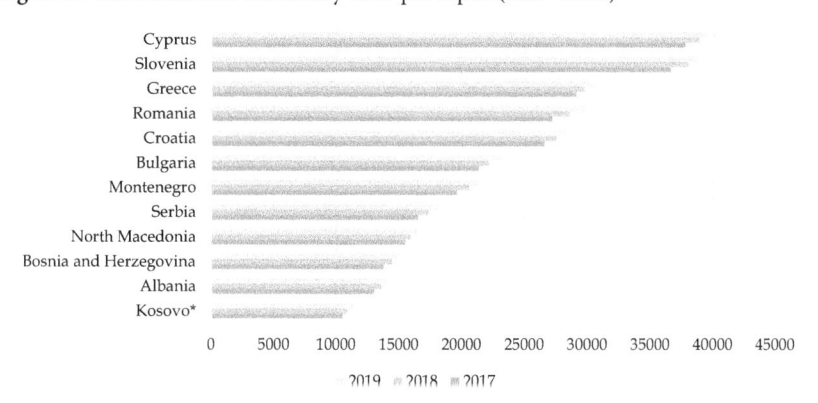

Note: Data visualization is based on the World Development Indicators database (2021).

**Table 2.** EBRD banking sector transition scores in Southeast Europe in 2016

| EU countries | Transition score |
|---|---|
| Croatia | 3+ |
| Greece | 3+ |
| Slovenia | 3 |
| Bulgaria | 3 |
| Cyprus | 3 |
| Romania | 3 |
| **Western Balkans** | **Transition score** |
| Albania | 3- |
| Bosnia and Herzegovina | 3- |
| Montenegro | 3- |
| North Macedonia | 3- |
| Serbia | 3- |
| Kosovo* | 2+ |

Note: The transition scores range from 1 to 4+. The higher the score, the higher the transition level in banking sector (EBRD, 2016).

# 3. Loan loss provisions

In this chapter, the main focus of the empirical research that follows, loan loss provisions, is explained in more detail. They are one of the indicators of credit risk, which has its non-discretionary and discretionary components that will be discussed in more detail. Regulations regarding LLPs have been continuously evolving in the last few decades, and it is interesting to note that changes in regulations have always been accompanied by major debates.

In this chapter, I also present the main questions of my empirical study, as well as the challenges of the comparability of data originating from different banking sectors and different banks.

## 3.1 Loan loss provisions as an indicator of credit risk

Credit or default risk is immanent to banks because lending is their main activity. "By definition, credit risk is the risk resulting from uncertainty in counterparty's ability or willingness to meet its contractual obligations" (Bandyopadhyay, 2016, p. 1). During upward economic cycles, banks' credit policies tend to be more liberal: the volume of new lending increases, credit covenants are more relaxed, the maturity of existing loans is easily extended, and the credit risk is underestimated. There are several likely reasons why banks pursue liberal lending policies during periods of economic expansion: disaster myopia may prevent banks from being more prudent (Guttentag & Herring, 1986); bank credit policies are interdependent because bank managers follow the same behavior pattern (Rajan, 1994); or fierce competition between banks encourages them to relax lending conditions, which increases loan growth, produces supply credit shifts and inevitably leads to high loan losses in subsequent periods (Keeton, 1999). Conversely, during economic downturns, banks follow a more conservative credit policy: as credit risks increase, the volume of new loans decreases and shifts to less risky and less profitable projects, which affects banks' interest income. If credit risks are not properly recognized in prior periods, during downturns they rise and materialize to a greater or lesser extent, thus amplifying expenses for the bank.

The cyclical character of the credit market is thus marked by recurring periods of liberal and conservative lending in the economy. Loans that are easily approved during the liberal lending phase later haunt the banks in the form of loan losses during the economic recession (Asea & Blomberg, 1997). Moreover, the theoretical and empirical literature demonstrates that credit markets oscillations may produce an "accelerator" effect on the economy (Asea & Blomberg, 1997; Bernanke & Gertler, 1989; Bernanke, Gertler, & Gilchrist, 1996; Bernanke et al., 1999; Gilchrist, Ortiz, & Zakrajsek, 2009). During economic upswings, the value of assets rises and so does the net worth of borrowers, banks are more willing to lend, and the credit supply grows, by which investments, production, and spending in the economy improve; during economic downturns, however, the value of assets declines and so does the net worth of the borrowers, banks are less willing to lend, and the credit supply drops so that investments, production, and spending in the economy decrease.

If there is no credit risk, which is a theoretical approach, there are no loan losses, so the economic value of loans is equal to their nominal value. In reality, however, as credit risk is inherent in banks' lending activity, loan losses occur and provisions for loan losses adjust the economic value of loans below their nominal value (Gebhardt & Novotny-Farkas, 2011). Due to loan losses, the banks' balance sheet channel is considered to be friction on the supply side of the credit market (Gertler & Karadi, 2011).

In general, credit market frictions, or imperfections, contribute to the *financial accelerator* effect on the macroeconomy (Bernanke et al., 1999, p. 1345) and the main cause of credit market frictions is asymmetric information between the lender and the borrower (Bernanke et al., 1999; Faia & Monacelli, 2007; Freixas & Rochet, 2008; Gilchrist et al., 2009). Borrowers have private information about the project for which they seek financing from a bank (Brauneis & Rausch, 2013; Freixas & Rochet, 2008). Due to their limited liability status, some corporate borrowers may be prone to engage in riskier projects or to exaggerate the positive outcomes of a project. Lenders are, however, unaware of the project type and borrower type and whether it is a creditworthy project and borrower or not. In the case of default, unless there is collateral, corporate borrowers are liable to their lenders only up to the amount of capital invested (Freixas & Rochet, 2008; Leland & Pyle, 1977). There is a moral hazard on the supply side of the credit market as well. Some systemically important banks ("too big to fail") may be prone to engage in the financing of riskier projects during economic upswings as they are accustomed to government protection (Gertler & Karadi, 2011). In any case, once the project is financed, lenders cannot observe the project returns unless they carry out a process of verification (auditing). Auditing a project's cash flows involves costs, which is why if debt repayments are regular, state verification is not performed; lenders mainly behave like a dormant partner (Freixas & Rochet, 2008).

Several variables may indicate credit risk developments. Variables such as *loan growth* or *share of loans in total assets* indicate whether credit growth is expansionary or contractionary. Although expansionary credit growth indicates higher credit risk, one should be careful. Credit risk is associated with expansionary credit growth more when such credit growth is the result of an aggressive increase in banks' credit supply than when it is the result of meeting increased demand (Keeton, 1999; Quagliariello, 2006). The variable *non-performing loans ratio* can also be an indicator of credit risk. However, non-performing loans are only occasionally reported in the notes to financial statements, which makes it difficult to collect data at the level of individual banks (Glen & Mondragón-Vélez, 2011). *Loan loss provisions* are a very suitable variable that indicates credit risk; actually, this variable indicates not only the credit risk but also its impact on the profitability and capitalization of banks, and data on it are available in banks' financial statements (Babouček & Jančar, 2005).

## 3.2 Components of loan loss provisions

There is no universal quantitative model to assess credit risk in a bank or to estimate loan losses with high precision (ECB, 2017; Knott, Richardson, Rismanchi, & Sen, 2014). When estimating the level of credit risk in banks, therefore, there may be a certain amount of discretion or management judgement. In theory, loan loss provisions are often assumed to encompass *non-discretionary* and *discretionary* components. In the literature, the non-discretionary component of loan loss provisions indicates the level of credit risk with respect to the business cycle while the discretionary component is found to contribute in realizing management objectives: *income smoothing*, *capital management*, or *signaling* (Beaver & Engel, 1996; Bouvatier & Lepetit, 2012a; Bouvatier et al., 2014; Gebhardt & Novotny-Farkas, 2011; Wahlen, 1994).

Wahlen (1994) explains that there is an asymmetry in the credit risk information available to bank managers on the one hand and investors and bank supervisors on the other: while bank managers are aware of the bank's loan portfolio quality, thorough verification of the loan portfolio quality in each period would be too expensive for investors and supervisors. Besides, accounting IFRS[12] guidelines

---

12 The International Accounting Standards Committee (IASC) was established in 1973 by the accounting bodies of 10 countries. The increasing number of multinational companies during the 1960s was the initial motivation to define some common accounting standards as there was a need to compare financial statements from different parts of the world. Along with the accelerated pace of globalization in 1980s and 1990s, the principal idea was taken more seriously: IAS increased in quality

are insufficiently precise in order to remain consistent in all economic branches. "Accounting standards, particularly under IFRS, also tend to be written in principle-based terms, requiring firms to disclose risk information, but usually not setting hard or industry-specific criteria around how that disclosure should be made" (Bholat, Lastra, Markose, Miglionico, & Sen, 2018, p. 40). Therefore, bank managers are in a position to apply their judgment in deciding when a credit risk will be recognized in the financial statements (Wahlen, 1994).

On the one hand, understanding the non-discretionary component of loan loss provisions is important in order to determine whether they are pro-cyclical and, if so, to promote the consistent implementation of prudential measures for forward-looking, counter-cyclical provisioning. On the other hand, it is important to determine whether the discretionary component of loan loss provisions occurs and, if so, which type. Certain types of discretion are acceptable, but not all (Bholat et al., 2018; Bushman & Williams, 2012). There are opinions in the literature that the motive of discretion makes a difference. Bank managers who use their discretion to apply more provisions in anticipation of a future deterioration in loan performance quality are far-sighted managers who use discretion wisely (Bushman & Williams, 2012; Gebhardt & Novotny-Farkas, 2011). However, if discretion is misused to gain bonuses, avoid paying taxes, attain profit targets and similar, it is considered unethical (Bischof et al., 2021; Ozili & Outa, 2017).

The aim of my empirical study is to determine whether both components of LLPs are present in SEE commercial banks. Specifically, I am interested in determining whether LLPs are pro-cyclical as well as whether certain types of discretionary decision making are present and, if so, which types. My analysis of outliers may indicate the likely motives of bank managers when deciding on provisions but separate research is still needed to determine their motives more precisely. Due to economic asymmetries between the EU and Western Balkans economies (Dabrowski & Myachenkova, 2018; Neck, 2012), I am also interested in determining whether commercial banks located in the Western Balkans practice provisioning in the same way as commercial banks located in the SEE EU member states. Finally, I am interested in whether there is a difference in provisioning practices between domestic and foreign-owned commercial banks.

---

while the number of national jurisdictions that permitted/required the use of these standards increased constantly (Camfferman & Zeff, 2007). In 2001, the IAS Board was formed as a successor to the IASC; the new body adopted the existing IAS but renamed them IFRS.

## 3.3 Evolution of loan loss provisioning regulations

In relation to disclosing their loan portfolio quality, banks have long been excluded from international accounting standards. In the UK, until the late 1970s, for example, too much transparency was considered negative, as it could lead to "bank runs" (Billings & Capie, 2009). The accounting approach to LLPs, therefore, varied from one European country to the next (Gebhardt & Novotny-Farkas, 2011). However, it was common practice for banks to record LLPs as the difference between the nominal value and the market or cost value of the non-performing loan; in addition, the 1988 Basel I Accord[13] allowed banks to make hidden reserves in the event of possible future loan losses (Gebhardt & Novotny-Farkas, 2011)[14]. Normally, there was a distinction between *specific* and *general* loan loss provisions. Banks set aside specific provisions for loan losses when non-performance (default) of individual loans had already materialized. General LLPs referred to provisions for latent risks in loan portfolios (Gebhardt & Novotny-Farkas, 2011).

In general, there is a conflicting approach to estimating LLPs from an institutional perspective. *Accounting standard setters* want financial reports to provide accurate information; *banking regulators* and *supervisors* consider early allocation of provisions to be desirable due to possible loan losses in the future; and *security regulators* believe that the use of LLPs to reduce the volatility of earnings affects prices on the stock market (Basel Committee on Banking Supervision, 2021; Bholat et al., 2018; Bushman & Williams, 2012; Gebhardt & Novotny-Farkas, 2011). Debates around loan loss provisioning continuously reoccur and are especially pronounced when they follow extreme examples of banks' practice or in the aftermath of crises.

In 1987, for example, Citicorp bank increased its loan loss provisions to around USD 3 billion. The reason for such a management decision was the expected loss stemming from loan exposures in Latin America. Beaver and Engel (1996) believe that Citicorp wanted to signal to the market how strong the performance of the bank is. This decision disturbed the stock market, and negatively affected the stock prices of some other banks that were insufficiently capitalized to

---

13  International banking regulations based on recommendations of the Basel Committee on Banking Supervision are named Basel I, Basel II, etc. for short.
14  In Germany, the legislator allowed deliberate underestimation of the value of loans up to a maximum of 4 % as a hidden reserve, to be revealed only to external auditors and supervisors but not to the public, who could only see loan loss reserves reported in the balance sheet (Bornemann, Homölle, Hubensack, Kick, & Pfingsten, 2014).

sustain higher loan loss provisions. In 1998, as another example, Suntrust bank addressed the United States Securities and Exchange Commission (SEC) in a regular process of getting approval for the acquisition of another bank. However, during the process, the SEC found that managers of Suntrust bank (using their discretionary judgment and favorable economic conditions) had been setting aside large amounts of loan loss reserves for several consecutive years. The SEC rejected the application for acquisition and requested Suntrust bank to release LLPs for the amount of around USD 100 million. The SEC was not in favor of excessive loan loss provisioning because it sends misleading signals to the market about the true value of a bank.

The debate became international and concluded in favor of accuracy and objectivity in financial statements (Knott et al., 2014). In 1991, the new accounting standard IAS 30 required banks to disclose the movement of their loan loss reserves and stop recording hidden reserves (Gebhardt & Novotny-Farkas, 2011). In 1998, the new accounting standard introduced the *"incurred" loss approach* to loan loss provisioning (Table 3). The main goal of the incurred loss approach was to reduce management judgement when estimating LLPs so that provisions are recorded only in the event of loan losses and not earlier (Knott et al., 2014).

The incurred loss approach was heavily criticized in the aftermath of the GFC. Criticisms primarily related to the pronounced pro-cyclical nature of provisions, or the fact that provisions were allocated too little and too late, and that loans were, therefore, generally under-provisioned, which contributes to uncertainty regarding the solvency of banks (Agénor & Zilberman, 2015; Bouvatier & Lepetit, 2012b; European Banking Authority, 2017; Gebhardt & Novotny-Farkas, 2011; Knott et al., 2014; Rigot & Demaira, 2020). In addition, the practice of banks of restructuring non-performing loans, coined "extend and pretend", was also criticized because such black-and-white regulations only contributed to hiding credit risk (Bholat et al., 2018).

As a result, the new accounting standard – the IFRS 9 – introduced the *"expected" loss approach* (Table 4), which replaced the incurred loss approach as of 2018. The goal of introducing the expected loss approach was to reduce the pro-cyclicality of loan loss provisions and thus contribute to financial stability (European Banking Authority, 2017; Financial Stability Forum, 2009). However, IFRS 9 allows for management judgement (European Banking Authority, 2017). The main difference when compared to the incurred loss approach is that in the new approach, loan loss provisions are to be calculated before the credit default materializes. More precisely, provisions for loan losses are to be calculated in reference to the loan stage and there are 3 stages in total. Although newly approved, healthy loans are classified in stage 1, banks are obliged to estimate the expected losses for such loans in the next 12 months and make provisions. Watch-list loans classified in stage 2 are those having certain repayment difficulties while non-performing loans are classified in stage 3. In reference to the exposures classified in stages 2 and 3, banks have to estimate loan losses expected during the entire lifetime horizon of such exposures and make provisions. Standard setters additionally granted a transitional period of five years for the banks to attenuate the initial impact of implementing IFRS 9 on their capital.

In addition to the warm welcome, there were also criticisms of the new approach to loan loss provisioning. Among the first to be voiced was the criticism that the new approach does not address the continuing lack of consistency in international practice; namely, as the new approach increases the importance of discretionary decision making, we can unfortunately expect growing divergences in the practice of provisioning (Bholat et al., 2018). Another criticism was that the principal interest of the expected loss approach – to cover for the credit risk expected in the future – is more appropriate for retail lending than other types of lending. The probability of future losses in loans granted to large corporations, for example, can rarely be detected in advance (Rigot & Demaira, 2020). With the emergence of the COVID-19 pandemic, which led to the global macroeconomic shock, additional criticism emerged. It has been said that if banks could predict the switching points of economic cycles on time then provisioning using the expected loss method would imply making additional buffers before the start of a crisis. "The sudden and unexpected nature of the pandemic, and the certainty that its implications will be less damaging for the economy if there is plenty of credit flowing towards the affected businesses and households, suggest the desirability of preventing the pro-cyclical damage that the new provisioning standards can cause in this crisis" (Abad & Suarez, 2020, p. 100). Huizinga and Laeven (2019) believe that the pro-cyclicality of loan loss provisions will remain a problem in Eurozone banks even after the introduction of the new standard. Additional criticism is that the new approach promotes "kitchen sinking accounting", a practice of constructing the worst possible financial statements in the current period without deferring the expenses/impairments to subsequent periods (Euromoney, 2020).

European financial authorities agreed, among others, on relaxing the application of IFRS 9 at the outbreak of the COVID-19 pandemic crisis (ECB, 2020; European Securities Markets Authority, 2020; IFRS, 2020). To prevent an increase in NPL stock, additionally, the European Commission published an action plan that comprises: (i) the development of secondary markets for non-performing loans; (ii) the establishment of asset management companies ("bad banks") at national levels; and (iii) an improvement of insolvency laws (European

Commission, 2020). It is obvious that the focus of EU institutions is, among other things, on preventing the negative impact of a macroeconomic shock on global financial stability. Measures of a similar nature can be seen in individual SEE economies, regardless of their EU members status, such as: relaxing regulatory requirements relative to capital, liquidity, asset classification and loan loss provisioning; introducing loan moratoria; loan guarantee schemes, etc. (IMF Policy Tracker, 2021).

My second empirical study seeks to answer the question as to how a macroeconomic shock would affect the movement of loan loss provisions in the SEE banking sectors. In particular, I am interested in the reaction of loan loss provisions to the negative shock in GDP growth and to the positive shock in the number of unemployed. A comparative analysis of the results of stress tests and of outliers indicates certain similarities and differences in the resilience of individual banking sectors. Macroeconomic stress tests as a focus of central bank research and academic research are constantly improving in an effort to implement the most appropriate policy measures to attenuate the effects of shock.

## 3.4 Loan loss provisions in Southeast Europe

During the first phase of economic transition, during the early 1990s, states began to withdraw from owning and supporting enterprises. At that time banks were reluctant to finance enterprises, not only because of general uncertainty about economic growth but also because of a lack of experience in assessing credit risks and the inherited stock of non-performing loans (Calvo & Kumar, 1994; EBRD, 1995; Gorton & Winton, 2002). Enterprises were forced to postpone investment decisions and had to rely on internal resources, which again negatively influenced economic growth and corporate credit supply (Calvo & Kumar, 1994; EBRD, 1995).

The authorities had to ameliorate banking regulations to address the stock of NPLs and to promote the supply of credit to potentially viable companies (Calvo & Kumar, 1994). The new or strengthened *prudential banking regulations* included, among other things, loan classifications and provisions for potential loan losses. Transition economies that advanced in the EU accession process adopted prudential banking regulations faster than others. Slovenia, Romania, and Bulgaria were among the first to adopt classes of loans to be assigned appropriate provisions (EBRD, 1995). Most of loans were newly classified as either healthy loans, watch list loans or doubtful loans. The quality of the loan portfolio was assessed according to the borrower's financial position and credit history (EBRD, 1995).

However, just because a prudential regulation had been adopted did not imply that it was implemented immediately. Realizing the goals of prudential regulation required strengthening supervision over banks as well as adequate accounting standards for non-performing loans and loan loss provisions (Borish et al., 1995; EBRD, 1995). Western-style banking regulations and supervision were promoted on the whole, but the implementation of prudential regulations required an understanding of the specific conditions in transition economies (Gorton & Winton, 2002). In some cases, the high level of recognized and provisioned non-performing loans was unsustainable and led to the failure of banks (Männasoo & Mayes, 2005). In other cases, banks used tactics to roll over loans to troubled borrowers to avoid the bankruptcy of both (Gorton & Winton, 2002). As troubled borrowers were mainly state-owned companies, in order to avoid a scenario of borrowers and banks alike going bankrupt, leading to rising unemployment, regulators opted to shore up existing loans to state-owned companies through subsidies (Gorton & Winton, 2002). Although introduced with positive motives, the subsidizing of state-owned companies influenced the misallocation of loans in credit markets (Gorton & Winton, 2002). It was a phase of inefficiency and instability in the banking sector in transition economies. Over time, however, the transition economies grew stronger, as did their bank regulations and supervision.

Different aspects of loan loss provisions have been analyzed by local authors, of which I mention only some of those that caught my attention. Under European Parliament regulation 1606/2002, banks were required to move from national to international accounting standards starting in 2006. However, when it came to calculating loan loss provisions, some central banks were hesitant to apply international methodology because it was much milder than national requirements (Chen, Sivec, & Volk, 2018; Lleshanaku & Üç, 2014). The Slovenian central bank, for example, was concerned that by decreasing loan loss provisions, banks would become more vulnerable. This is why a transitional solution was implemented that helped control the level of bank capitalization (Chen et al., 2018). In Albania, the application of both IAS/IFRS methodology and Albanian central bank methodology was allowed, the latter being considered to result in a higher level of provisions (Lleshanaku & Üç, 2014). An empirical analysis of the banking sector of the Federation of Bosnia and Herzegovina[15] in the period

---

15   Bosnia and Herzegovina consists of the two entities, the Federation of Bosnia and Herzegovina and the Republic of Srpska. There is a dual financial system: "Both entities have their own parliament, government, judicial system and stock exchange. Similarly, regulatory and supervisory responsibilities for banking, insurance, and capital markets lie at the entity level by Constitution" (IMF, 2015, p. 11).

2000–2012 raises doubts about hidden losses in the balance sheets, especially in 2009, due to underestimated loan loss provisions (Jović, 2014). But Jović (2014) also warns of the problem with short time series for proper statistical inferences. Finally, loan loss provisions in the Romanian banking sector during the 2001–2010 period were influenced by unemployment and credit expansion in both the short and the long run (Nikolaidou & Vogiazas, 2013).

Indeed, as Jović (2014) indicates, time series are generally short: for example, time series of loan loss provisions in the SEE banking sectors are available since 2006 only in Croatia, North Macedonia, and Bosnia and Herzegovina (Figure 2). In other SEE banking sectors they are even shorter, and for some they do not exist in the IMF Financial Soundness Indicators (FSI) database (2021). Figure 2 presents data on provisions for losses on non-performing loans as a share in total loans (a stock variable). Looking at the LLP movements, we notice a growth trend after the GFC in all economies, which, after reaching its peak, turns into a downward trend. It is also noticeable that since 2018, when the new "expected loss" approach replaced the old "incurred loss" approach in the assessment LLPs, there have been no significant changes in the LLP trend except in Slovenia. Also, I would like to comment (although this period is not included in my empirical study) that except in Greece and Cyprus, the COVID-19 pandemic did not have a significant impact on the level of loan loss provisions, most likely under the influence of stabilizing macroeconomic policies.

Another topic worth analyzing is the share of non-performing loans in total loans and, equally importantly, the coverage of non-performing loans by loan loss provisions. According to the IMF, these two indicators are among the core Financial Soundness Indicators as they indicate the quality of banks' assets (IMF, 2019). Various terms are used to denote non-performing loans (NPL), such as problematic loans, bad loans, defaulted assets, doubtful loans, non-accrual loans, restructured loans, delinquent loans, forbearance, impaired loans, distressed assets, etc. Different terms correspond to different approaches to the phenomenon because NPLs can be viewed from the aspect of repayment status as well as from the legal, accounting, and regulatory aspect. The definition of non-performing loans[16] often differs across banking sectors or over time for

---

16  In October 2013, ahead of the EU-wide asset quality review, the European Banking Authority published a definition of non-performing loans to be applied on a best effort basis (European Banking Authority, 2014). In July 2016, the Basel Committee provided a complete definition of non-performing loans (Basel Committee on Banking Supervision, 2016).

the same banking sector (Bholat et al., 2018). According to established practice, however, it is common to consider all those loans to be non-performing which are more than 90 days late in payment and/or which are unlikely to be fully repaid, and where banks expect loan recovery by activating loan collateral.

Although banks do not systematically disclose information on their NPL stocks in their financial statements, they do inform relevant national institutions. Therefore, it is possible to collect data on non-performing loans and the coverage of non-performing loans at the level of the national banking sector rather than at the level of individual banks. The *NPL ratio* indicates the share of non-performing loans in total gross loans.[17] It is considered an indicator of asset quality and an ex-post indicator of credit risk: a higher NPL ratio means lower asset quality and higher credit risk, and vice versa. Non-performing loans should be timely and adequately covered by loan loss provisions to ensure the safety and stability of a banking sector. The *NPL coverage ratio* indicates the level of non-performing loans covered by loan loss provisions and as such measures the ability to absorb future loan losses: a higher NPL coverage ratio means a higher ability to absorb future loan losses. Given the different practices in EU member states, the European Parliament adopted a proposal for minimum NPL coverage under the uniform provisioning calendar and published it in April 2019 (Stamegna, 2019). According to this calendar, the minimum level of NPL coverage depends on the collateral; unsecured non-performing loans should be 100 % provisioned in the second year while secured non-performing loans should be provisioned progressively as time goes on.

A visual analysis of the movement of both ratios in the observed banking sectors (Figures 3 and 4) reveals the following:

– In the years following the sovereign debt crisis, NPL ratios were substantially higher in the Greek and Cypriot banking sectors than in all others. Almost half of total loans were non-performing in these banking sectors.[18]

---

17  According to the IMF definition, total gross loans represent the total loan portfolio including gross non-performing loans (IMF, 2019). Gross NPLs are NPLs from which loan loss provisions have not been deducted.

18  Indeed, the breakdown of NPL ratios by counterparty for EU countries for Q2 2016 shows that Greece and Cyprus are the leaders in all segments: in the segment of small and medium sized enterprises (NPL ratios are 66.2 % in Greece and 64.7 % in Cyprus), in the segment of large enterprises (37.4 % and 61.1 %), and the segment of households (46.4 % and 55.9 %) (Enria, 2017).

- If the NPL ratio of 5 % is considered a reference (European Banking Authority, 2018), then only a few SEE banking sectors have managed to reduce their NPL ratio below the threshold, namely in Slovenia, Romania, North Macedonia, and Serbia. However, although all other SEE banking sectors have an NPL ratio of more than 5 %, it has been slowly declining as their banking sectors gradually recover from the GFC.
- In June 2018, the average NPL coverage ratio in the EU was 46 % (Stamegna, 2019). If we consider it as a benchmark, then we find that Greek banking sector had lower coverage ratios, indicating lower absorption power for future potential loan losses. Despite the unavailable data in the IMF database, it can be added that the Bulgarian banking sector had the same problem, as one of the main findings of the IMF mission in 2017 was that the NPL coverage ratio in Bulgaria should be at least 20 percentage points higher (IMF Monetary and Capital Markets Department, 2017).
- The example of the North Macedonian banking sector is particularly interesting as for almost the entire observed period it had an NPL coverage ratio of more than 100 %, meaning that provisions covered not only losses on non-performing loans but also partially on performing loans.
- In most cases it seems that there is an inverse relationship between the share of NPLs in total loans and their coverage by provisions (suggesting that when the NPLs increase, their coverage by provisions decreases). This relationship is, however, not historically stable because there are periods when the relationship between the two variables is not an inverse one.
- Following the outbreak of the COVID-19 pandemic crisis, the NPL ratio continued a slight downward trend or remained stable in the banking sectors observed, which can be explained by both the positive impact of stabilizing macroeconomic measures and the continued implementation of the NPL reduction strategies. The NPL coverage ratio remained relatively stable, too, with the exception of a significant increase in the North Macedonian and Albanian banking sectors, which are perceived as being less integrated in the global financial markets (Nenovski & Smilkovski, 2012; Sojli, 2009).

Historical trends for NPL ratios and especially NPL coverage ratios provide additional valuable information that help explain the characteristics of credit risks in the individual banking sectors of Southeast Europe.

## 3.5 Comparability of the data

From the accounting point of view, loan loss provisions are recorded as a flow and as a stock variable in the banks' financial statements. As a flow variable, loan loss provisions are recorded as an expense in the *income statement*, and as a stock variable, accumulated loan loss provisions from previous accounting periods reduce the value of loans in the *balance sheet* (Gebhardt & Novotny-Farkas, 2011). In my empirical research, I use loan loss provisions as a flow variable in the first study and as a stock variable in the second study.

In general, all empirical research raises the question of the comparability of data from different national banking sectors and even different banks within the same national banking sector (Bholat et al., 2018; Ozili & Outa, 2017). International accounting standards (IAS) were adopted by the EU in 2002 and became valid in 2006. The application of IAS in SEE banking sectors was mostly *required* during the observed period (European Commission, 2019; IFRS, 2021). However, the accounting standard IAS 39, which introduces the incurred approach in estimating provisions for loan losses, is complex and has been refined and revised several times (Gebhardt & Novotny-Farkas, 2011). Furthermore the application of the new IFRS 9, which replaced IAS 39 in 2018, leaves the option of a 5-year transition period and, in addition, it was relaxed when the 2020 COVID-19 pandemic began (ECB, 2020; European Securities Markets Authority, 2020; IFRS, 2020). The data comparability question arises not only because of the potentially inconsistent application of the IFRS but also due to not fully harmonized definitions of non-performing loans in different countries (Bholat et al., 2018) as well as different assumptions and methods of loan loss provision estimations applied by managers of different banks (Ozili & Outa, 2017). When analyzing the results of various empirical studies, and this is not limited to SEE credit markets, this caveat should be kept in mind. However, in general, the available data indicate a trend in loan loss provisions, which is why there is so much research interest and quantitative studies.

I used several databases in my research, among which Standard & Poor's Global Market Intelligence is a private database, while all other databases were publicly available at the time I used them as a data source. For estimations within my first empirical study I used Stata, within the second study EViews and only for outlier analysis R statistical program. Details are available upon request (ksenijapo@edu.aau.at).

**Table 3.** The incurred loan loss approach (simplified)

| Unimpaired loans | Impaired loans |
|---|---|
| Minimal general loan loss provisions | Loan loss provisions calculated based on incurred and expected loss during lifetime horizon |

Source: Restoy and Zamil (2018)

**Table 4.** The expected loan loss approach (simplified)

| Stage 1: Performing loans | Stage 2: Underperforming loans | Stage 3: Non-performing loans |
|---|---|---|
| Loan loss provisions calculated based on expected loss during 12 month horizon | Loan loss provisions calculated based on expected loss during loan lifetime horizon | Loan loss provisions calculated based on incurred and expected loss during loan lifetime horizon |

Source: Restoy and Zamil (2018)

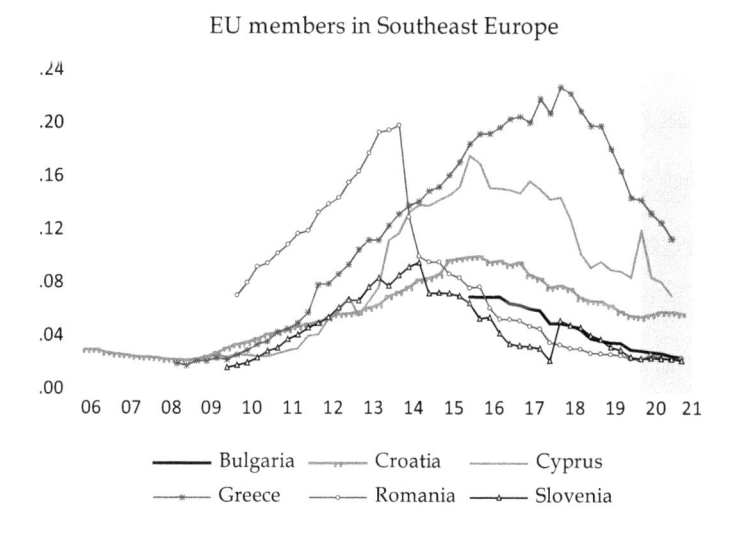

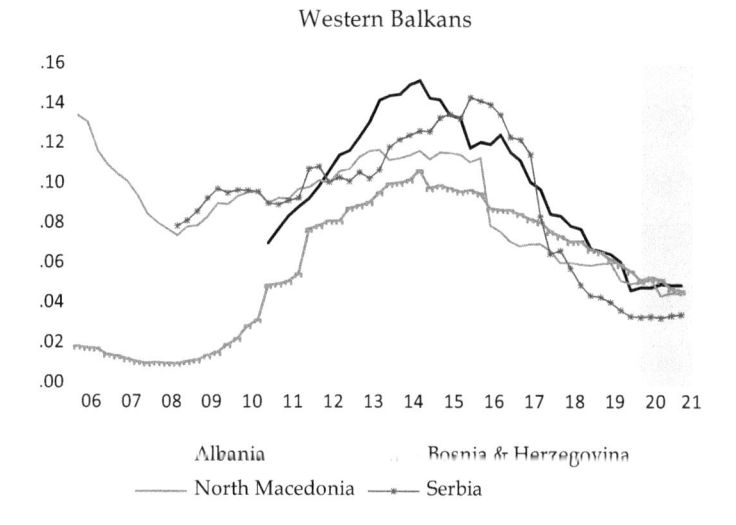

**Figure 2.** Loan loss provisions across SEE banking sectors

Note: The X-axis represents the years and the Y-axis represents the measurement of loan loss provisions as a percentage of total loans. There are no data on the Montenegrin and Kosovo* banking sectors, while data for the Bulgarian banking sector are scarce. The shaded area refers to the time of the COVID-19 pandemic. The data source is the IMF FSI database (2021).

**Figure 3.** NPL ratio and NPL coverage ratio in the SEE EU countries

Note: The X-axis represents the years. The Y-axis on the left hand scale (LHS) represents the measurement of non-performing loans as a percentage of total assets, while the Y-axis on the right hand scale (RHS) represents the coverage of non-performing loans by loan loss provisions. The shaded area refers to the time of the COVID 19 pandemic. The data source is the IMF FSI database (2021). There are insufficient data on the Bulgarian banking sector.

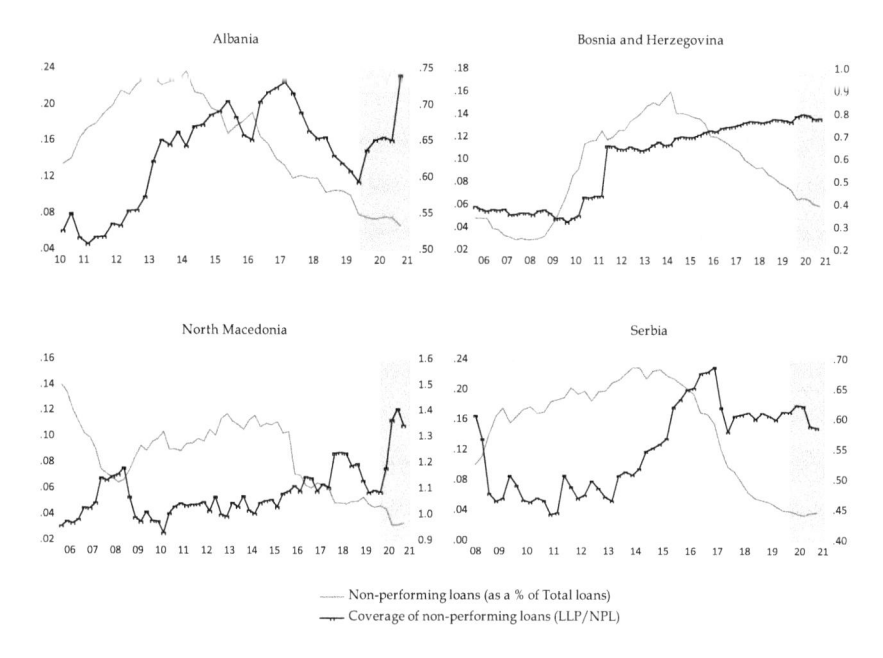

**Figure 4.** NPL ratio and NPL coverage ratio in the Western Balkans

Note: The X-axis represents the years. The Y-axis on the LHS represents the measurement of non-performing loans as a percentage of total assets, while the Y-axis on the RHS represents the coverage of non-performing loans by loan loss provisions. The shaded area refers to the time of the COVID-19 pandemic. The data source is the IMF FSI database (2021). There are no data on the Montenegrin and Kosovo* banking sectors.

# 4. Non-discretionary and discretionary components of loan loss provisions in Southeast Europe

In this chapter, the first of two empirical studies is presented which aims to determine the characteristics of loan loss provisioning practices from the perspective of non-discretionary and discretionary components in SEE commercial banks. Before the empirical analysis, I present research that examines the pro-cyclicality of loan loss provisions (the non-discretionary component) as well as hypotheses on capital and income management and signaling with the use of loan loss provisions (the discretionary component) in banks from different (mostly economically developed) countries.

## 4.1 Theoretical framework

Many empirical and theoretical papers have been written about loan loss provisions (Anandarajan et al., 2005; Basel Committee on Banking Supervision, 2021; Ozili & Outa, 2017; Wall & Koch, 2000), but knowledge about different experiences, improved methodologies for estimations, and motives for management judgement are still being developed. In this chapter, I present selected empirical and theoretical literature that expands our knowledge of the non-discretionary and discretionary components of loan loss provisions in banks from the developed part of the world.

The contribution of my study is in expanding our knowledge of the non-discretionary and discretionary components of loan loss provisions in commercial banks located in the SEE EU periphery and less developed, non-EU members (i.e. the Western Balkans). In addition, my work contributes to our understanding of some motives for management judgement on loan loss provisions, although further research is needed in this area.

### 4.1.1 Capital management

There were two prevailing trends in the financial markets of developed countries from the 1970s to 1990s: deregulation and integration. As a result of credit market liberalization, competition in the banking industry increased. Although competition enhances allocational efficiency, the question arises as to whether there is a negative trade-off between competition and financial stability (Allen

& Gale, 2004; Freixas & Rochet, 2008; Hellmann, Murdock, & Stigliz, 2000). If more banks compete in the same market, profits decline, and the banks gradually enter more lucrative but, at the same time, riskier projects. It is unlikely that all of the projects will turn out to be successful at generating profits, thus converting a portion of bank loans into larger or smaller losses.

In order to ensure both competition and financial stability, the EU regulators introduced a minimum capital requirement in the 1988 Basel I Accord. It was expected that if banks maintain adequate minimum levels of their capital, they will be less inclined to enter risky investments. Later upgrades of the regulation (Basel II and Basel III), although more complex, remained focused on the two tiers of bank equity and a minimum defined level of adequate capital ratio. Tier 1 is the core capital that encompasses the bank shareholders' equity and retained earnings while tier 2 capital encompasses supplementary bank capital, such as revaluation reserves, stock of general loan loss provisions,[19] etc. Without going into detail on the Basel banking regulations,[20] let me highlight that banks are required to keep adequate capital ratios above a certain minimum level. Loan loss provisions affect bank capital as higher loan loss provisions decrease retained earnings and, consequently, decrease tier 1 capital.

The capital management hypothesis tests whether LLPs are used to ensure that regulatory obligations concerning bank capital are fulfilled. The results of empirical analyses in that respect are not unique. Some findings confirm the capital management hypothesis and some do not. There is evidence for capital management using LLPs in banks in emerging Europe[21] during the 1997–2010 period (Bonin & Košak, 2013) as well as in Greece between 2001 and 2012

---

19  My empirical study mainly covers the period when Basel II and the IAS 39 (incurred loss approach) were in force. Basel II gives the opportunity to some banks to incorporate general loan loss reserves into their tier 2 capital.

20  In short, Basel I regulated the bank's minimum capital requirements, hidden reserves were allowed, and general loan loss reserves were part of tier 2; Basel II ensured that loan loss provisions cover *expected* loan losses while *unexpected* losses are covered by bank capital; Basel III expanded the scope of loan loss provisions to include potential losses on newly approved loans (Gebhardt & Novotny-Farkas, 2011; Ozili & Outa, 2017). Ozili and Outa (2017) point out that the two different approaches to loan loss provisioning are reflected in the somewhat conflicting requirements of Basel II (i.e. approach of banking regulators and supervisors) and the IAS 39 (i.e. approach of accounting standard setters). A type of reconciliation is the introduction of IFRS 9 with the expected loan loss approach as of 2018.

21  *Emerging Europe* designates CESEE countries that became members of the EU in 2004 and 2013.

(Makri & Papadatos, 2014). Bikker and Metzemakers confirm capital management in the banks of some OECD countries analyzed during the 1991–2001 period (Bikker & Metzemakers, 2005). Capital management has also been determined in USA banks prior to the adoption of Basel I regulations (Moyer, 1990). However, in the empirical research of Bouvatier, Lepetit, and Strobel (2014), capital management using LLPs is not found in the commercial banks of 17 Western European countries between 2004 and 2009. Capital management is not found in US banks after the adoption of the Basel I regulations either (Kim & Kross, 1998). Due to the stricter regulations regarding provisioning in Spain, it is not surprising that capital management was not found in the panel of 142 banks observed during the period 1986–2002 either (Pérez, Salas, & Saurina, 2006). Therefore, there is no unified conclusive finding referring to bank practices of capital management. The results differ depending on the country, time span, and due to "the diverging legal, regulatory or institutional frameworks" (Bikker & Metzemakers, 2005, p. 15).[22]

As suggested by the literature, motives to influence capital through accounting decisions are connected to the avoidance of timely and costly searches for additional equity during economic downturns (Bikker & Metzemakers, 2005) or the avoidance of high regulatory costs associated with the lack of being able to abide by minimum capital requirements (Moyer, 1990). Managers of undercapitalized banks are more inclined to manage capital, especially if a bank also has high levels of non-performing loans (Bikker & Metzemakers, 2005; Gebhardt & Novotny-Farkas, 2011).

### 4.1.2 Income smoothing

When analyzing income smoothing, I focus on accounting income smoothing that in comparison to real[23] income smoothing neither affects cash flow nor produces an economic event. In the accounting view, using certain financial reporting methods and estimates, managers "window-dress" financial reports. Accounting income smoothing is a recognized practice in both industry and banking.

---

22  The findings of Brandao-Marques, Correa, and Sapriz's empirical study (2020), which includes banks from 54 countries around the world before and after the GFC, indicate that government support encourages banks to take on more risk (measured by the level of loan loss provisions), but if banks are subject to a stricter supervisory regime, then this moral hazard effect is offset.
23  Real income smoothing alters business operations in order to manage earnings.

Normally, income smoothing operates by accounting shifts of cost or revenues from one period to another (Eckel, 1981). In bad times, according to Merchant (1990), income is pulled from a subsequent period to the current one by deferring expenses and/or accelerating revenues. These accounting transferals are possible due to "the flexibility allowed in the generally accepted accounting procedures" (Fudenberg & Tirol, 1995, p. 76).

It is well understood that income smoothing is not sustainable in the long run because actual and reported earnings have to be equal in the long run. However, from the inter-temporal point of view, managers may perform income smoothing by increasing reported earnings above actual values when times are bad or decreasing reported earnings below actual values in good times. The differences between actual and reported earnings are named "hidden savings" if positive or "hidden dis-savings" if negative. In a common business setup, where present performance is always more valued than past or future performance, managing hidden savings or hidden dis-savings ensures the stability of reported earnings over time (Fudenberg & Tirol, 1995; Merchant, 1990). Additionally, reporting earnings lower than they actually are helps avoid more ambitious income targets in future periods (Merchant, 1990).

Despite the fact that it may be perceived as unethical, Lambert (1984) finds that income smoothing is a rational equilibrium behavior that managers (as rational economic agents) may perform. Managers care about decreasing the volatility of earnings. In relation to managers' bonuses and employment stability, reporting stable earnings is more favorable than reporting volatile, fluctuating earnings. Merchant finds that managers who operate in a milieu of relatively high uncertainty and under pressure to achieve income targets, are more inclined to use income smoothing. On the contrary, if an operating milieu is relatively stable and predictable, income smoothing becomes less unobservable and, therefore, riskier to implement (Merchant, 1990).

The fact that bank managers use loan loss provisions when practicing income smoothing is recognized by the market so that in some cases "stakeholders are [...] likely to anticipate (and tolerate) a certain amount of earnings management" (Healy & Wahlen, 1999, p. 369). Regulators and standard-setters are aware of and tolerate moderate bank income smoothing because the "elimination of management judgment in financial reporting is not optimal (or even feasible) for investors, and unlimited judgment is not practical given audit limitations and the costly nature of ex post settling up after misleading or fraudulent reporting" (Healy & Wahlen, 1999, p. 367). However, if the size and frequency of income smoothing is large, it deceives the market by misreporting the level of risk in the banking industry (Bouvatier et al., 2014) and affects resource allocation in the economy (Healy & Wahlen, 1999). Hidden savings in banking are enabled by "cookie jar" reserves,[24] or accumulated reserves. On the other side, hidden dissavings in banks are activated during economic downturn episodes: reported earnings are made higher than actual earnings by, for example, releasing previously accrued loan loss reserves.

The income smoothing hypothesis tests whether loan loss provisions are used in order to manage bank income. A dominant finding in the empirical literature is that income smoothing using loan loss provisions occurs. Arpa, Giulini, Ittner, and Pauer (2001), for example, determined that Austrian banks had a tendency to smooth their income by using LLPs during the period 1990–1999. Based on an empirical analysis of bank provisioning behavior in Western European countries between 2004 and 2009, Bouvatier, Lepetit, and Strobel (2014) found that income smoothing was more pronounced in those banks that had more concentrated ownership and that operated in an environment of weak supervision and low quality of external audits. Income smoothing was empirically determined in emerging Europe from 1997 to 2010 (Bonin & Košak, 2013). Fonseca and González (2008) analyzed bank provisioning behavior in 40 countries worldwide between 1995 and 2002; they determined that income smoothing was practiced more in those banks operating in market-oriented financial systems characterized by weaker investor protection, weaker supervision and regulation, and weaker legal enforcement. Huizinga and Laeven (2019) pointed out that the practice of income smoothing was more pronounced in the banks of the Eurozone, compared to other developed economies. However, after analyzing the US banking sector during the period 1986–1995, it was found that no income smoothing occurred after the 1990 change in regulations (Ahmed, Takeda, & Thomas, 1998). Similarly, Pérez et al. (2006) ascertained that after the introduction of new regulations in 2000, income smoothing became less important in Spanish banks. Finally, based on a panel data set consisting of 211 banks from 11 emerging European countries observed over the period 2003–2014, Skala (2021) observed that state-owned banks did not perform income smoothing using loan loss provisions.

---

24  The name was coined by Arthur Levitt, chairman of the SEC, during the 1998 examination of the financial reports of the Suntrust Bank (Gebhardt & Novotny-Farkas, 2011; Healy & Wahlen, 1999). The Suntrust Bank accumulated loan loss reserves during several previous good years even though the loans for which the loss provisions were reported as likely to be repaid. It was noticed that the practice of creating "cookie jar" reserves during economic upswings is shared by other banks as well.

Some managers' incentives for income smoothing have already been mentioned, namely to stabilize earning fluctuations (Fudenberg & Tirol, 1995; Lambert, 1984; Merchant, 1990); to avoid over-ambitious plans in periods after those with high earnings (Merchant, 1990); to protect their job stability and reward schemes (Healy & Wahlen, 1999; Lambert, 1984). Other evidence suggests that income smoothing achieves short-run effects on stock prices on the capital market, like reporting downward accounting income before management buyouts or upward accounting income before stock-financed acquisitions (Healy & Wahlen, 1999).

### 4.1.3 Signaling

Audited financial statements (along with press releases, official websites, and various financial media, etc.) also represent a way for managers to disclose or signal the financial performance of a bank (Healy & Palepu, 2001). Annual bank financial statements accompanied by the unqualified opinion of an external auditor as well as favorable assessment by rating agencies potentially contribute to reducing information asymmetry – and distinguishing the bank from "lemons" on the same market (Akerlof, 1970; Healy & Palepu, 2001). Moreover, investors on the stock market tend to trust more established auditors, the so-called Big 4 when it comes to information about loan loss provisions (Kanagaretnam, Krishnan, & Lobo, 2009). The signals are addressed not only to potential investors but also to current shareholders, competition, providers of labor, customers, etc. (Healy & Wahlen, 1999). In this view, signaling and communicating strengths both aim to provide the same effect (Wahlen, 1994).

The signaling hypothesis tests whether banks use financial statements to communicate strengths with respect to their provisions for loan losses (that have the character of an expense). The selected empirical literature on bank signaling in reference to loan loss provisions does not convey a unique conclusion: some authors confirm the bank signaling hypothesis while others reject it. Wahlen (1994) finds signaling to be an unexpected, one-off discretionary increase in loan loss provisions that is interpreted by investors as "good news": bank managers have private information about significant future cash flows, which is why the bank can sustain a current increase in expenses. Distressed commercial banks in 18 EU countries during the 1999–2008 period were more prone to signal strength than healthy commercial banks because the benefits of signaling are greater than the costs (Leventis, Dimitropoulos, & Anandarajan, 2012). Similarly, managers of undervalued banks in America were found to be more likely to signal strength (Kanagaretnam, Lobo, & Yang, 2004). On the other hand, no evidence of bank signaling was found in Western European countries during the 2004–2009 period (Bouvatier et al., 2014) or in Australian banks during the 1991–2001 period (Anandarajan, Hasan, & McCarthy, 2007).

### 4.1.4 Pro-cyclicality

> *The willingness to lend is greater than usual at the commencement of a period of speculation, and much less than usual during the revulsion which follows.*
>
> (Mill, [1848] 2009, p. 515)

The pro-cyclicality hypothesis tests whether loan loss provisions increase during economic downturns and decrease during economic upturns. The wording of the hypothesis may sound odd because pro-cyclicality normally indicates the movement of an economic variable in the same direction as the movement of an aggregate economic activity. However, a large body of empirical research on loan loss provisions accepts the causal dimension of pro-cyclicality, as defined by the Financial Stability Forum (2009). Pro-cyclicality is thus defined as a dynamic interaction between the financial and real sectors that amplifies business cycle oscillations and, consequently, affects financial stability (Financial Stability Forum, 2009). Lending and economic activity have a dynamic interaction; in a period of growth, loan loss provisioning is mostly irrelevant. However, in a period of economic recession, it becomes important whether loan loss provisioning amplifies pro-cyclicality through an additional impact on credit supply contraction as well as whether provisioning influences financial instability (Basel Committee on Banking Supervision, 2021).

In most of the literature, regardless of the geographical space and time covered by the empirical research, loan loss provisions estimated using the incurred loss approach were found to be pro-cyclical and, therefore, backward looking (Arpa et al., 2001; Bikker & Metzemakers, 2005; Bonin & Košak, 2013; Bouvatier et al., 2014; Laeven & Majnoni, 2003; Makri & Papadatos, 2014). The pro-cyclicality of loan loss provisions is even higher in Eurozone banks than in banks in other developed countries such as Canada, Norway, Switzerland, and the USA (Huizinga & Laeven, 2019). The opposite practice, forward-looking provisioning, means that loan loss provisions should increase during times of economic expansion as the stock of loan loss provisions is intended to be used during economic downturns. Mario Quagliariello, Director of Supervisory Strategy and Risk at the ECB, strongly advocates a greater allocation of loan loss provisions during economic expansion as otherwise loan loss provisions would just amplify the effects of the negative macroeconomic indicators (Quagliariello, 2006). Spain is one of the rare countries whose bank regulators introduced forward-looking provisioning in 2000 (Saurina, 2009). Saurina, therefore, recommends using forward-looking provisioning in emerging economies: "Dynamic provisions could be an important prudential instrument for emerging economies, where there is greater macroeconomic volatility and the banking system plays a dominant role in financial intermediation. An anticyclical buffer should help strengthen the solvency of each bank and increase the stability of the system as a whole" (Saurina, 2009, p. 5).

There is also an opinion that income smoothing practiced by bank managers contributes to attenuating the pro-cyclicality of loan loss provisions (Bikker & Metzemakers, 2005; Bonin & Košak, 2013). However, as previously explained, this may be only one of the motives for income smoothing.

## 4.2 Empirical research

In this chapter, I describe my empirical study conducted to examine the non-discretionary and discretionary use of loan loss provisions in commercial banks in Southeast Europe. Understanding the non-discretionary component of loan loss provisions is important in order to determine whether they act pro-cyclically and, therefore, backward looking. In that case, there is a need to promote the consistent implementation of prudential measures for forward-looking, counter-cyclical provisioning in the future. It is also important to determine which type of the discretionary component of loan loss provisions occurs. In that respect, in addition to estimations, outlier analysis complements the empirical study as it indicates likely motives for certain provisioning decisions; however additional research is needed to further examine motivations for management judgements. Finally, answers to the questions as to whether the practice of provisioning is different in the EU compared to non-EU members, as well as whether it is different in domestic compared to foreign banks, also help to understand the specifics of the banking sectors in Southeast Europe.

### 4.2.1 Data

My panel dataset is balanced and it encompasses commercial banks over the eight-year period from 2010 to 2017 in Albania, Bosnia and Herzegovina, Bulgaria, Croatia, Cyprus, Greece, Montenegro, North Macedonia, Romania, Serbia, Slovenia, and Kosovo*. More precisely, the commercial banks included in Standard and Poor's Global Market Intelligence database are included in the panel.[25] In the case of Cyprus, commercial banks from the (internationally not recognized) Turkish Republic of Northern Cyprus are exempted, due to the lack of data. In the case of Serbia, commercial banks from (internationally partially recognized) Kosovo* are in the panel, due to the availability of data. In the case of Bosnia and Herzegovina, commercial banks are taken on an entity level, i.e. the Federation of Bosnia and Herzegovina and the Republic of Srpska,[26] while macroeconomic data are taken on an aggregate level.

As the aim of my study is to establish whether the behavior of commercial banks located in the EU member countries of Southeast Europe differ from the ones located in the Western Balkans, I use panels named *All commercial banks* for the SEE EU (Table 7) and for the Western Balkans (Table 14). It should be noted that Croatia is treated as an SEE EU member state despite the fact that it did not officially enter the EU until 2013, the reason being that Croatia closed its EU accession negotiations officially in June 2011. Prior to 2011, the process of accession was slowed down due to a border dispute with Slovenia.

Due to the need to observe loan loss provisioning in domestic compared to foreign-owned banks, the dataset of commercial banks was reduced by banks whose ownership changed from domestic to foreign, or vice versa, during the observed time span while banks that changed from one to another foreign owner or from one to another domestic owner remained in the panels. It is evident that foreign-owned banks dominate the credit markets of Southeast Europe, as in the SEE EU member states, 59 out of 88 banks are foreign owned (Table 7) and in the Western Balkans, 68 out of 85 banks are foreign owned (Table 14).

In the period after the GFC, certain commercial banks on a global level, including in Southeast Europe, went through a consolidation process initiated by the extraordinary intervention of national or international authorities. Namely, monetary authorities pledged to do "whatever it takes" to address financial instability (Brunnermeier, 2023). Although the goals were to preserve financial stability, restore confidence in the banking sector, improve its resilience, and support overall economic recovery, the consolidation of problematic banks created market shortcomings such as impacts on the rating of financial banks, distortion of competition, etc. (Fitch Ratings, 2013a, 2013b). It was only in

---

25  Data for some commercial banks were not available in Standard & Poor's Global Market Intelligence database.
26  There are several foreign-owned banks operating as subsidiaries in both entities, for example NLB bank d.d. Sarajevo in the Federation of Bosnia and Herzegovina and NLB bank a.d. Banja Luka in the Republic of Srpska.

August 2013 that the rules of the European Commission for state aid to the financial sector came into force (European Court of Auditors, 2020). The reason for introducing written rules was that it had been established that state aid gave an advantage to the beneficiary compared to the competition.

The above-mentioned processes of consolidation represent an extraordinary activity that restricts the observation of usual market behavior during the business cycles. My study, therefore, additionally analyzes the total banking sector without commercial banks that went through consolidation in the observed period.[27] For this purpose, I formed panels named *Selected commercial banks* for the SEE EU (Table 8) and for the Western Balkans (Table 15). Although 45 consolidated banks (24 in the SEE EU and 21 in the Western Balkans) seem like a large number, in fact the majority in that number are consolidated international banking groups and their subsidiaries located in most of the observed economies such as Alpha bank, Eurobank, Hypo Alpe Adria bank, NBG bank, and Piraeus bank. Therefore, analyses based on the panel *Selected commercial banks* are useful as they indicate loan loss provisioning practices that are motivated by market and macroeconomic conditions, without the direct effects of assistance by the monetary authorities.

*4.2.1.1 Variables*

The *current value of loan loss provisions* ($LLP_{i,t}$) (flow variable) is a dependent variable tested against several independent variables (Table 5). The expected signs of the coefficients of the independent variables, based on theoretical foundations, are summarized in Table 6. In my study, I use independent variables that capture the difference, as closely as possible, between the non-discretionary and discretionary components of the LLPs. Sometimes, due to the lack of a sufficient number of observations for the independent variable that best indicates a certain phenomenon, I had to use another independent variable as the second best option. Other authors encountered the same challenge in their empirical studies, which is why I explicitly mention the independent variables that I used in my empirical research and compare them with the solutions of other authors.

The *first lag value of a dependent variable* $\left(LLP_{i,t-1}\right)$ as an independent variable indicates the dynamic nature of the panel. LLPs today should have predictive power to forecast LLPs tomorrow. The "lagged values capture the speed of

---

27  Banks that went through commercially motivated mergers and acquisitions remained in the panels.

adjustment of loan loss provisions to an equilibrium level" (Laeven & Majnoni, 2003, p. 16). The coefficient needs to be below 1; if it is above 1, it signifies an unstable dynamic exploding away from equilibrium (Roodman, 2009). Other authors also use lagged values of LLP as a regressor and find its coefficient to be positive but below 1 (Bikker & Metzemakers, 2005; Bonin & Košak, 2013; Bouvatier et al., 2014; Fonseca & González, 2008).

The non-discretionary component of LLP serves to cover expected credit losses and, therefore, the ratio of non-performing loans represents a natural candidate for capturing this phenomenon, especially if backward-looking practices prevail in banks (Bouvatier & Lepetit, 2012a). However, since commercial banks do not systematically report their NPL ratios, the authors use other indicators of non-discretionary LLPs, such as business cycle variables or credit cycle variables. Therefore, the pro-cyclicality hypothesis is tested empirically using either the *real GDP growth rate* $\left(\Delta GDP_{j,t}\right)$ or the *growth rate of real GDP per capita* $\left(\Delta GDPpc_{j,t}\right)$ as an independent variable. The same macroeconomic aggregates are used by other authors; Fonseca and González (2008) and Laeven and Majnoni (2003), for example, use the annual growth rate of real GDP per capita while Bouvatier et al. (2014) and Bikker and Metzemakers (2005) use the real GDP growth rate. Similar to other authors (Bonin & Košak, 2013; Bouvatier et al., 2014; Laeven & Majnoni, 2003), I additionally use the *growth rate of net lending*[28] $\left(\Delta L_{i,t}\right)$ as an independent variable that indicates the causal relationship between LLPs and the credit cycle. Besides, the Basel Committee on Banking Supervisions (2021) recommends that lending is included when testing the pro-cyclical hypothesis in order to better understand the dynamic interaction between economic activity and lending that tends to amplify business cycle oscillations.

As suggested by the literature (Bonin & Košak, 2013; Bouvatier & Lepetit, 2012a; Bouvatier et al., 2014; Fonseca & González, 2008), only one independent variable is relevant to test the income smoothing hypothesis, namely *earnings before effects of taxes and loan loss provisions* $\left(I_{i,t}\right)$. Data on this variable are readily available, so there is no debate about the best way to capture income smoothing behavior. The positive coefficient of this variable indicates the use of LLP to reduce income volatility.

In empirical research, different bank variables are used to test the capital management hypothesis, such as equity to total assets (Anandarajan et al., 2005; Bikker & Metzemakers, 2005; Bonin & Košak, 2013; Bouvatier et al., 2014), Tier

---

28  Net lending is the result of the difference between gross lending and loan loss reserves.

2/RWA[29] (Fonseca & González, 2008), the lagged value of regulatory capital (Pérez et al., 2006), or (Tier 1+Tier 2)/RWA (Bonin & Košak, 2013; Bouvatier & Lepetit, 2012). A good variable to indicate capital management behavior would be the one that is closest to the formula for calculating the amount of capital a bank must have, as required by bank regulators. This formula is usually named the capital adequacy ratio, that is, the amount of core capital (Tier 1 + Tier 2) as a percentage of risk-weighted assets. Bearing in mind that tier 1, tier 2 capital, and RWA data are not reported systematically, the authors resort to variables that are second-best indicators. Similarly, in my study either *total equity to total assets* $\left(EQ_{i,t}\right)$ or *total equity to risk weighted assets* $\left(EQ/RWA_{i,t}\right)$ is taken as a regressor to test the capital management hypothesis. The higher the share of equity in total assets, and especially in relation to risk-weighted assets, the better the bank's solvency. According to theory, the negative coefficient of equity indicates the use of LLP for capital management.

In order to verify the signaling hypothesis, I use *income from net fees and commissions* $\left(FCI_{i,t}\right)$ and *1-year ahead change in bank earnings before effects of taxes and LLP* $\left(SIGN_{i,t}\right)$. Some empirical research takes the regressor *income from net fees and commissions* to test the signaling hypothesis (Anandarajan et al., 2005, 2007; Bouvatier et al., 2014; Leventis et al., 2012). The expected sign is positive, indicating evidence for the use of LLP to signal the strength of the bank. High income from net fees and commissions indicates the strength of a bank to sustain additional provisions from loan losses. The bank's strength comes from diversified bank activities, not only from interest-bearing products (Ozili & Outa, 2017). In some other empirical studies, the authors use the variable *1-year ahead change in bank earnings (before effects of taxes and LLP)* to indicate the signaling hypothesis (Ahmed et al., 1998; Anandarajan et al., 2007; Bouvatier & Lepetit, 2012; Kanagaretnam et al., 2004). In this case, similarly, the banks want to signal that they can sustain higher LLPs since they expect higher earnings. Given that the credit markets of the Western Balkans are dominated by subsidiaries of foreign banks, and not by banks listed on the stock exchange, the question is whether these banks have any need to signal financial strength by using LLPs.

The *ownership dummy variable* used in estimations tends to determine whether there is a difference between provisioning practices in domestic and

---

29  RWA or risk weighted assets are bank assets (bank loans and other types of exposure) that are weighted according to the connected level of the risk of default.

foreign banks. It takes the value of 1 for a domestic bank and otherwise it is zero. *Time dummy variables* have to be included to prevent correlations across banks as individuals in the idiosyncratic errors (Roodman, 2009). There are seven time dummy variables, from 2011 to 2017. The time dummy variable for 2011 takes a value of 1 if the year is 2011 and otherwise it is zero. The same rule is applied for the other time dummies.

The source for bank data is Standard & Poor's Global Market Intelligence (more precisely, bank data are taken from the unconsolidated financial statements), and the source for macroeconomic data is the World Development Indicators (The World Bank. World Development Indicators, 2019). Bank variables are standardized by total assets in order to neutralize the effect of different currencies and different bank sizes. The same type of normalization is used in most empirical literature (Anandarajan et al., 2007; Bouvatier et al., 2014; Fonseca & González, 2008).

### 4.2.1.2 Analysis of outliers

Outlying observations occur under the influence of unusual factors, making them differ radically from other observations (Maddala, 1992). An analysis of outliers helps understand unusual factors or rare events that generate unusual observations. That is why, prior to providing descriptive statistics and correlations between variables, I analyze outliers in the panel datasets. I decided to conduct the outlier analysis at the level of Selected commercial banks panels; otherwise the outlier analysis at the level of All commercial banks panels would point to banks that were consolidated under the extraordinary interventions of the monetary authorities, thus obscuring market motivations for the management of loan loss provisions.

My focus is the detection of interesting outliers, or "accurate (i.e. nonerror) data points that lie at a distance from other data points and may contain valuable or unexpected knowledge" (Aguinis, Gottfredson, & Joo, 2013, p. 276), and influential outliers, outliers that impact the estimation output. For outlier identification, I use three distance techniques (residual vs. fitted, normal q-q, and scale-location) and one influence technique (residuals vs. leverage). Technically, pairs of variables are regressed in such a way that LLP is a dependent variable in each ordinary least square (OLS) regression and independent variables are alternately (a) the growth rate of net lending, (b) earnings before LLPs and taxes, and (c) bank equity. The applied techniques are reported for the SEE EU in Figure 6 and the Western Balkans in Figure 8. The upper left graph reports residual vs. fitted, which indicates those observations that deviate significantly from the fitted model. The upper right graph represents normal q-q, which detects outlying observations based on cross-plotting the standardized residuals[30] of empirical distribution on the y-axis and the theoretical quantiles calculated based on assumed normal distribution on the x-axis. Scale location is provided in the lower left graph, it is similar to residual vs. fitted, the only difference being that the square root of standardized residuals is on the y-axis instead of the ordinary residuals. The lower right graph includes residuals vs. leverage, which indicates influential outliers, i.e. those data points that lie outside the upper and lower lines.

The main outlying observations identified in the SEE EU are TBI Bank Bulgaria in 2010, Praxia bank Greece in 2015–2017, Erste bank Romania in 2014, Idea bank Romania in 2014, Patria bank Romania in 2013, and Gorenjska bank Slovenia in 2013 (Figure 6), while main outliers in the Western Balkans are Capital bank North Macedonia in 2012, API bank Serbia in 2014, JUBMES bank Serbia in 2015 and NLB bank Serbia in 2013 (Figure 8). For each of these outlying observations, I tried to find reasons from the available sources why they appeared:

- In July 2011, *TBI bank Bulgaria* changed owners from the Slovenian NLB group to the Dutch TBI Financial services (SEENews, 2020). Based on the financial statements in Standard & Poor's database, in 2011, compared to the previous reporting year, the following items were lower: non-performing loans, loan loss provisions, net loans, and net loss while bank capital improved. This may be an example of an accounting "clean-up" motivated by a change in bank ownership.
- Following the recommendation of the Romanian central bank in 2014, *Erste bank* decided to "clean up" its balance sheets through an accelerated reduction in non-performing loans (SEENews, 2014).
- In February 2017, *Praxia bank Greece* changed owners from the French Crédit Agricole group to the investor group Atlas Merchant Capital Fund LP (Praxia bank, 2018). The accounting year 2016 was the last prepared under the ownership of the French group, and in this year a large amount of loans was written off, loan loss provisions reversed subsequently, net loans decreased substantially, as did interest income and income from fees and commission. Due to these "clean-up" activities, bank capital improved while the net loss

---

30 The standardized residual is equal to dividing an ordinary residual by an estimate of its standard deviation.

from the previous year turned into net income in 2016 (Credicom Consumer Finance Bank SA, 2017)
- At the end of 2013, *Idea bank Romania* changed owners from an American family to the Polish Getin group (Romania-Insider.com, 2013). Based on banking data from Standard & Poor's database, in 2014, compared to the previous reporting year, "clean-up" activities of the balance sheet are noticeable: loan loss provisions became significantly lower and net loans significantly higher, net loss turned into net income, and bank capital increased.
- From June 2014, the main shareholder of the *Patria bank Romania* became the Emerging Europe Accession Fund, which bought the majority share from MKB Bank Zrt Magyarska (Business Review, 2014) and changed its name from Nextebank to Patria bank. As soon as the following year, the bank's financial statements revealed a reduction in loan loss provisions, better profitability, and higher equity.
- The GFC hit Slovenian banks hard in 2013, including *Gorenjska bank*, which suffered an increase in non-performing loans, an increase in provisions for loan losses, and a decrease in equity, and so the bank's management adopted a restructuring plan (Gorenjska bank, 2013).
- Based on the limited data from the Annual Report (Capital bank, 2013), it can only be determined that in 2011 the central bank of North Macedonia ordered *Capital Bank* to improve its equity. The majority owner of the bank, Alfa Finance Holding from Bulgaria, provided a capital injection in 2013.
- In 2013, VTB Bank acquired 100 % of Moskovska bank (Market Screener, 2013) and changed its name to *API Bank Serbia*. The change in ownership was accompanied by an increase in loan loss provisions but also by an increase in equity.
- In 2015, *JUBMES bank Serbia*, a domestic bank, substantially increased its loan loss provisions while interest income and income from fees and commissions decreased. The bank finalized the reporting year 2015 with an increased net loss in comparison to the previous year while bank capital decreased by 1/3 in comparison to the previous year (MS Auditor's Report, 2016). The bank was sold in 2019.
- In 2013, *NLB bank Serbia* also recognized a higher level of non-performing loans for which a substantial amount of loan loss provisions was recorded. As a result, the bank finalized the accounting year 2013 with a net loss. In order to meet regulatory capital levels, the owner re-capitalized the bank (NLB banka AD Beograd, 2014, p. 47).

Based on the analysis of identified outlying observations, it may be concluded that significant changes in loan loss provisions occur due to:
- A change in ownership/management
- The recognition of increased loan losses on its own initiative
- The recognition of increased loan losses at the request/on the recommendation of a regulator

The first reason may be considered the discretionary part of loan loss provisions, as Healy and Wahlen also found that income smoothing follows a change in bank ownership (Healy & Wahlen, 1999). The remaining two reasons show the à posteriori practice of managing loan loss provisions, as bank managers decided to increase provisions during the period of economic recession instead of increasing them in the period preceding the economic recession. In addition, the recognition of loan loss provisions at the request of the regulator also indicates that even the refined panel of *Selected commercial banks* contains management decisions motivated by the indirect or direct recommendations of the monetary authorities. However, more extensive research is needed to better understand the motives influencing decision making on loan loss provisions. Besides, residual-based techniques are maybe not perfect for panel datasets, although they are able to indicate main outliers in a panel, as OLS estimation is susceptible to large outliers (Wooldridge, 2009).

The difference GMM estimator used in my research is sensitive to outliers (Arellano & Bond, 1991), which is why their treatment is a valid option. Since the presence of outliers in the Western Balkans is much more noticeable,[31] my decision is to estimate in parallel: (i) panel data as is, without outlier treatment, and (ii) panel data with some variables winsorized. Winsorizing diminishes the effect of outliers. It denotes the transformation of outlying values to a specified quantile: in other words, outlying values are replaced by a maximum or minimum cap. In my study, data on several variables above the 95$^{th}$ percentile were transformed to this percentile and, at the same time, data on the same variables below the 5$^{th}$ percentile were transformed to this percentile. I winsorized only four variables: loan loss provisions, bank equity, income from fees and commissions, and income before loan loss provisions and taxes. In similar empirical studies, the authors also opted for the treatment of outliers

---

[31] The greater heterogeneity of the Western Balkans panel datasets in relation to those of the SEE EU can be observed by analyzing descriptive statistics.

before estimation (Bonin & Košak, 2013; Bouvatier et al., 2014; Huizinga & Laeven, 2019; Laeven & Majnoni, 2003).

### 4.2.1.2 Descriptive statistics and correlations

Descriptive statistics are provided for the panel *All commercial banks* and for the panel *Selected commercial banks* in the SEE EU (Tables 9 and 12) and the Western Balkans (Tables 16 and 19). Comparisons of descriptive statistics are, therefore, possible within and between these two regions. Considering that I use the same variables as Bouvatier et al. (2014) do to test income smoothing, capital management, signaling, and procyclicality hypotheses in the developed part of Europe in the period covering the first wave of the GFC, a comparison is also possible with descriptive statistics from this interesting empirical study.

To follow the in-depth analysis of descriptive statistics more easily, it is good to itemize types of banks that are excluded from the groups of all commercial banks in order to obtain groups of selected banks. These are: (i) international banking groups under restructuring, with a remark that restructuring processes had a different impact on the subsidiaries compared to the parent bank; (ii) banks that had to be resolved due to their insolvency; and (iii) banks that had to take over healthy parts of resolved banks.

The higher mean values of loan loss provisions (*LLP*) in the panel *All commercial banks* compared to the panel *Selected commercial banks* in both regions (i.e. 0.014 compared to 0.012 in the SEE EU and 0.013 compared to 0.009 in the Western Balkans) indicate that, on average, the group of all commercial banks has a worse risk profile than the group of selected banks. This is because the group of all commercial banks had higher loan default rates on average and had to set aside a higher level of LLPs, which is not surprising considering that the group of all commercial banks also includes those banks that had to be consolidated.

The higher mean values of LLP in the panels of banks from the SEE EU compared to the equivalent panels of banks from the Western Balkans (i.e. 0.014 is higher than 0.013 when comparing groups of all commercial banks, and 0.012 is higher than 0.009 when comparing groups of selected banks) indicate that, on average, banks in the first region have a worse risk profile compared to banks in the second region. Indeed, by comparing the individual economies of the two regions (Figures 5 and 7), one can notice that there are three economies in the SEE EU region compared to only one economy in the Western Balkans where banks have mean values of LLP over 0.015. However, the very high standard deviation in the *All commercial banks* panel in the Western Balkans compared to the equivalent panel in the SEE EU (i.e. 0.041 is higher than 0.018) indicates that there is greater variability around the mean value of LLPs in the Western Balkans. In addition, the much wider range of maximum and minimum values of observations in the panel *All commercial banks* in the Western Balkans compared to the equivalent panel in the SEE EU indicates a more pronounced presence of outliers. Given that this affects the estimation results, as previously elaborated, I decided to treat the outliers by applying winsorization in the Western Balkans panels.

The empirical study by Bouvatier et al. (2014) reports that the mean value of LLP was 0.0032 in commercial banks in Western European countries observed from 2004 to 2009. The impact of the GFC certainly plays a role in the interpretation of the results, as they suggest that banks in Southeast Europe had, on average, a worse risk profile after the second wave of the GFC compared to banks in the developed part of Europe after the first wave of the GFC (0.014 in the SEE EU and 0.013 in the Western Balkans compared to 0.0032 in Western European countries).

Growth rates of net lending ($\Delta L$) had lower mean values in the group of all commercial banks compared to the group of selected banks in both regions (i.e. 0.02 compared to 0.045 in the SEE EU and 0.087 compared to 0.110 in the Western Balkans). This may suggest that the banks in the consolidation phase, which enter the *All commercial banks* panels, were, on average, less inclined to new lending. The same lower tendency towards new lending can also be concluded for banks in the SEE EU, which had lower mean values of the growth rate of net lending compared to the equivalent banks from the Western Balkans (i.e. 0.02 is lower than 0.087 when comparing groups of all commercial banks, and 0.045 is lower than 0.110 when comparing groups of selected banks): this is understandable given the major challenges that the Cypriot and Greek economies faced after the GFC and the sovereign debt crisis.

The variable income from fees and commissions (*FCI*) indicates that part of the bank's income that is generated on top of interest income. More precisely, it indicates a greater diversification of the bank's operations that goes beyond traditional lending. Given that, on average, the FCI was 0.008 in the group of all commercial banks and 0.009 in the group of selected banks in the SEE EU, this suggests that the latter are stronger. On the contrary, the FCI was, on average, 0.010 in the group of all commercial banks and 0.0099 in the group of selected banks in the Western Balkans, signaling the slightly greater strength of the former. In addition, as measured by the FCI variable, on average, the strength of all commercial banks in the SEE EU is lower compared to all commercial banks from the Western Balkans: 0.008 is lower than 0.009. However, the opposite holds when comparing groups of selected banks as 0.010 is higher than 0.0099. This asymmetry in the results has a similar explanation as the asymmetry in the results related to capital, as explained in the next paragraphs. On average, commercial banks in Western Europe had even greater strength, where the FCI variable was 0.0136 (Bouvatier et al., 2014).

Earnings before taxes and loan loss provisions ($I$), a variable that indicates profitability, had lower mean values in the group of all commercial banks compared to the group of selected banks in both regions (i.e. 0.011 compared to 0.012 in the SEE EU and 0.013 compared to 0.016 in the Western Balkans). This may suggest that banks in the consolidation, which enter the panel of *All commercial banks*, were less profitable on average. The same lower profitability of banks in the SEE EU can be concluded, as they had lower mean values of earnings before taxes and LLP than their peers in the Western Balkans (i.e. 0.011 is lower than 0.013 when comparing groups of all commercial banks, and 0.012 is lower than 0.016 when comparing groups of selected banks). According to the study by Bouvatier et al. (2014), the profitability of banks in the developed part of Europe was the same as in the Western Balkans and higher than in the SEE EU, as the mean value of earnings before taxes and LLPs amounted to 0.013.

When we consider the capital of banks, whether it is measured with equity to total assets ($EQ$) or equity to risk weighted assets ($EQ/RWA$), we notice that the mean values are lower in the group of all commercial banks compared to the group of selected banks in the SEE EU countries (0.011 is lower than 0.012 when it comes to EQ, and 0.123 is lower than 0.126 when it comes to EQ/RWA). This suggests that when consolidated banks are excluded from the group of all commercial banks, the remaining selected banks show, on average, a higher level of capitalization and thus higher solvency. However, the opposite phenomenon can be observed in the equivalent panels in the Western Balkans, namely, the group of all commercial banks reports, on average, higher capitalization than the group of selected banks because their mean values of EQ and EQ/RWA are higher (0.163 is higher than 0.148 when it comes to EQ, and 0.264 is higher than 0.224 when it comes to EQ/RWA). The consolidated banks primarily comprise subsidiaries of foreign-owned banks, such as Marfin Bank from Cyprus, Hypo Alpe Adria Bank from Austria, and Eurobank, NBG bank, Piraeus bank, and Alpha Bank from Greece. Their parent banks faced solvency problems in their home countries and not at the level of their subsidiaries in the host countries of the Western Balkans. Even more, to address solvency problems in their home countries, their parent banks adopted a strategy of gradually selling subsidiaries, divesting non-core assets, and exiting non-core markets (i.e. exiting the Western Balkans).

On average, the capitalization of banks in the SEE EU member states is lower compared to banks from the Western Balkans: (i) when it comes to EQ: 0.123 is lower than 0.163 when comparing groups of all commercial banks, and 0.126 is lower than 0.148 when comparing groups of selected banks; (ii) when it comes to EQ/RWA: 0.197 is lower than 0.264 when comparing groups of all commercial banks, and 0.204 is lower than 0.224 when comparing groups of selected banks. The analysis of this part of the descriptive statistics demonstrates very well how different the impact of the GFC was on the credit sectors of the SEE EU compared to the Western Balkans. It should be added that the mean value of EQ of 0.00949 (Bouvatier et al., 2014) suggests that commercial banks in Western Europe were, on average, less well capitalized than commercial banks in the SEE EU and the Western Balkans.

During the 8-year period covered by my empirical study, from 2010 to 2017, the mean values of the GDP growth rate and the GDP per capita growth rate were lower in the SEE EU compared to the Western Balkans. Based on these results, it seems that the GFC did not, on average, affect economic growth in the Western Balkans as much as it affected EU members from SEE[32].

Pairwise correlations between sets of variables indicate the direction and strength of the linear relationship between them. To determine the collinear relationship, correlation matrices are provided for the panel *All commercial banks* in both regions, in the SEE EU region (Table 10) and in the Western Balkans region (Table 17).

Although the coefficients showing pairwise correlations between variables in the SEE EU panel are not high, they nevertheless show that LLPs have a negative linear association with the credit cycle and business cycle, as well as with the level of a bank's equity, while they have a positive linear association with the level of a bank's earnings. The greater presence of outliers in the panel of all commercial banks in the Western Balkans prevents a credible interpretation of the determined correlation coefficients. However, the value of correlation matrices analysis is such that high collinearity between pairs of variables is not established.

---

32  Commercial banks in the Western Balkans were confronted with indirect effects of the GFC (Fabris, 2009) (and later the sovereign debt crisis) through various channels: (i) due to the rise in reference interest rates on the global financial market, compounded by the fact that the majority of credit exposures were denominated in euros; (ii) a psychological reaction led to some deposit withdrawals; and (iii) the situation was exacerbated as foreign banks from developed countries reduced the inflow of capital to the Western Balkans or even withdrew their subsidiaries entirely.

Unlike correlation matrices, which indicate the correlation between pairs of variables, Variance Inflation Factors measure the correlation between each individual regressor with other regressors in the model. The values of the Variance Inflation Factors calculated for the regressors in the panel *All commercial banks in the SEE EU* (Table 11) and the regressors in the Western Balkans (Table 18) are far below 10, which means that multicollinearity is not established.

### 4.2.2 Method

The basic equation to be estimated in the panel form:

$$\begin{aligned} LLP_{i,t} = &\beta_0 + \beta_1 LLP_{i,t-1} + \beta_2 \Delta L_{i,t} + \beta_3 FCI_{i,t} + \beta_4 I_{i,t} \\ &+ \beta_5 EQ_{i,t} + \beta_6 \Delta GDP_{j,t} + \beta_7 FCI_{i,t} * D_{i,t} + \beta_8 I_{i,t} * D_{i,t} \\ &+ \beta_9 EQ_{i,t} * D_{i,t} + \beta_{10} \Delta GDP_{j,t} * D_{i,t} + T_t + \epsilon_{i,t} \end{aligned} \quad (1)$$

$$\epsilon_{i,t} = a_i + u_{i,t} \quad (2)$$

where:

| | |
|---|---|
| $LLP_{i,t}, LLP_{i,t-1}, \Delta L_{i,t},\ldots$ | Denotes variables explained in Table 5 |
| $i = 1,\ldots,N$ | Number of cross sections in the panel |
| $t = 1,\ldots,T$ | Number of time periods in the panel |
| $\beta_0$ | Constant |
| $\beta_1, \beta_2,\ldots,\beta_{10}$ | Coefficients of independent variables |
| $D_{i,t}$ | Ownership dummy variable that takes value of 1 if ownership is domestic, otherwise it is zero. |
| $T_t$ | Time dummy variable. There are seven time dummy variables, from 2011 to 2017. The time dummy for 2011 takes a value of 1 if the year is 2011, otherwise it is zero, and so on. |
| $\epsilon_{i,t}$ | Error term that is equal to the sum of $(a_i)$ unobserved individual fixed effects and $(u_{i,t})$ unobserved idiosyncratic part of the error term, as in equation (2). |

In a generalized way, for the purpose of clarifying the steps in the estimation, the equations (1) and (2) may take a simplified form, i.e. one that excludes exogenous and dummy variables:

$$Y_{i,t} = \beta_0 + \beta_1 Y_{i,t-1} + a_i + u_{i,t} \qquad (3)$$

where:

$Y_{i,t}$    Denotes dependent variable

Equation (3) represents a *dynamic panel* whose characteristic is that a lagged value of a dependent variable, which acts as an independent variable, is correlated with the unobserved individual fixed effects (Baltagi, 2005). This variable is called an endogenous variable; having an endogenous independent variable in a dynamic panel model violates the basic orthogonality assumption in OLS estimation:[33] "The problem with dynamic panels is that the traditional OLS estimators are biased and therefore different methods of estimation need to be introduced" (Asteriou & Hall, 2016, p. 458). Nickell clarifies that estimation bias depends negatively on the time dimension: the larger (smaller) the time dimension in a panel data, the lower (higher) the OLS estimation bias (Nickell, 1981). Normally, OLS estimation should be used in macro panels and instrumental variable estimation in micro panels.[34] In the dynamic micro panel, the instrumental variable type of estimator called the Generalized Methods of Moments (GMM) is considered to be the most appropriate (Judson & Owen, 1999; Kiviet & Bun, 2006).

As the panels in my empirical study have the number of observed commercial banks ($N$) greater than the number of observed years ($T$), these panels are considered to be *dynamic micro panels* ($N>T$), where a lagged value of loan loss provisions $\left(LLP_{i,t-1}\right)$ acts as an independent variable. In similar empirical studies involving dynamic micro panels, the authors used either the difference GMM (Bonin & Košak, 2013; Fonseca & González, 2008) or the system GMM

---

33    The main orthogonality assumption for OLS estimation is that none of the (exogenous) independent variables is correlated with the error term (Wooldridge, 2002, p. 56).
34    Micro panels have a large number of cross-sections and a short time dimension ($N>T$) while macro panels have a large time dimension in comparison to the number of cross-sections ($T>N$).

estimator (Bouvatier & Lepetit, 2012a; Bouvatier et al., 2014). The difference GMM estimator uses the levels of dependent variables as instruments while the system GMM estimator uses the transformed (differenced) dependent variables as instruments. The basic estimator in my empirical study is the two-step difference GMM. To perform robustness checks, the two-step system GMM and the pooled OLS estimator are additionally used.

*4.2.2.1 The two-step difference GMM estimation*

The GMM estimation of equation (3) starts by first differencing:

$$(Y_{i,t} - Y_{i,t-1}) = (\beta_0 - \beta_0) + \beta_1(Y_{i,t-1} - Y_{i,t-2}) + (a_i - a_i) + (u_{i,t} - u_{i,t-1}) \quad (4)$$

As a result of first differencing, (i) the unobservable individual fixed effects are removed; (ii) the constant is removed; (iii) the valid instruments for estimating $\beta_1$, *lagged values of dependent variable,* are obtained; but (iv) the endogeneity problem remains because $u_{i,t-1}$ is part of $Y_{i,t-1}$.

Equation (1) can be also written in the general form of a matrix without constant and dummy variables for the simplicity of explaining the assumptions of the GMM estimator:

$$Y_{i,t} = \beta X_{i,t} + \epsilon_{i,t} \quad (5)$$

where:

$Y_{i,t}$      Denotes the 1x$G$ vector of dependent variables ($G$ is a number of time periods)

$X_{i,t}$      Denotes the $G$x$K$ matrix of regressors, including exogenous and endogenous variables ($K$ is a number of independent variables)

$\epsilon_{i,t}$      Denotes the 1x$G$ vector of error terms

The first necessary condition for identification in the GMM estimation of equation (5) is an *orthogonality condition*, which means that instruments are uncorrelated with the error terms (Wooldridge, 2002):

$$E[Z'\epsilon] = 0 \quad (6)$$

where:

E         Denotes expectation operator
Z         Represents the matrix of instrumental variables

More precisely, in the case of the first difference GMM, instruments are uncorrelated with the idiosyncratic part of the error term, which is also a moment condition (Roodman, 2009):

$$E[Z'\Delta u] = 0 \qquad (7)$$

The second necessary condition for identification is a rank condition: a matrix $(Z'X)$ should have a full column rank, where K signifies the number of columns, i.e. the number of independent variables (Wooldridge, 2002):

$$\operatorname{rank} E(Z'\Delta X) = K \qquad (8)$$

$E(Z_i' \Delta X_i)$ is an $LxK$ matrix so prior to rank condition, *order condition* must be fulfilled: there should be at least as many instruments as independent variables, $L \geq K$ (where $L$ is the number of instrumental variables). If $t = 3$, for example, then equation (4) takes the form:

$$(Y_{i,3} - Y_{i,2}) = \beta_1 (Y_{i,2} - Y_{i,1}) + (u_{i,3} - u_{i,2}) \qquad (9)$$

where $Y_{i,1}$ is the valid instrument for $(Y_{i,2} - Y_{i,1})$. Therefore, if $t = 3$, there is one valid instrument. If $t = 4$, there are two valid instruments for $(Y_{i,3} - Y_{i,2})$, namely $Y_{i,1}$ and $Y_{i,2}$, and so on. There is a system of equations, one equation for each period $t$ along with its own instruments. By increasing the time dimension, the number of instruments increases while the matrix of instruments $Z$ takes the following form:

$$Z = \begin{bmatrix} Y_{i,1} & & & & & & \cdots \\ & Y_{i,1} & Y_{i,2} & & & & \cdots \\ & & & Y_{i,1} & Y_{i,2} & Y_{i,3} & \cdots \\ \cdots & \cdots & \cdots & \cdots & \cdots & \cdots & \cdots \end{bmatrix}$$

In $t=3$, $Y_{i,1}$ as an instrument is highly correlated with $(Y_{i,2} - Y_{i,1})$ and not correlated with the future error terms $(u_{i,3} - u_{i,2})$. There are $K = T-2$ number of independent variables represented by the differenced lagged values of the dependent variables. At the same time, there are $L = \frac{1}{2}(T-1)(T-2)$ number of instruments represented by the lagged values of the dependent variables. If $t=3$, then $K=L=1$, the model is just-identified, and the equation has a unique solution. However, for any $t > 3$, $L$ is higher than $K$, the model is over-identified. In any situation in which $L > K$ the estimation is more complicated, as there are more columns in the matrix $Z$ than necessary for a unique solution.

Third, the estimated *weighting matrix* converges in probability to an optimal weighting matrix as N increases (Wooldridge, 2002):

$$\widehat{W} \xrightarrow{p} W \text{ as } N \to \infty$$

$W$ is a positive, symmetric $LxL$ matrix. This is why the GMM estimation requires panel data where N>T. The GMM estimator is *consistent* because under the above three assumptions, the vector of estimated coefficients $\hat{\beta}$ converges in probability to its true value as N increases; $\hat{\beta}$ is asymptotically normally distributed (Wooldridge, 2002).

The fourth assumption states that *instruments are weighted in inverse proportion to their variances and covariances* (Roodman, 2009; Wooldridge, 2002). In matrix $W$ moments with larger variance are weighted less and moments with smaller variance are weighted more:

$$W = \Omega^{-1} \qquad (10)$$

Before estimating $\hat{\beta}$, the variance-covariance matrix $\Omega$ needs to be estimated. It is done in two steps within the difference GMM estimator (Arellano & Bond, 1991). In the first step, based on an arbitrary variance-covariance matrix, the suboptimal weighting matrix $H$ is created and then used to estimate the $\hat{\beta}_1$ vector of coefficients. The minimizing problem is resolved by differentiating the function with respect to $b$ and then solving the first-order conditions.

$$\min_b \left[\sum_{i=1}^{N}(Z'(\Delta Y - \Delta Xb))\right]' H \left[\sum_{i=1}^{N}(Z'(\Delta Y - \Delta Xb))\right]$$

The solution for the vector of sample coefficients $\hat{\beta}_1$ is given by the equation:

$$\hat{\beta}_1 = \left(\Delta X' Z H Z' \Delta X\right)^{-1} \left(\Delta X' Z H Z' \Delta Y\right) \quad (11)$$

In the second step, the residuals obtained from the previous estimation are used to construct the variance-covariance matrix $\widehat{\Omega}$. Its inverse value is the optimal weighting matrix $\widehat{W}$, which is then used to calculate a unique solution for the vector of sample coefficients $\hat{\beta}_2$:

$$\hat{\beta}_2 = \left(\Delta X' Z \widehat{W} Z' \Delta X\right)^{-1} \left(\Delta X' Z \widehat{W} Z' \Delta Y\right) \quad (12)$$

The two-step difference GMM estimator is an efficient GMM estimator, robust to heteroscedasticity and serial correlation in the error terms. However, when the sample is small and the number of instruments is large, the original two-step GMM estimator used to produce standard errors that are downward biased. Nowadays all the statistical software packages include the corrected Windmeijer formula for calculating the variance of $\hat{\beta}_2$ (Windmeijer, 2005).

The diagnostic check of estimations comprises:

- The *Hansen specification test* (Hansen, 1982) that verifies the validity of the instruments used. Failure to reject the null hypothesis gives support to the choice of instruments.
- The *Arellano-Bond test* (Arellano & Bond, 1991) that verifies the null hypothesis of no first or second order autocorrelation of the error term (the idiosyncratic part of the error term, to be precise). Failure to reject the null hypothesis of no *second* order autocorrelation implies that the error term is not serially correlated and the moment conditions are correctly specified. The

Arellano-Bond test requires that time dummies are included in the regression as they prevent the contemporaneous cross individual correlation of the idiosyncratic part of the error term (Roodman, 2009, p. 121).

All models are tested and estimated in Stata. When using the two-step difference GMM and the two-step system GMM estimator, all available LLP lag values from lag 2 onwards were considered as instruments. Other independent variables were considered as strictly exogenous.

## 4.3 Results

The estimation results are presented separately for commercial banks located in the SEE EU (Table 13) and for those located in the Western Balkans (Table 20). The interpretation of the estimation results is provided first for each region individually, then through a comparison of the two observed regions, as well as through a comparison of the two regions observed in my study with other regions that were observed in similar empirical studies. Both tables (Tables 13 and 20) present the results of seven different estimations: the first four estimations refer to the panels *All commercial banks*, and the last three estimations refer to the panels *Selected commercial banks* (i.e. panels that omit banks included in the consolidation processes ordered by the monetary authorities). In the lower section of both tables, in addition to basic information about the number of observations and the presence of time dummy variables, the results of diagnostic checks are included: the number of instruments, the number of groups, the Hansen specification test, the Arellano-Bond test of the first and second order autocorrelation of the error term, F-statistics, and the coefficient of determination.

### 4.3.1 Within regions

The panel dataset *All commercial banks* in the **SEE EU region** was estimated with four regressions, of which the two-step difference GMM estimator was applied in the first three regressions and the two-step system GMM estimator in the fourth regression (Table 13). The first and fourth regressions refer to the basic equation (1); only the type of estimator is different. In the second and third regressions, compared to the basic regression, some independent variables were replaced in order to additionally check the robustness of the estimation results. Thus, for example, in the second regression compared to the basic regression, the *FCI* variable was replaced by the *SIGN* variable, the *EQ* variable was replaced by the *EQ/RWA* variable, and the *ΔGDP* variable was replaced by the *ΔGDPpc* variable, with a change in the corresponding interaction terms. In the third regression compared to the basic regression, the *EQ* variable was replaced by the *EQ/RWA* variable, and the *ΔGDP* variable was replaced by the *ΔGDPpc* variable, with a change in the corresponding interaction terms.

Findings from all four regressions show that:

- A one unit increase in past LLPs is associated with a unit increase of around 0.3 in the current value of LLPs, ceteris paribus. Statistical significance of 1 % in all four regressions indicates that this positive relationship is robust.
- A one unit increase in the growth rate of net lending is associated with a unit decrease of around 0.014 in LLPs, ceteris paribus. Statistical significance of 1 % in all four regressions indicates that this negative relationship is robust, also suggesting that the group of all commercial banks in the SEE EU tends to provision less during credit expansion and, conversely, tends to provision more during credit contraction.
- A one unit increase in the bank's equity is associated with a decrease in LLPs (with decreases in LLP ranging from 0.03 to 0.1), ceteris paribus. The statistical significance of 1 % in all four regressions indicates that this negative relationship is robust, which also suggests that the group of all commercial banks in the SEE EU tends to reduce LLPs to influence the increase in their regulatory capital.

There are also several findings that are weakly robust:

- In two out of the four regressions, there is weakly robust evidence that domestic banks are more inclined to signal their strength and to manage their capital using LLPs.
- In one out of the four regressions, there is weakly robust evidence that banks tend to smooth their income using LLPs.

The above-mentioned findings were determined in the group of all commercial banks, which is influenced by those banks that, due to financial instability, had to enter the consolidation process at the request of the monetary authorities. When such banks are excluded from the panel dataset, a new panel *Selected commercial banks* is obtained. I performed three different regressions in the panel *Selected commercial banks* from the SEE EU: the fifth regression refers to the basic equation (1) and uses the two-step difference GMM estimator; in the sixth regression compared to the basic regression, *EQ/RWA* was taken instead of *EQ* with a change in the corresponding interaction term and using the two-step system GMM estimator; finally, in the seventh regression compared to the basic regression *EQ/RWA* was taken instead of *EQ* and *ΔGDPpc* instead of *ΔGDP* with a change in the corresponding interaction terms and using the pooled OLS estimator.

Findings from all three regressions show that:

- A one unit increase in past LLPs is associated with a unit increase of around 0.2 in the current value of LLPs, ceteris paribus. As before, statistical significance of 1 % in all three regressions indicates that this positive relationship is robust. However, the value of the coefficients is lower than before, indicating that LLPs in the panel *Selected commercial banks* are less persistent over time.
- As before, a one unit increase in the growth rate of net lending is associated with a 0.011 unit decrease in LLPs, ceteris paribus. Statistical significance of 1 % in all regressions indicates that this negative relationship is robust, also suggesting that even the group of selected commercial banks in the SEE EU tends to provision less during credit expansion and, conversely, tends to provision more during credit contraction. Moreover, a one unit increase in the growth rate of GDP or growth rate of GDP per capita is associated with a 0.0009 unit decrease in LLPs, ceteris paribus. Statistical significance of 1 % in all regressions indicates that this negative relationship is robust, also suggesting that in the group of selected commercial banks in the SEE EU, loan loss provisioning is pro-cyclical as banks tend to provision less during economic expansion and, conversely, tend to provision more during economic recession.
- A one unit increase in earnings is associated with a 0.2 unit increase in LLPs, ceteris paribus. As the statistical significance of 1 % in all regressions demonstrates that this positive relationship is robust, the empirical study suggests that the group of selected banks in the SEE EU practices income smoothing. Banks tend to use LLPs to reduce the volatility of earnings (by lowering LLPs, for example, banks increase their earnings, and, thus, also to some extent, reduce the pro-cyclicality of LLPs).
- In the group of selected banks, the estimates do not indicate the robustness of the use of LLPs to manage the level of regulatory capital. This demonstrates how strong the influence of consolidated banks is because when they are removed from the panel, the remaining selected banks are clearly more solvent. Indeed, data from the descriptive statistics also show a higher level of capitalization in the group of selected banks.

Additionally, as before, there is weak evidence that domestic banks in the group of selected banks are more inclined to signal their strength using LLPs.

Finally, it should be mentioned that the constant term is statistically significant in all relevant estimations and in both panels in the SEE EU region. This suggests that even when there is no influence of independent variables, there is always a certain level of LLPs as a share of total assets ranging from 1.5 % in the group of all commercial banks to 1.3 % in the group of selected banks.

Carrying out regressions in the panel *All commercial banks* in the **Western Balkans region** was more demanding due to the stronger effect of outliers (Table 20). For example, the first regression, which was performed following the basic equation (1) and using the two-step difference GMM estimator, outputs an illogical finding suggesting the absence of any influence of past LLPs on their current level. For this reason, I decided to continue conducting regressions on this panel with winsorized data. Therefore, the second regression refers to the basic equation (1) as well, only that the panel *All commercial banks* with winsorized data is used.

Model specification is the same in the third and fourth regressions, only that in the third regression the two-step difference GMM estimator is used, while in the fourth regression the two-step system GMM estimator is used on the panel *All commercial banks* with winsorized data. Compared to the basic regression, the model in the third and fourth regressions takes *EQ/RWA* instead of *EQ*, and $\Delta GDPpc$ instead of $\Delta GDP$ with a change in the corresponding interaction terms.

In the interpretation of the findings, I refer only to the regressions performed on the panel with winsorized data.

- The finding that is the same in all three regressions is that past values of LLPs affect their current values, with a one unit increase in the past LLPs being associated with an increase of around 0.4 in the current value of LLPs in the group of all commercial banks in the Western Balkans, ceteris paribus. Statistical significance of 1 % in all three regressions indicates that this positive relationship is robust.

There are also several findings that are considered to be weakly robust due to the fact that the coefficients are statistically significant in one or two out of the three regressions:

- A one unit increase in earnings is associated with a 0.2 unit increase in LLPs, ceteris paribus. Statistical significance of 5 % was only found in the regression using the two-step system GMM estimator. The identification of income smoothing obviously depends on the type of estimator.
- A one unit increase in equity is associated with a 0.08 unit decrease in LLPs, ceteris paribus. Statistical significance of 10 % was only found in the second regression. More interestingly, other findings suggest that domestic banks in the Western Balkans are more inclined to manage their capital by

using LLPs, with all regressions that take EQ/RWA producing estimates that are statistically significant at the 5 % level. It should be reiterated that EQ/RWA as a variable better represents capital management practice more accurately.

The next part of the interpretations refers to the panel *Selected commercial banks*, which was obtained when the banks that were in consolidation at the request of the monetary authorities were excluded from the group of all commercial banks in the Western Balkans. When interpreting the findings, it should be kept in mind that the excluded consolidated banks in the Western Balkans mostly include subsidiaries of foreign banks whose parent banks were faced with solvency problems in their home countries. Although some of these subsidiaries in the Western Balkans did not necessarily have problems with solvency, the consolidation of their parent banks also affected their operations.[35]

I performed three different regressions in the panel *Selected commercial banks* from the Western Balkans: the fifth and seventh regressions compared to the basic regression take $\Delta GDPpc$ instead of $\Delta GDP$ with a change in the corresponding interaction terms, only that in the fifth regression the two-step difference GMM estimator is used, while in the seventh regression the pooled OLS estimator is used on the panel *Selected commercial banks* with winsorized data. Finally, the sixth regression compared to the basic regression takes $EQ/RWA$ instead of $EQ$ with a change in the corresponding interaction term and uses the two-step system GMM estimator on the panel *Selected commercial banks* with winsorized data. The robust findings are:

- A one unit increase in past LLPs is associated with a unit increase of around 0.5 in the current value of LLPs, ceteris paribus. As before, statistical significance of 1 % in all regressions indicates that this positive relationship is robust. However, the value of the coefficients is higher, indicating that LLPs in the panel *Selected commercial banks* are more persistent over time compared to the group of all commercial banks in the Western Balkans.
- Selected banks in the Western Balkans tend to use LLPs for regulatory capital management. Statistical significance of 1 % and 5 % in the regressions indicate that this negative relationship is robust. This finding demonstrates how strong the influence of consolidated banks is because when they are removed from the panel, the remaining selected banks are clearly less solvent. Indeed, data

---

35 Most of these subsidiaries now have new owners as they were divested in the process of consolidation of their parent banks.

from the descriptive statistics show a lower level of capitalization in the group of selected banks compared to the group of all commercial banks in the Western Balkans.

Other findings, although weakly robust, should be noted:

- In two out of the three regressions, the findings suggest that selected banks in the Western Balkans tend to use LLPs for income smoothing. In fact, the findings additionally suggest that domestically owned banks are more inclined to carry out this practice.
- In two regressions, the findings suggest that selected banks in the Western Balkans tend to provision more during periods of decreases in GDP per capita growth rates and vice versa, indicating that loan loss provisioning is pro-cyclical with respect to living standards. One regression additionally finds that the tendency to provision more during economic downturn is more pronounced in domestic banks.

Finally, the constant term is statistically significant at 1 % level in all relevant estimations in both panels of the Western Balkans. This suggests that there is always a certain level of LLPs as a share of total assets ranging from 1.5 % in the group of all commercial banks to 0.6 % in the group of selected banks.

### 4.3.2 Between regions

With regard to each hypothesis, I analyze and compare findings from three different sources. First, the empirical study by Bouvatier et al. (2014) provides insights into loan loss provisioning in the Western Europe during the period 2004–2009. More precisely, the study covers 873 commercial banks from countries: Austria, Belgium, Denmark, Finland, France, Germany, Greece, Ireland, Italy, Luxembourg, Netherlands, Norway, Portugal, Spain, Sweden, Switzerland, and the UK. Second, the empirical study by Bonin and Košak (2013) provides insights into loan loss provisioning in emerging Europe during the period 1997–2010. More precisely, this study covers 318 banks from 11 countries that joined the EU at a later stage: Bulgaria, Czech Republic, Croatia, Estonia, Hungary, Latvia, Lithuania, Poland, Romania, Slovakia, and Slovenia. Third, my empirical study provides insights into loan loss provisioning in the EU periphery and the Western Balkans during the period 2010–2017. More precisely, my study covers 88 commercial banks from the SEE EU region (Bulgaria, Croatia, Greece, Cyprus, Romania, and Slovenia) and 85 commercial banks from the Western Balkans (Albania, Bosnia and Herzegovina, Montenegro, North Macedonia, Serbia, and Kosovo*).

In short, the first two empirical studies can be considered to indicate the behavior of banks from Western and Eastern Europe in the first wave of the GFC, while my study indicates the behavior of banks from the EU periphery and the Western Balkans covering the second wave of the GFC.

*(i) Capital management*

The findings suggest that banks in Eastern Europe (Bonin & Košak, 2013), the SEE EU region, and the Western Balkans tend to use LLPs to manage their capital. Specifically, robust capital management is evident in both all commercial banks in the SEE EU and in selected banks in the Western Balkans. Notably, these bank groups also exhibit lower average capitalization.[36] Bouvatier et al. (2014) write: "banks with low regulatory capital could be more inclined to make loan loss provisions to keep their capital ratio adequate", which seems to be evidenced by my study. In addition, my study has a weakly robust finding that domestic banks (in groups of all commercial banks in both regions) tend to manage capital more than foreign banks. The findings related to the capital management hypothesis in my empirical study demonstrate very well how the impact of the GFC and sovereign debt crisis differed for banks in Southeast Europe. On the one hand, international banking groups were more vulnerable during the crises in their home countries, but on the other hand their subsidiaries contributed to financial stability in the Western Balkans. However, due to the consolidation processes of and subsequent abandonment of the credit markets of the Western Balkans, the question arises as to what impact this will have on financial stability in the Western Balkans in the future.

*(ii) Income smoothing*

The findings of all three studies indicate that banks use LLPs to influence the reduction in the volatility of earnings. The only difference is that the findings on income smoothing in the compared studies are robust, while in my study it is robust only for one group of banks (the group of selected banks in the SEE EU) and weakly robust for the others. Since my empirical study takes the same variable as the study by Bouvatier et al. (2014),[37] the findings on income

---

36 Descriptive statistics from my study reveal lower capitalization levels among all commercial banks in the SEE EU and, similarly, lower capitalization levels among the selected banks in the Western Balkans.

37 This variable is earnings before taxes and loan loss provisions as a percentage of total assets.

smoothing from these two studies can be compared even more closely: A one unit increase in earnings is associated with a 0.06 unit increase in loan loss provisions in Western Europe (Bouvatier et al., 2014) and a 0.2 unit increase in loan loss provisions in the group of selected banks in the SEE EU, ceteris paribus. This indicates that banks in Western Europe are less inclined to practice income smoothing using loan loss provisions. As banks in Western Europe have a higher level of profitability on average,[38] this additionally suggests that banks with more profitability could be less inclined to reduce the volatility of their earnings using loan loss provisions. In addition, my study has a weakly robust finding that domestic banks in the group of selected banks from the Western Balkans seemed to be more engaged in income smoothing using loan loss provisions.

*(iii) Signaling*

My empirical study provides a weakly robust finding that domestic banks in the SEE EU are more prone to signal their strength to sustain potentially higher loan loss provisions. A one unit increase in income from fees and commissions is associated with a 1.4 unit increase in LLPs in domestic banks from the group of all commercial SEE EU banks and it is associated with a 1.19 unit increase in LLPs in domestic banks from the group of selected SEE EU banks, ceteris paribus. Since the mentioned domestic banks are also those banks that have a lower level of strength as measured by the mean value of the FCI variable,[39] this finding from my study is consistent with the finding from an empirical study by Leventis, Dimitropoulos, and Anandarajan (2012) that distressed banks have a greater tendency to signal their strength in comparison to healthier banks. It should be noted that banks' strength signaling does not appear in any other region, neither in the Western Balkans nor in Western Europe (Bouvatier et al., 2014).

---

38   The results of the descriptive statistics indicate that, on average, the level of profitability is lower in the group of selected banks in the SEE EU, compared to banks in Western Europe.
39   The mean value of FCI in *domestic* banks in the group of all commercial SEE EU banks as well as in the group of selected SEE EU banks is the same and amounts to 0.002 (data available upon request). This is lower than the mean value of FCI in the group of all commercial SEE EU banks (0.008) and lower than the mean value of FCI in the group of selected SEE EU banks (0.009).

## *(iv) Pro-cyclicality*

The findings suggest that banks in Western Europe (Bouvatier et al., 2014) as well as the group of selected banks in the SEE EU tend to provision more during both economic and credit contractions. Another robust finding from my study suggests that group of all commercial banks in the SEE EU tend to increase their LLPs during episodes of credit contraction. In contrast, empirical studies indicate that banks in Eastern Europe (Bonin & Košak, 2013) and selected banks in the Western Balkans tend to increase provisions based on economic rather than credit contraction. More precisely, banks in Eastern Europe provision more during economic downturns (Bonin & Košak, 2013), while a group of selected banks in the Western Balkans (from my study) provision more when living standards decline. There is also one weakly robust finding in my study, according to which domestic banks in the group of selected banks from the Western Balkans tend to provision more during episodes of economic downturn. This also adds to the impression that banks from the Western Balkans refer more to the economic than to the credit cycle when deciding on provisions for loan losses.

## *(v) Additional findings*

Although they go beyond the analyzed hypotheses, a few noteworthy findings from my study refer to the dynamics and level of LLPs. By comparing the coefficients of the first lag value of LLP, it can be seen not only that the finding about the influence of past values of LLP on their current values is robust with high statistical significance but also that it is most pronounced in the Western Balkans. LLPs are, therefore, more persistent over time in commercial banks in the Western Balkans in comparison to banks in the SEE EU, Eastern Europe (Bonin & Košak, 2013), and Western Europe (Bonin & Košak, 2013).

By comparing the constants through different regressions in my study, it can be evidenced that they are robust and highly statistically significant, demonstrating that, regardless of the effect of independent variables, there is always a certain level of LLPs in banks, which is somewhat higher in groups of all commercial banks than in groups of selected banks in both the SEE EU and the Western Balkans. Indeed, in the descriptive statistics, it was also evident that, on average, the groups of all commercial banks had a worse risk profile than the groups of selected banks, and that this is most likely because the consolidated banks had higher loan default rates and had to set aside larger LLPs.

Finally, it seems that the discretionary component of regulatory capital management stands out as the dominant component of LLPs in the group of *all* commercial banks in both the SEE EU and the Western Balkans. In the group of selected banks, i.e. those that function according to market principles without much state intervention, the non-discretionary component of LLPs and income smoothing as its discretionary component stand out as dominant.

Interesting findings follow in the second study of my research, which provides further insights into the differences in the macroeconomic aspects of LLPs in the SEE EU compared to the Western Balkans.

Table 5. Dependent and independent variables

| Symbol | Description |
| --- | --- |
| $LLP_{i,t}$ | Loan loss provisions to total assets in bank $i$ and year $t$ |
| $LLP_{i,t-1}$ | Loan loss provisions to total assets in bank $i$ and year $t-1$ |
| $\Delta L_{i,t}$ | Growth rate of net loans in bank $i$ and year $t$ |
| $FCI_{i,t}$ | Income from net fees & commissions to total assets in bank $i$ and year $t$ |
| $SIGN_{i,t}$ | 1-year ahead change in earnings before taxes and LLP in bank $i$ and year $t$ |
| $I_{i,t}$ | Income before taxes and LLP to total assets in bank $i$ and year $t$ |
| $EQ_{i,t}$ | Total equity to total assets in bank $i$ and year $t$ |
| $\Delta GDP_{j,t}$ | Real GDP growth rate in country $j$ and year $t$ |
| $EQ/RWA_{i,t}$ | Ratio of total equity to risk weighted assets in bank $i$ and year $t$ |
| $\Delta GDPpc_{j,t}$ | GDP per capita growth rate in country $j$ and year $t$ |

Note: Standard & Poor's Global Market Intelligence for bank data and the World Development Indicators (2019) for macroeconomic data.

Table 6. Expected sign of independent variables

| Independent variable | Expected sign of coefficient | Confirmed hypothesis | |
|---|---|---|---|
| $LLP_{i,t-1}$ | Positive, but less than 1 | Dynamic nature of LLP | |
| $\Delta GDP_{j,t}$ | Negative | Pro-cyclicality of LLP with respect to business cycle | Indicators of the non-discretionary component |
| $\Delta GDPpc_{j,t}$ | | | |
| $\Delta L_{i,t}$ | Negative | Pro-cyclicality of LLP with respect to credit cycle | |
| $FCI_{i,t}$ | Positive | Signaling | |
| $SIGN_{i,t}$ | | | Indicators of the discretionary component |
| $I_{i,t}$ | Positive | Income smoothing | |
| $EQ_{i,t}$ | Negative | Capital management | |
| $EQ/RWA_{i,t}$ | | | |

Table 7. SEE EU: Panel All commercial banks

| Country | Total banks | S&P[a] database | Domestic banks | Foreign banks | Ownership change[b] | Panel All commercial banks |
|---|---|---|---|---|---|---|
| | (A) | (B) | (D) | (E) | (F) | (B)-(F) |
| Bulgaria | 22 | 21 | 7 | 13 | 1 | 20 |
| Croatia | 24 | 22 | 8 | 12 | 2 | 20 |
| Cyprus | 11 | 10 | 1 | 8 | 1 | 9 |
| Greece | 7 | 7 | 5 | 1 | 1 | 6 |
| Romania | 27 | 23 | 3 | 19 | 1 | 22 |
| Slovenia | 12 | 12 | 5 | 6 | 1 | 11 |
| Total | 103 | 95 | 29 | 59 | 7 | 88 |

[a] Standard & Poor's Global Market Intelligence.
[b] Banks that changed ownership from domestic to foreign, or vice versa.

Table 8. SEE EU: Panel Selected commercial banks

| Country | Total banks | S&P database | Consolidation[a] | Domestic banks | Foreign banks | Ownership change | Panel Selected commercial banks |
|---|---|---|---|---|---|---|---|
| | (A) | (B) | (C) | (D) | (E) | (F) | (B)-(C)-(F) |
| Bulgaria | 22 | 21 | 3 | 7 | 10 | 1 | 17 |
| Croatia | 24 | 22 | 3 | 7 | 10 | 2 | 17 |
| Cyprus | 11 | 10 | 4 | 1 | 5 | | 6 |
| Greece | 7 | 7 | 5 | 1 | 1 | | 2 |
| Romania | 27 | 23 | 5 | 3 | 14 | 1 | 17 |
| Slovenia | 12 | 12 | 4 | 3 | 5 | | 8 |
| Total | 103 | 95 | 24 | 22 | 45 | 4 | 67 |

[a] Banks that went through a consolidation process initiated by the intervention of national or international authorities

Table 9. SEE EU: Panel All commercial banks. Summary statistics

| | N | Mean | SD | Median | Min | Max |
|---|---|---|---|---|---|---|
| $LLP_{i,t}$ | 656 | .014 | 0.018 | .010 | -.112 | .171 |
| $\Delta L_{i,t}$ | 568 | .02 | 0.246 | -.005 | -.669 | 3.918 |
| $FCI_{i,t}$ | 656 | .008 | 0.005 | .008 | -.001 | .038 |
| $SIGN_{i,t}$ | 568 | -.001 | 0.019 | .000 | -.140 | .106 |
| $I_{i,t}$ | 656 | .011 | 0.021 | .012 | -.250 | .085 |
| $EQ_{i,t}$ | 656 | .123 | 0.076 | .113 | -.162 | .904 |
| $EQ/RWA_{i,t}$ | 635 | .197 | 0.122 | .179 | -.201 | 1.614 |
| $\Delta GDP_{j,t}$ | 704 | 1.259 | 3.073 | 1.733 | -10.149 | 8.197 |
| $\Delta GDPpc_{j,t}$ | 704 | 1.584 | 3.203 | 2.173 | -10.016 | 8.824 |

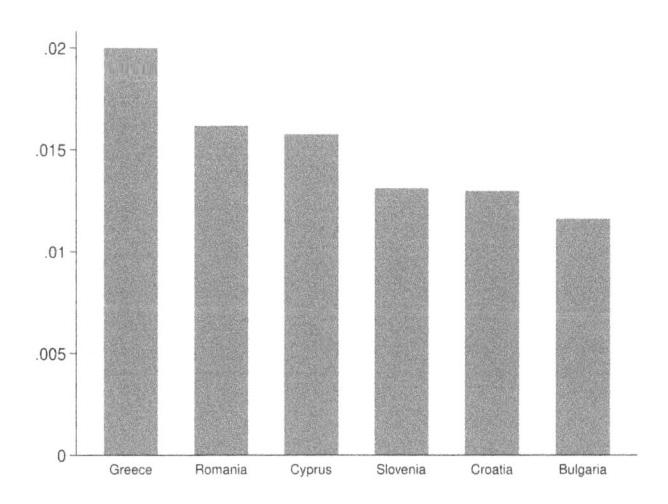

Non-discretionary and discretionary components 91

**Figure 5.** SEE EU: Panel All commercial banks. Average LLPs

**Table 10.** SEE EU: Panel All commercial banks. Correlation matrix

|  | $LLP_{i,t}$ | $\Delta L_{i,t}$ | $FCI_{i,t}$ | $I_{i,t}$ | $EQ_{i,t}$ | $\Delta GDP_{j,t}$ |
|---|---|---|---|---|---|---|
| $LLP_{i,t}$ | 1 | | | | | |
| $\Delta L_{i,t}$ | -0.171*** | 1 | | | | |
| $FCI_{i,t}$ | -0.032 | 0.048 | 1 | | | |
| $I_{i,t}$ | 0.151*** | 0.214*** | 0.282*** | 1 | | |
| $EQ_{i,t}$ | -0.272*** | -0.123** | 0.113** | -0.245*** | 1 | |
| $\Delta GDP_{j,t}$ | -0.190*** | 0.091* | 0.132** | 0.182*** | 0.038 | 1 |

* $p < 0.05$, ** $p < 0.01$, *** $p < 0.001$.

**Table 11.** SEE EU: Panel All commercial banks. Variance inflation factor

| Variable | VIF | 1/VIF |
|---|---|---|
| $LLP_{i,t-1}$ | 1.04 | 0.963 |
| $\Delta L_{i,t}$ | 1.06 | 0.939 |
| $FCI_{i,t}$ | 1.14 | 0.881 |
| $I_{i,t}$ | 1.26 | 0.795 |
| $EQ_{i,t}$ | 1.15 | 0.871 |
| $\Delta GDP_{j,t}$ | 1.05 | 0.951 |
| Mean VIF | 1.12 | |

**Table 12.** SEE EU: Panel Selected commercial banks. Summary statistics

|  | N | Mean | SD | Median | Min | Max |
|---|---|---|---|---|---|---|
| $LLP_{i,t}$ | 496 | .012 | 0.015 | .009 | -.112 | .095 |
| $\Delta L_{i,t}$ | 429 | .045 | 0.264 | .017 | -.669 | 3.918 |
| $FCI_{i,t}$ | 496 | .009 | 0.005 | .009 | -.001 | .032 |
| $I_{i,t}$ | 496 | .012 | 0.021 | .013 | -.250 | .085 |
| $EQ_{i,t}$ | 496 | .126 | 0.082 | .112 | -.004 | .904 |
| $EQ/RWA_{i,t}$ | 476 | .204 | 0.132 | .178 | -.007 | 1.614 |
| $\Delta GDP_{j,t}$ | 536 | 1.430 | 2.847 | 1.925 | -10.149 | 8.197 |
| $\Delta GDPpc_{j,t}$ | 536 | 1.784 | 2.986 | 2.212 | -10.016 | 8.824 |

**Figure 6.** SEE EU: Panel Selected Commercial banks. Outliers

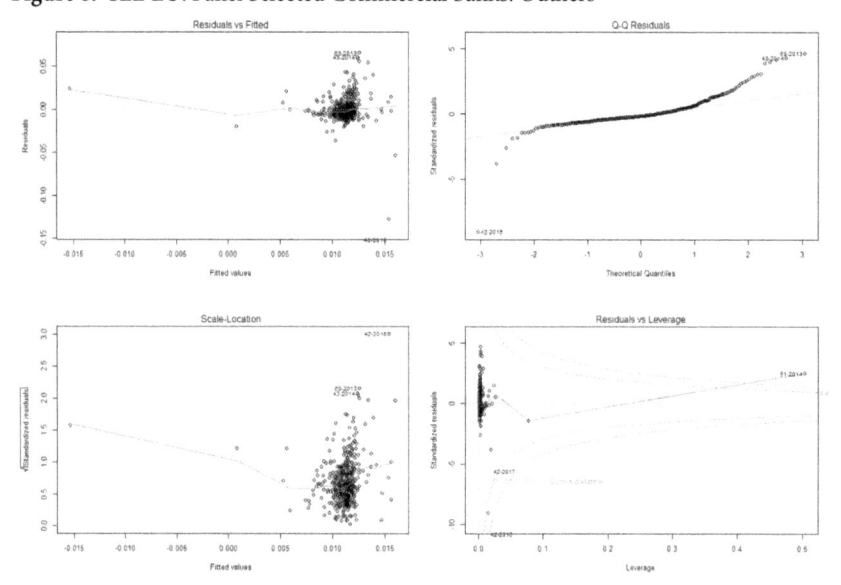

Outliers in the regression LLP ~ Growth rate of net lending

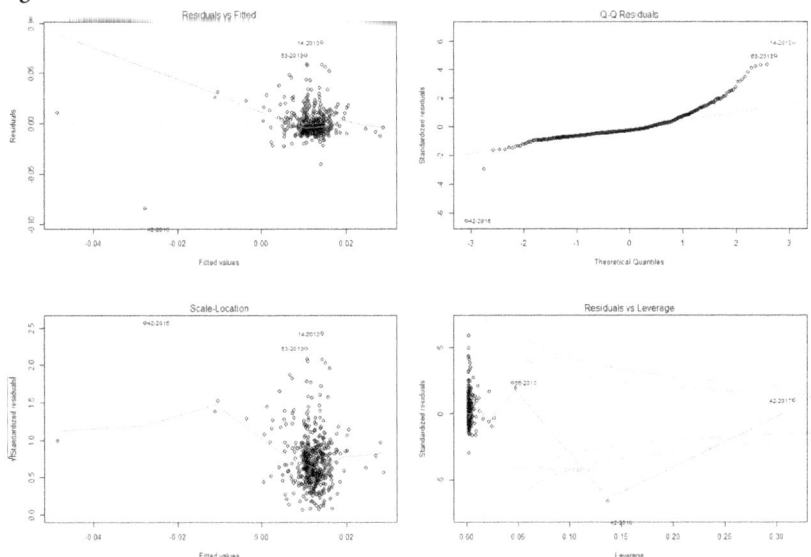

Non-discretionary and discretionary components 93

**Figure 6.** Continued

Outliers in the regression LLP ~ Income before LLP and taxes

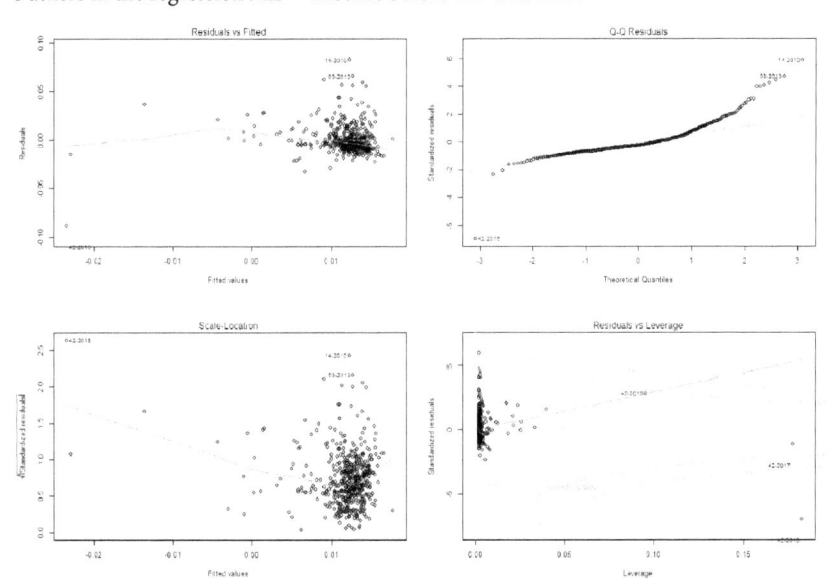

Outliers in the regression LLP ~ Equity

Identified outliers are: TBI bank Bulgaria in 2010 (id: 14–2010), Praxia bank Greece (id: 42–2015, 2016 & 2017), Erste bank Romania in 2014 (id: 43–2014), Idea bank Romania in 2014 (id: 51–2014), Patria bank Romania in 2013 (id: 56–2013), and Gorenjska bank Slovenia in 2013 (id: 63–2013).

**Table 13.** SEE EU Panels: Estimations

| $LLP_{i,t}$ | All commercial banks ||||  Selected commercial banks |||
|---|---|---|---|---|---|---|---|
|  | (1) Diff. GMM | (2) Diff. GMM | (3) Diff. GMM | (4) System GMM | (5) Diff. GMM | (6) System GMM | (7) Pooled OLS |
| $LLP_{i,t-1}$ | .3441*** | .3249*** | .3448*** | .2947*** | .2412*** | .2328*** | .2019*** |
|  | (.0746) | (.0646) | (.0738) | (.100) | (.0733) | (.0719) | (.0425) |
| $\Delta L_{i,t}$ | -.0136*** | -.0166*** | -.0144*** | -.0148*** | -.0112*** | -.0116*** | -.0105*** |
|  | (.0043) | (.0044) | (.0044) | (.0048) | (.0035) | (.0039) | (.0024) |
| $FCI_{i,t}$ | .0269 |  | -.0104 | 1.124 | -.3771 | -.1403 | -.2593 |
|  | (.4111) |  | (.4832) | (.9538) | (.5018) | (.6522) | (.1824) |
| $SIGN_{i,t}$ |  | -.0602 |  |  |  |  |  |
|  |  | (.115) |  |  |  |  |  |
| $I_{i,t}$ | .1664* | .1195 | .1397 | .0390 | .2427*** | .2265*** | .2393*** |
|  | (.0857) | (.1276) | (.0957) | (.1290) | (.0804) | (.0626) | (.0454) |
| $EQ_{i,t}$ | -.0543*** |  |  | -.0907*** | -.0492*** |  |  |
|  | (.0164) |  |  | (.0341) | (.0158) |  |  |
| $EQ/RWA_{i,t}$ |  | -.1019*** | -.0338** |  |  | -.0101 | -.0097 |
|  |  | (.0364) | (.0141) |  |  | (.0125) | (.0078) |
| $\Delta GDP_{j,t}$ | -.0003 |  |  | -.0003 | -.0009** | -.0009** |  |
|  | (.0003) |  |  | (.0005) | (.0004) | (.0004) |  |
| $\Delta GDPpc_{j,t}$ |  | .0004 | -.0002 |  |  |  | -.0009*** |
|  |  | (.0005) | (.0003) |  |  |  | (.0003) |
| $FCI_{i,t} * D$ | 1.4497* |  | 1.4407* | .6627 | 1.1937* | 1.102 | .0032 |
|  | (.8344) |  | (.8409) | (1.232) | (.6252) | (1.011) | (.2775) |
| $SIGN_{i,t} * D$ |  | -.3429 |  |  |  |  |  |
|  |  | (.3073) |  |  |  |  |  |
| $I_{i,t} * D$ | .0031 | -.3776 | .0164 | .1352 | .0237 | .0274 | -.0098 |
|  | (.1604) | (.2673) | (.1697) | (.2309) | (.1482) | (.1205) | (.0958) |
| $EQ_{i,t} * D$ | -.1584** |  |  | -.1196 | -.0473 |  |  |
|  | (.0741) |  |  | (.0913) | (.0603) |  |  |
| $EQ/RWA_{i,t} * D$ |  | -.0342 | -.0849* |  |  | -.0521 | -.0095 |
|  |  | (.0465) | (.0434) |  |  | (.0349) | (.0093) |
| $\Delta GDP_{j,t} * D$ | .0001 |  |  | -.0013 | .0001 | .0003 |  |
|  | (.0007) |  |  | (.001) | (.0006) | (.0007) |  |
| $\Delta GDPpc_{j,t} * D$ |  | -.0005 | .0000 |  |  |  | .0004 |
|  |  | (.0008) | (.0006) |  |  |  | (.0005) |
| Constant |  |  |  | .015** |  | .0129** | .0127*** |
|  |  |  |  | (.0066) |  | (.0061) | (.0019) |
| Year dummies | Yes | Yes | Yes | Yes | Yes | Yes | No |
| Observations | 480 | 380 | 464 | 568 | 362 | 414 | 414 |
| No. of groups | 87 | 85 | 86 | 88 | 66 | 67 |  |

Table 13. Continued

| $LLP_{i,t}$ | All commercial banks ||||| Selected commercial banks |||
|---|---|---|---|---|---|---|---|
| | (1) Diff. GMM | (2) Diff. GMM | (3) Diff. GMM | (4) System GMM | (5) Diff. GMM | (6) System GMM | (7) Pooled OLS |
| No. of instruments | 21 | 19 | 21 | 23 | 21 | 23 | |
| Hansen test, p-value | 0.104 | 0.204 | 0.107 | 0.247 | 0.136 | 0.228 | |
| AR(1), p-value | 0.003 | 0.011 | 0.004 | 0.004 | 0.005 | 0.005 | |
| AR(2), p-value | 0.258 | 0.908 | 0.317 | 0.292 | 0.473 | 0.617 | |
| F-statistics | | | | 16.04 | | 20.18 | 15.55 |
| F-statistics, p-value | | | | 0.000 | | 0.000 | 0.000 |
| $R^2$ | | | | | | | 0.278 |

Variables: loan loss provisions ($LLP_{i,t}$), 1st lag of loan loss provisions ($LLP_{i,t-1}$), loan growth ($\Delta L_{i,t}$), income from fees and commissions ($FCI_{i,t}$), change in 1-year ahead bank income ($SIGN_{i,t}$), income before LLP and taxes ($I_{i,t}$), equity ($EQ_{i,t}$), equity to RWA ($EQ/RWA_{i,t}$), growth rate of real GDP ($\Delta GDP_{j,t}$), growth rate of GDP per capita ($\Delta GDPpc_{j,t}$), ownership dummies (D takes the value 1 for a domestically owned bank, otherwise it is 0). T-statistics is reported in brackets; significance levels are *** p<.01, ** p<.05, * p<.1

Table 14. Western Balkans: Panel All commercial banks

| Country | | Total banks | S&P[a] database | Domestic banks | Foreign banks | Ownership change[b] | Panel All commercial banks |
|---|---|---|---|---|---|---|---|
| | | (A) | (B) | (D) | (E) | (F) | (B)-(F) |
| Albania | | 16 | 16 | 2 | 13 | 1 | 15 |
| Bosnia & Herzegovina | Federation | 16 | 15 | 4 | 10 | 1 | 14 |
| | Srpska Republic | 8 | 7 | 1 | 6 | | 7 |
| Montenegro | | 14 | 10 | 2 | 8 | | 10 |
| North Macedonia | | 14 | 13 | 1 | 11 | 1 | 12 |
| Serbia | | 27 | 24 | 5 | 16 | 2 | 21 |
| Kosovo* | | 6 | 6 | 2 | 4 | | 6 |
| Total | | 100 | 90 | 17 | 68 | 5 | 85 |

[a]Standard & Poor's Global Market Intelligence.
[b]Banks that changed ownership from domestic to foreign, or vice versa.

## 96  Non-discretionary and discretionary components

Table 15. Western Balkans: Panel Selected commercial banks

| Country | | Total banks | S&P database | Consolidation[a] | Domestic banks | Foreign banks | Ownership change | Panel Selected commercial banks |
|---|---|---|---|---|---|---|---|---|
| | | (A) | (B) | (C) | (D) | (E) | (F) | (B)-(C)-(F) |
| Albania | | 16 | 16 | 4 | 2 | 9 | 1 | 12 |
| Bosnia & Herzegovina | Federation | 16 | 15 | 5 | 1 | 9 | | 10 |
| | Srpska Republic | 8 | 7 | 1 | 1 | 5 | | 6 |
| Montenegro | | 14 | 10 | 1 | 2 | 7 | | 9 |
| North Macedonia | | 14 | 13 | 2 | 1 | 9 | 1 | 10 |
| Serbia | | 26 | 23 | 8 | 2 | 11 | 2 | 13 |
| Kosovo* | | 6 | 6 | | 2 | 4 | | 6 |
| Total | | 100 | 90 | 21 | 11 | 54 | 4 | 65 |

[a]Banks that went through a consolidation process initiated by the intervention of national or international authorities.

Table 16. Western Balkans: Panel All commercial banks. Summary statistics

| | N | Mean | SD | Median | Min | Max |
|---|---|---|---|---|---|---|
| $LLP_{i,t}$ | 648 | .013 | 0.041 | .008 | -.064 | .918 |
| $\Delta L_{i,t}$ | 566 | .087 | 0.229 | .063 | -.942 | 1.794 |
| $FCI_{i,t}$ | 652 | .010 | 0.006 | .009 | -.023 | .065 |
| $I_{i,t}$ | 648 | .013 | 0.030 | .016 | -.548 | .109 |
| $EQ_{i,t}$ | 652 | .163 | 0.087 | .141 | .036 | .706 |
| $EQ/RWA_{i,t}$ | 560 | .264 | 0.222 | .211 | .050 | 2.210 |
| $\Delta GDP_{j,t}$ | 680 | 2.164 | 1.708 | 2.350 | -2.724 | 6.320 |
| $\Delta GDPpc_{j,t}$ | 680 | 2.670 | 1.657 | 2.792 | -2.806 | 7.372 |
| Winsorized $LLP_{i,t}$ | 648 | .010 | 0.011 | .008 | -.006 | .042 |
| Winsorized $FCI_{i,t}$ | 652 | .010 | 0.005 | .009 | .003 | .019 |
| Winsorized $I_{i,t}$ | 648 | .011 | 0.014 | .016 | -.024 | .037 |
| Winsorized $EQ_{i,t}$ | 652 | .157 | 0.064 | .141 | .079 | .310 |
| Winsorized $EQ/RWA_{i,t}$ | 560 | .244 | 0.114 | .211 | .107 | .516 |

In the second part of the table, summary statistics is reported for LLP, FCI, I, EQ and EQ/RWA that are winsorized to the 5th and 95th percentiles.

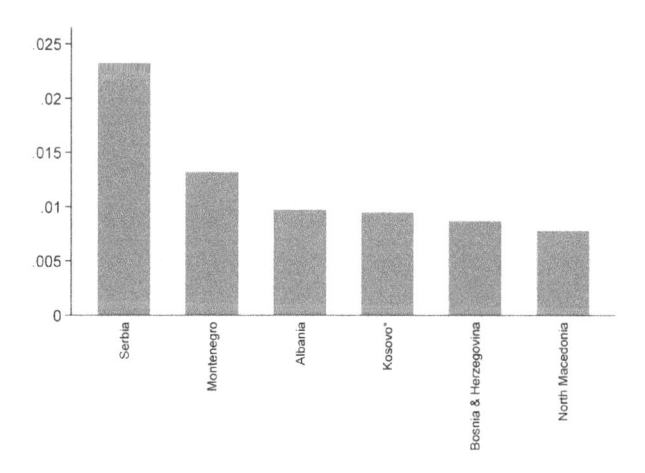

Non-discretionary and discretionary components 97

Figure 7. Western Balkans: Panel All commercial banks. Average LLPs

Table 17. Western Balkans: Panel All commercial banks. Correlation matrix

|  | $LLP_{i,t}$ | $\Delta L_{i,t}$ | $FCI_{i,t}$ | $I_{i,t}$ | $EQ_{i,t}$ | $\Delta GDP_{j,t}$ |
|---|---|---|---|---|---|---|
| $LLP_{i,t}$ | 1 | | | | | |
| $\Delta L_{i,t}$ | -0.299*** | 1 | | | | |
| $FCI_{i,t}$ | 0.022 | -0.084* | 1 | | | |
| $I_{i,t}$ | 0.044 | -0.015 | 0.176*** | 1 | | |
| $EQ_{i,t}$ | -0.020 | 0.037 | 0.002 | -0.121** | 1 | |
| $\Delta GDP_{j,t}$ | -0.154*** | 0.016 | -0.067 | 0.029 | -0.230*** | 1 |

* $p < 0.05$, ** $p < 0.01$, *** $p < 0.001$. The matrix reports on winsorized data for LLP, FCI, I and EQ.

Table 18. Western Balkans: Panel All commercial banks. Variance inflation factor

| Variable | VIF | 1/VIF |
|---|---|---|
| $LLP_{i,t-1}$ | 1.13 | 0.889 |
| $\Delta L_{i,t}$ | 1.12 | 0.893 |
| $FCI_{i,t}$ | 1.05 | 0.956 |
| $I_{i,t}$ | 1.05 | 0.954 |
| $EQ_{i,t}$ | 1.07 | 0.933 |
| $\Delta GDP_{j,t}$ | 1.07 | 0.935 |
| Mean VIF | 1.08 | |

The VIF reports on winsorized data for LLP, FCI, I and EQ.

98  Non-discretionary and discretionary components

**Table 19.** Western Balkans: Panel Selected commercial banks. Summary statistics

|  | N | Mean | SD | Median | Min | Max |
|---|---|---|---|---|---|---|
| $LLP_{i,t-1}$ | 496 | .009 | 0.008 | .007 | -.004 | .029 |
| $\Delta L_{i,t}$ | 435 | .110 | 0.207 | .076 | -.450 | 1.794 |
| $FCI_{i,t}$ | 500 | .0099 | 0.004 | .010 | .003 | .018 |
| $I_{i,t}$ | 496 | .016 | 0.013 | .018 | -.018 | .038 |
| $EQ_{i,t}$ | 500 | .148 | 0.065 | .130 | .077 | .326 |
| $EQ/RWA_{i,t}$ | 422 | .224 | 0.114 | .188 | .104 | .566 |
| $\Delta GDP_{j,t}$ | 519 | 2.270 | 1.747 | 2.545 | -2.724 | 6.320 |
| $\Delta GDPpc_{j,t}$ | 519 | 2.737 | 1.687 | 2.822 | -2.806 | 7.372 |

Data for LLP, FCI, I, EQ and EQ/RWA are winsorized to the 5th and 95th percentiles.

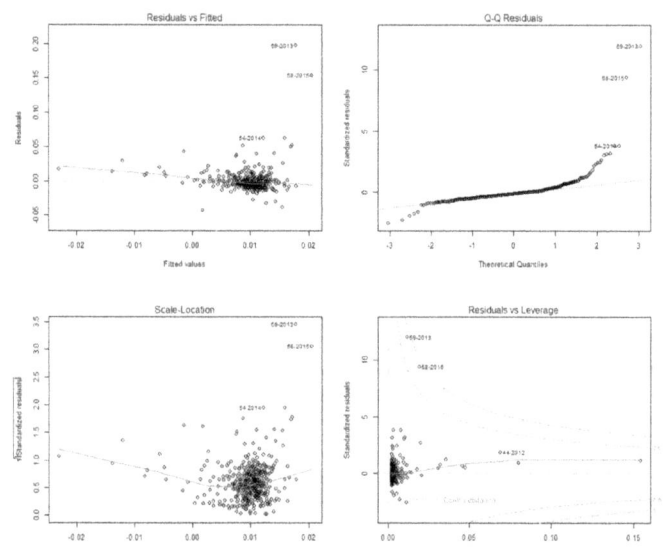

**Figure 8.** Western Balkans: Panel Selected Commercial banks. Outliers

Outliers in the regression LLP – Growth rate of net lending

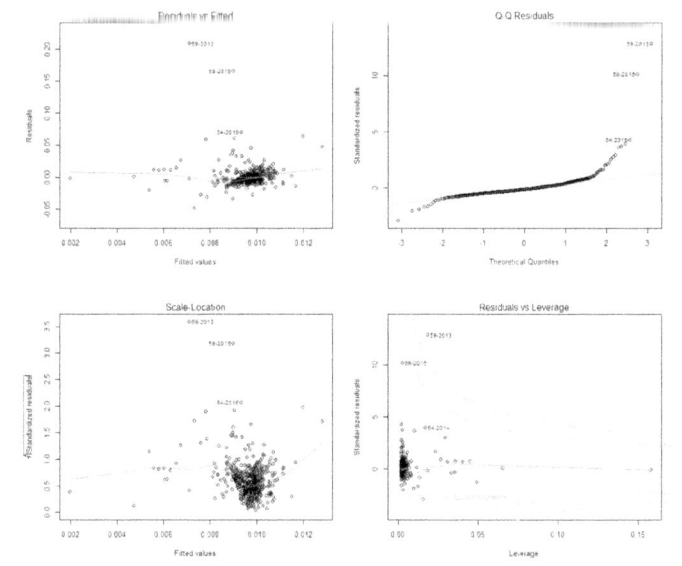

Non-discretionary and discretionary components 99

**Figure 8.** Continued

Outliers in the regression LLP ~ Earnings before LLP and taxes

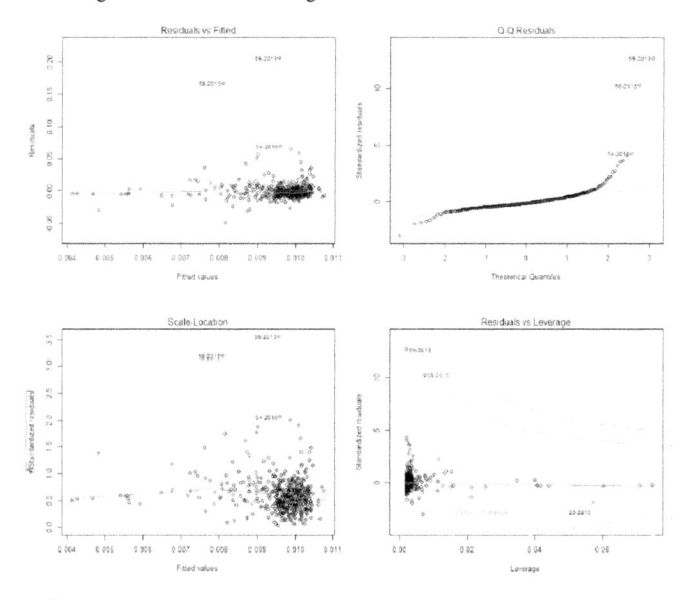

Outliers in the regression LLP ~ Equity

Identified outliers are: Capital bank North Macedonia in 2012 (id: 44–2012), API bank Serbia in 2014 (54–2014), JUBMES bank Serbia in 2015 (id: 58–2015), and NLB bank Serbia in 2013 (id: 59–2013).

**Table 20.** Western Balkans Panels: Estimations

|  | All commercial banks |  |  |  | Selected commercial banks |  |  |
|---|---|---|---|---|---|---|---|
| $LLP_{i,t}$ | (1) Diff. GMM | (2) Diff. GMM | (3) Diff. GMM | (4) System GMM | (5) Diff. GMM | (6) System GMM | (7) Pooled OLS |
| $LLP_{i,t-1}$ | .0612 | .4225*** | .5026*** | .4732*** | .4791*** | .6153*** | .4832*** |
|  | (.1712) | (.1168) | (.1566) | (.162) | (.0881) | (.0938) | (.0412) |
| $\Delta L_{i,t}$ | -.0147 | -.0048 | -.0084 | -.0088 | -.0028 | -.0019 | -.0018 |
|  | (.0174) | (.0044) | (.006) | (.0057) | (.0022) | (.0026) | (.0015) |
| $FCI_{i,t}$ | -.6567 | -.2121 | -.4194 | -.3727 | -.0861 | -.1065 | -.0127 |
|  | (.7934) | (.4239) | (.4993) | (.4885) | (.1935) | (.0932) | (.0809) |
| $I_{i,t}$ | .1847* | .1803 | .1892 | .2001** | .1867** | .028 | .0497* |
|  | (.103) | (.1217) | (.1197) | (.0995) | (.0709) | (.0503) | (.0285) |
| $EQ_{i,t}$ | -.092* | -.0887* |  |  | -.0427*** |  | -.0115** |
|  | (.0487) | (.0458) |  |  | (.014) |  | (.0058) |
| $EQ/RWA_{i,t}$ |  |  | -.0239 | -.0198 |  | -.0066** |  |
|  |  |  | (.0303) | (.0192) |  | (.003) |  |
| $\Delta GDP_{j,t}$ | -.0008 | -.0008 |  |  | -.0004 |  |  |
|  | (.0012) | (.0006) |  |  | (.0003) |  |  |
| $\Delta GDPpc_{j,t}$ |  |  | -.0005 | -.0005 | -.0004* |  | -.0006*** |
|  |  |  | (.0006) | (.0006) | (.0003) |  | (.0002) |
| $FCI_{i,t} * D$ | 1.6742 | 1.0801 | .607 | .4778 | .4243 | .077 | -.0032 |
|  | (2.1478) | (1.1614) | (1.363) | (1.2738) | (1.0215) | (.1831) | (.1461) |
| $I_{i,t} * D$ | -1.8025*** | .0448 | .1507 | .1695 | .0518 | .1857** | .1798*** |
|  | (.1147) | (.2182) | (.282) | (.2805) | (.1332) | (.0881) | (.0591) |
| $EQ_{i,t} * D$ | -.1631 | -.0553 |  |  | .0228 |  | -.0006 |
|  | (.1651) | (.075) |  |  | (.065) |  | (.0085) |
| $EQ/RWA_{i,t} * D$ |  |  | -.0732** | -.0802** |  | -.0028 |  |
|  |  |  | (.0364) | (.0332) |  | (.0096) |  |
| $\Delta GDP_{j,t} * D$ | -.0012 | -.0008 |  |  | -.001* |  |  |
|  | (.0021) | (.0009) |  |  | (.0005) |  |  |
| $\Delta GDPpc_{j,t} * D$ |  |  | -.0003 | -.0003 | -.0007 |  | -.0006 |
|  |  |  | (.0009) | (.0009) | (.0008) |  | (.0003) |
| Constant |  |  |  | .0155* |  | .0058*** | .0066*** |
|  |  |  |  | (.0078) |  | (.002) | (.0014) |
| Year dummies | Yes | Yes | Yes | Yes | Yes | Yes | No |
| Observations | 477 | 477 | 418 | 502 | 366 | 377 | 430 |
| No. of groups | 84 | 84 | 82 | 85 | 64 | 62 |  |
| No. of instruments | 21 | 21 | 21 | 23 | 36 | 23 |  |
| Hansen test, p-value | 0.130 | 0.243 | 0.129 | 0.172 | 0.555 | 0.175 |  |

Table 20. Continued

| $LLP_{i,t}$ | All commercial banks ||||  Selected commercial banks |||
|---|---|---|---|---|---|---|---|
| | (1) Diff. GMM | (2) Diff. GMM | (3) Diff. GMM | (4) System GMM | (5) Diff. GMM | (6) System GMM | (7) Pooled OLS |
| AR(1), p-value | 0.094 | 0.000 | 0.001 | 0.001 | 0.001 | 0.000 | |
| AR(2), p-value | 0.468 | 0.446 | 0.393 | 0.435 | 0.115 | 0.312 | |
| F-statistics | | | | 11.01 | | 79.11 | 24.79 |
| F-statistics, p-value | | | | 0.000 | | 0.000 | 0.000 |
| $R^2$ | | | | | | | 0.371 |

Variables: loan loss provisions ($LLP_{i,t}$), 1$^{st}$ lag of loan loss provisions ($LLP_{i,t-1}$), loan growth ($\Delta L_{i,t}$), income from fees and commissions ($FCI_{i,t}$), income before LLP and taxes ($I_{i,t}$), equity ($EQ_{i,t}$), equity to RWA ($EQ/RWA_{i,t}$), growth rate of real GDP ($\Delta GDP_{j,t}$), growth rate of GDP per capita ($\Delta GDPpc_{j,t}$), ownership dummies ($D$ takes the value 1 for a domestically owned bank, otherwise it is 0). The first estimation is with original data, the others are based on winsorized data for LLP, FCI, I, EQ and EQ/RWA. T-statistics is reported in brackets; significance levels are *** p<.01, ** p<.05, * p<.1

## 5. The effect of macroeconomic shocks on loan loss provisions in Southeast Europe

In this study, the aim is to simulate two types of macroeconomic shocks, negative shock to GDP and positive shock to unemployment, and to determine their transmission to loan loss provisions. Therefore, the findings of this empirical study contribute to the understanding of the different levels of resilience of the observed banking sectors in relation to the impact of macroeconomic shocks on the growth of loan loss provisions. The applied structural vector autoregression (SVAR) model, which requires a theoretical foundation, is based on the Keynesian supply shock.

The simulation of macroeconomic shocks is based on historical quarterly data, which are not equally long for each country but which end on the eve of the COVID-19 pandemic crisis. However, the aim of my study is not to forecast the trend of credit risk after the pandemic but it does, unintentionally, coincide with real events. Unlike my previous study, which focused on individual commercial banks, now the focus is on individual banking sectors.

### 5.1 Theoretical framework

The research idea is to simulate a macro stress test to find out how loan loss provisions would respond to a negative GDP shock and a positive unemployment shock in the Western Balkans in comparison to the other countries in Southeast Europe. The SVAR used for this purpose requires economic theory to identify the restrictions in the model. Namely, the variables in the SVAR model should be ordered to reflect causal priority. The principle to follow is that the first variable in order is affected only after a lag by succeeding variables; the next variable in order affects the preceding variable after a lag and the succeeding variables instantly; the last variable affects the preceding variables only after a lag.

For the purpose of identifying restrictions in the SVAR model, I adhere to the literature that analyzes the impact of negative macroeconomic shocks on credit risk caused by the COVID-19 pandemic. The economic theory of Keynesian supply shocks argues that the aggregate supply shock resulting from the sudden business shutdowns and citizen lockdowns at the outbreak of the pandemic caused an inevitable increase in unemployment as well as an even greater shock in aggregate demand (Guerrieri, Lorenzoni, Straub, & Werning, 2020; Nomura Research Institute, 2020). Faria-e-Castro (2020) extends the concept of the Keynesian supply shock further to the financial sector in a dynamic equilibrium setting; he argues that a negative productivity shock and increased unemployment during the pandemic weakened borrowers' capacities to repay their debts because their disposable income became lower and subsequently the overall loan default rate increased. The non-linear Dynamic Stochastic General Equilibrium (DSGE) model of Faria-e-Castro (2020) forecasts how the Keynesian supply shock caused by the pandemic is transmitted to credit spreads and default rates. The parameterization of this nonlinear model is based on data related to the USA economy.

Economic theory suggests, therefore, that the loan loss provisions is ordered first as both GDP and unemployment affect it after a lag. Real GDP should be ordered second as it affects unemployment contemporaneously and the loan loss provisions after a lag. Indeed, in empirical literature that uses vector autoregression (VAR) modeling for macro-financial stress testing, a similar ordering of the variables is used (De Bock & Demyantes, 2012; Hoggarth, Logan, & Zicchino, 2005; Hristov & Roth, 2022; Klein, 2013; Marcucci & Quagliariello, 2008; Pool et al., 2015). In the empirical literature just mentioned, either LLPs or a similar variable used to indicate the credit risk are ranked first.

Marcucci and Quagliariello (2008) examine, for example, the dynamism between the default rate of corporate borrowers and macroeconomic indicators such as output gap, inflation, interbank interest rate, and real exchange rate in Italy based on data that cover the 1990–2004 period. The specification of their parsimonious VAR model is based on the macro stress test of UK banks (Hoggarth, Logan, & Zicchino, 2005), that is, it is based on the VAR model constructed from variable bank write-offs and the same four macroeconomic indicators.

De Bock and Demyantes (2012) estimate impulse response functions in emerging Asian, Latin American, and East European economies based on the 1996–2010 period. Their SVAR model includes five macro-financial variables arranged in the following order: NPL ratio, credit, foreign portfolio and bank flows, real GDP, and exchange rate.

Nir Klein (2013) focuses on 16 economies of CESEE and the dynamism between the NPL ratio, credit, unemployment, GDP, and inflation based on historical data during the 1998–2011 period. In arranging the variables, this study resorts to VAR model specifications from De Bock and Demyanets (2012) as well as Marcucci and Qualiariello (2008). The difference in the ordering of variables in my model compared to Nir Klein's (2013) model stems from the assumption that the COVID-19 pandemic crisis first caused the closure of businesses, then the growth in unemployment, transferring the effects from the real sector to the financial sector.[40]

The SVAR model of Pool et al. (2015) encompasses 12 developed OECD countries during the 1980–2010 period and examines the dynamics between the variables arranged as follows: LLPs, output gap, inflation, interest rate, and credit. In creating this model specification, the authors relied on the economic theory of Bernanke et al. (1999), Bouvatier and Lepetit (2012b), Christiano, Motto, and Rostagno (2014), Cúrdia and Woodford (2010), and Freixas and Rochet (2008).

In the recent panel SVAR study, which encompasses the four largest euro area economies during the 1995Q1-2020Q1 period, it was found that after a period of lower economic uncertainty, credit risk is likely to increase (Hristov & Roth, 2022). The model specification is based on the following variables: systemic risk indicator, GDP, inflation, stock market index, and an uncertainty measure. The study uses several variables alternately as an indicator of systematic risk, such as debt service ratio, household debt, mortgage loans, house prices, and early warning indicators. The study of Hristov and Roth (2022) is additionally interesting as it applied the jackknife-type procedure to check whether the findings change significantly after excluding certain countries from the panel.

These empirical studies are based on parsimonious VAR models, where the number of variables is limited even though either the time dimension, or the number of cross-sections, or both are quite large, especially in comparison with my study. My empirical study is also based on the parsimonious SVAR model, but in proportion to the size of the time series and cross sections, it includes three endogenous variables.

Despite the fact that the above-mentioned empirical studies refer to different countries, they find evidence of macro-financial linkages; more precisely, they find evidence that the credit risk increases after a negative GDP shock and/or a positive unemployment shock. A credit risk is indeed the main, immediate concern of bank board members[41] as shown in the survey carried out by Ernst and Young and the Institute for International Finance (2021) that lasted from

---

40  Even if the places of GDP and unemployment are swapped in the SVAR models of my study, the response impulse functions are largely the same (my empirical study also provides a robustness check of the results based on the swapped order of the mentioned two variables).

41  Nearly three quarters (73 %) of the bank board members surveyed identified credit risks as the main concern in the next 12 months. The next two immediate concerns were cyber security (71 %) and digital transformation (47 %) (Ernst and Young & Institute for International Finance, 2021).

November 2020 to January 2021 and covered 62 systemically important banks from 33 countries worldwide. Most of them expect changes in post-pandemic bank regulations connected to stress-testing scenarios (Ernst and Young & Institute for International Finance, 2021). During the COVID-19 pandemic crisis, authorities undertook a set of fiscal and monetary policy measures to mitigate the consequences of macroeconomic shocks. Some of the measures relating to the banking sector are: reducing the cost of borrowing by subsidizing interest rates, facilitating new lending by loan guarantee schemes, mitigating the budget constraints of households and businesses by loan moratoria, reducing the negative impact on banks' balance sheets by relaxing regulatory requirements relative to asset classification, loan loss provisioning, etc. (IMF Policy Tracker, 2021). Due to these measures, the decline in economic activity and the increase in unemployment during the pandemic in individual SEE countries has not had a major impact so far on the credit risk measured by LLPs (the pandemic is shown as the shaded area in Figures 9, 11, 13, 15, 17,19, 21, 23, and 25).

The non-linear character of the macroeconomic shocks[42] coupled with the stabilizing effect of state measures reduce the predictive power of traditional macro-financial stress models. It should be noted that the traditional models based on historical data and existing economic theory are being augmented by additional data and additional models to capture non-linear features of reality. Nevertheless, their main purpose is to reveal the dynamism between selected macro-financial variables and to indicate the magnitude and persistence of responses to various types of shocks in a simplified linear way following existing economic theory.

## 5.2 Empirical research

In this empirical study, by constructing the SVAR models and applying the OLS estimator, evidence is found of the dynamic interaction between selected macro-financial variables. Understanding the response of loan loss provisions to the negative GDP shock and the positive unemployment shock is important for understanding the specifics of individual economies and their banking sectors as well as the level of vulnerability of individual banking sectors.

---

42 The non-linearity stems from the fact that the contact-intensive sector of the economy was more exposed to the influence of macroeconomic shocks.

## 5.2.1 Data

Unlike the first empirical study, which is based on data from individual commercial banks, the second study is based on aggregate data for the entire banking sectors of the observed economies (including, thus, not only commercial banks but all other financial institutions as well like savings banks, cooperative banks, etc.).

The variables used in the baseline SVAR models are loan loss provisions, real GDP, and number of unemployed persons (Table 21). The bank data are from the IMF's FSI database (2021) and their Ecofin FSI database (IMF. Dissemination Standards Bulletin Board, 2021), the GDP data are from the IMF's International Financial Statistics (IFS) database (2021a) and unemployment data are from the International Labor Organization (ILO) database (2021). Only in the case of Bosnia and Herzegovina, due to the scarcity of data in the ILO database, is the IMF's IFS database the source for unemployment data. The quarterly data series have different time lengths across countries, depending on data availability: LLP data are unavailable for Bulgaria and Kosovo* while GDP data are unavailable for Montenegro. Therefore, these economies are not included in my estimations.

A visual representation of the time series is provided for the individual countries in Figures 9, 11, 13, 15, 17, 19, 21, 23 and 25. For each country, I prepared a pair of graphs showing two time series: (i) the first graph shows time series of the log of GDP and LLP as a percentage of total loans and (ii) the second graph shows time series of the log of number of unemployed and LLP as a percentage of total loans. The time series are created using dual axis scaling, the LLP scale is always on the right axis while the GDP scale and number of unemployed scale are on the left axis.

By visual inspection of the presented time series, it seems that two observations can be distinguished. First, in general it seems that there is an inverse relationship between GDP and LLP, suggesting that when economic activity falls, the stock of LLP increases; as well as a direct relationship between unemployment and LLP, suggesting that when the number of unemployed increases, the stock of LLP increases. However, these relations are not historically stable, not surprisingly, as some other authors, such as Quagliariello in Italy or Pain in the UK, have noted the same for their economies (Pain, 2003; Quagliariello, 2006). Second, although the time frame of my empirical study does not include the years of the COVID-19 pandemic (the shaded area on the graphs), it should be reiterated that, in order to preserve macro-financial stability, state interventions were substantial. As a result, the stock of LLPs remained stable in most countries observed.

As the next step, the stationarity of the level data was examined, that is, the stationarity of the LLP as a percentage of total loans, real GDP, and the number of unemployed. Stationarity is connected with the economic concept of a long-term equilibrium, as stationary series converge to their constant mean, making them valuable for forecasting purposes. Testing the stationarity of time series was carried out at the level of each country individually, and presented for Croatia in Table 22, with Cyprus in Table 25, Greece in Table 28, Romania in Table 31, Slovenia in Table 34, Albania in Table 37, Bosnia and Herzegovina in Table 40, North Macedonia in Table 43, and Serbia in Table 46. Each of these tables is divided into two parts: The upper part reports on the results of unit root tests on level data, and the lower part reports on the results of unit root tests on transformed data. Considering that all unit root tests on level data confirmed non-stationarity, data transformation had to be done in order to reach stationarity as required in the construction of SVAR models.[43] The level data of LLP were transformed by applying the first difference ($\Delta$ LLP), the level data of real GDP were transformed by applying the first difference to the natural logarithm of the level data ($\Delta$ ln GDP), and the transformation of the number of unemployed level data was performed in the same way, that is, by applying the first difference to the natural logarithm of the level data ($\Delta$ ln Unemployment). In order to examine the presence of a unit root, two types of tests were used, the Augmented Dickey-Fuller (ADF) test and the Phillips-Perron test. As all the time series show quarterly data, a maximum of 4 lags was taken in testing the presence of a unit root. Since all transformed time series have reached stationarity, in the next step I perform an in-depth analysis of their summary statistics, before creating SVAR models individually for each country.

In addition, in order to compare the transmission of macroeconomic shocks to credit risk, i.e. LLPs, in the SEE EU region in comparison with the Western Balkans region, two corresponding panel SVAR models were also created. The SEE EU panel comprises Southeast European countries that are EU members: Croatia, Cyprus, Greece, Romania, and Slovenia. The Western Balkans panel comprises countries that are either EU candidates (Albania, North Macedonia, and Serbia) or potential EU candidates (Bosnia and Herzegovina). The first characteristic of the two panels is that they are macro panels because their time dimension is

---

43   There was only one exception, which is the stationary GDP time series in Romania. However, as the SVAR model could not be created on mixed I(0) and I(1) data, the transformation of this time series was also carried out.

greater than the number of cross-sections (*T*>*N*). Another characteristic is that they are unbalanced because their cross sections have different lengths of the time dimension.

This means that my study contains an analysis of the transmission of macroeconomic shocks to credit risk at the level of each country individually as well as at the level of the SEE EU region and the Western Balkans region. The small sample size is the main caveat, as there are only 4–5 countries in each region, while their variables have short series. This is because the publicly available IMF and ILO databases do not contain data for all the economies in Southeast Europe and even for those economies where data were available, in some cases they had to be treated additionally, such as data conversion from bi-annual to quarterly frequency or seasonal adjustment. Nevertheless, even under this caveat, my study conducts the stress tests of the observed banking sectors quite well, indicating those whose vulnerability (resilience) is somewhat higher compared to others.

*5.2.1.1 Descriptive statistics*

Descriptive or summary statistics are provided for transformed data, considering that SVAR models are built exclusively on transformed data, i.e. stationary time series. Summary statistics are presented for each country individually corresponding to the individual SVAR models created, and also at panel level to correspond to the panel SVAR models created. As mentioned, one caveat is that the time series are generally short as they do not go back further than 2006. In the case of Albania, for example, the time series for the number of unemployed is much shorter than the other two observed variables. Nevertheless, and especially in the case of Bosnia and Herzegovina and Croatia, the time series are long enough to incorporate economic upward and downward cycles. Summary statistics provide information on the number of observations, mean, median, maximum and minimum values, and standard deviation.

Comparing the summary statistics of LLPs in the SEE EU, it is evident that they record, on average, a positive change per quarter in all countries, except Romania. On average, the largest increase in LLPs per quarter was recorded in Greece and Cyprus, while in Romania they even decreased. When comparing summary statistics for GDP data, it is noticeable that GDP, on average, increases from one quarter to the next in all countries except Greece, where it decreases. The highest average quarterly GDP increase is recorded in Romania and the lowest in Cyprus and Croatia. Finally, when comparing summary statistics for unemployment data, it is noticeable that the number of unemployed increases, on average, from one quarter to the next only in Greece and Cyprus, while it decreases in all other countries, most notably in Romania.

In the next few paragraphs, summary statistics are interpreted for each observed SEE EU country. Overall, the movement of the three selected macro-financial indicators was more favorable in Romania than in other countries.

Summary statistics for *Croatia* (Table 23): (i) the positive mean value of Δ LLP indicates a positive change in LLPs (as a percentage of total gross loans) over the observed period by 0.0004 per quarter. The average deviation from the mean of 0.0033 indicates a somewhat higher volatility during the observed period. Positive macroeconomic trends are also visible during the given time span as (ii) on average, real GDP increased from one quarter to the next by 0.2 %, with 1.28 % deviations on average; and (iii) on average, the number of unemployed decreased from one quarter to the next by 0.88 %, although with higher volatility as deviations from the mean are 7.25 % on average and most likely due to the seasonality of employment in tourism.

Summary statistics for *Cyprus* (Table 26): (i) on average, LLPs recorded a positive change by 0.0014 as a share of total loans per quarter, while the average deviation from the mean of 0.0103 also indicates a somewhat higher volatility; (ii) on average, real GDP increased from one quarter to the next by 0.25 %, with 1.19 % deviations on average; (iii) on average, the number of unemployed increased from one quarter to the next by 1.5 %, although with higher volatility as deviations from the mean are 9.49 % on average.

Summary statistics for *Greece* (Table 29): (i) on average, LLPs recorded a positive change by 0.0026 as a share of total loans per quarter, while the average deviation from the mean was 0.009; (ii) on average, real GDP decreased from one quarter to the next by 0.68 %, with 1.66 % deviations on average; (iii) on average, the number of unemployed increased from one quarter to the next by 1.4 %, although with volatility as deviations from the mean are 4.9 % on average.

Summary statistics for Romania (Table 32): (i) on average, LLPs recorded a negative change by 0.0012 as a share of total loans per quarter, while the average deviation from the mean of 0.0138 indicates a somewhat higher volatility during the observed period. Positive macroeconomic trends are evident during the observed time span, as (ii) on average, real GDP increased from one quarter to the next by 0.78 %, while (iii) on average, the number of unemployed decreased from one quarter to the next by 1.58 %.

Summary statistics for *Slovenia* (Table 35): (i) on average, LLPs recorded a positive change by 0.0002 as a share of total loans per quarter, while the average deviation from the mean of 0.008 indicates a somewhat higher volatility during the observed period. Positive macroeconomic trends are also visible during the given time span, as (ii) on average, real GDP increased from one quarter to the next by 0.3 %, while (iii) on average, the number of unemployed decreased from one quarter to the next by 1.12 %.

Since the reasons for the negative trends in macro-financial variables in Greece and Cyprus are explained in Section 2.2, it would be interesting to provide likely reasons for the positive trends in macro-financial variables in Romania. During the period from 2008 to 2013, NPLs in Romania accumulated, which is why, at the beginning of 2014, the central bank of Romania issued a set of recommendations for their resolution. In 2014, for example, more than EUR 2 billion worth of NPLs were sold (Bauze, 2019; Montes-Negret & Cloutier, 2016). Consequently, LLPs started to decrease sharply (Figure 15). Besides, in 2012, the Romanian authorities undertook a number of extensive measures to reduce unemployment, and the result of the application of these measures can be seen in the unemployment time series in Figure 15, which has showed a remarkable downward trend since 2012 (Totîlca & Bratu, 2014; World Bank, 2013). All these interventionist measures change the trend of macro-financial variables and affect their mutual causal relationship.

Comparing the summary statistics of LLPs **in the Western Balkans**, it is evident that they record, on average, a negative change per quarter in all countries, except Bosnia and Herzegovina. The highest negative change in LLP per quarter on average was in North Macedonia, which is totally opposite reporting in relation to the SEE EU region. When comparing summary statistics for GDP data, it is noticeable that GDP, on average, increases from one quarter to the next in the Western Balkans. Finally, when comparing summary statistics for unemployment data, it is noticeable that number of unemployed decreases on average from one quarter to another in the Western Balkans. In the next few paragraphs, summary statistics are provided in detail for each observed economy in the Western Balkans.

Summary statistics for *Albania* (Table 38): (i) the negative mean value of Δ LLP indicates a negative change in LLPs (as a percentage of total gross loans) over the observed time by 0.0006 per quarter. The average deviation from the mean of 0.0068 indicates a somewhat higher volatility during the observed period; (ii) on average, real GDP increased from one quarter to the next by 0.5 %, with 1.96 % deviations on average; (iii) on average, the number of unemployed decreased from one quarter to the next by 0.17 %, although with higher volatility as deviations from the mean are 5.49 % on average.

Summary statistics for *Bosnia and Herzegovina* (Table 41): (i) on average, LLPs recorded a positive change by 0.0007 as a share of total loans per quarter, while the average deviation from the mean of 0.0048 indicates a somewhat lower volatility during the observed period; (ii) on average, real GDP increased from one quarter to the next by 0.285 %, with 1.66 % deviations on average; (iii) on average, the number of unemployed decreased from one quarter to the next by 0.4 %, although with volatility as deviations from the mean are 1.71 % on average.

Summary statistics for *North Macedonia* (Table 44): (i) on average, LLPs recorded a negative change by 0.0011 as a share of total loans per quarter, while the average deviation from the mean of 0.0059 indicates volatility during the observed period; (ii) on average, real GDP increased from one quarter to the next by 0.64 %, with 2.15 % deviations on average; (iii) on average, the number of unemployed persons decreased from one quarter to the next by 1.4 %, although with volatility as deviations from the mean are 5.6 % on average.

Summary statistics for Serbia (Table 47): (i) on average, LLPs recorded a negative change by 0.0009 as a share of total loans per quarter, while the average deviation from the mean of 0.0074 indicates volatility during the observed period; (ii) on average, real GDP increased from one quarter to the next by 0.37 %, with 1.06 % deviations on average; (iii) on average, the number of unemployed decreased from one quarter to the next by 0.84 %, although with volatility as deviations from the mean are 5.2 % on average.

Based on an analysis of the summary statistics by country, it can be asserted that the movement of the three selected macro-financial indicators was better in the Western Balkans then in the SEE EU member states. The likely reason for this difference is that the GFC had a limited negative effect on some of the observed economies of the Western Balkans compared to the observed economies of the SEE EU in the period concerned. This can also be asserted on the basis of a comparison of the descriptive statistics at the level of the SEE EU panel and the Western Balkans panel (Table 49). To begin with, on average, LLPs recorded a positive change by 0.0007 as a share of total loans per quarter in the SEE EU region, while they recorded a negative change by 0.0004 as a share of total loans per quarter in the Western Balkans region. On average, real GDP increased by 0.19 % per quarter in the SEE EU region and by 0.45 % in the Western Balkans region. Finally, on average, the number of unemployed decreased by 0.11 % in the SEE EU region and by 0.77 % in the Western Balkans region.

Despite these assertions, it should be kept in mind that in the Western Balkans, compared to the SEE EU region, unemployment is more persistent even though there is a greater average downward trend per quarter in the observed period, the economic strength is lower even though there is a greater average positive GDP trend per quarter in the observed period, the standard of living is lower, and the integration of the Western Balkans into global financial markets is weaker.

## 5.2.1.2 Analysis of outliers

Before forecasting the transmission of macroeconomic shocks to credit risk, I analyze the outlier observations in the SEE EU and Western Balkans panels. Pairs of previously transformed variables are linearly regressed using OLS estimation in panels. Δ LLP is used as a dependent variable in each regression, and alternately independent variables are first lag values of Δ LLP, as well as Δ ln GDP, and Δ ln number of unemployed. During linear regressions, residual-based techniques are applied to detect outliers: (i) residuals vs. fitted; (ii) normal q-q; (iii) scale location; and (iv) residuals vs. leverage. The main outliers are identified in the SEE EU panel (Figure 30) and the Western Balkans panel (Figure 31). The following is a brief analysis of the most likely reasons for the identified outliers' occurrences:

- *Romania in 2014Q2 and 2014Q3.* Due to the negative effects of the GFC, during the 2008–2013 period, Romanian banks experienced a progressive build-up of NPLs. The peak of this phase was in December 2013, when nearly one quarter of the banks' loan portfolios were non-performing. At the beginning of 2014, the National Bank of Romania issued a set of recommendations for active NPL resolution. As a result, in 2014 alone, banks sold more than EUR 2 billion worth of non-performing loans (Bauze, 2019; Montes-Negret & Cloutier, 2016). Subsequently, LLPs dropped in a short period of time.
- *Cyprus in 2013Q4.* The 2013 sovereign debt crisis in Cyprus was marked by a steep increase in both non-performing loans and LLPs. The two contributing reasons were the wind-down of two systemically important banks and the EUR 7.8 billion bail-in of uninsured deposits (Georghadji, 2017).
- *Cyprus in 2015Q4.* Cooperative banks increased provisions for their stock of non-performing loans supported by a significant state capital injection (IMF European Department, 2016).
- *Croatia in 2006H2.* Credit expansion in 2005 and 2006 occurred because a high number of foreign banks entered the domestic credit market. The central bank of Croatia undertook several measures to address credit expansion based on foreign borrowing. Among others, the amended regulation on capital adequacy ratio, which took effect in June 2006, caused an immediate increase in LLPs and a decline in capital adequacy. A slight decrease in net lending and a wave of bank recapitalizations followed (Gardo, 2008; Krznar, 2009).
- *Slovenia in 2018Q1.* In January 2018 the new accounting standards on provisioning (IFRS 9) started to be implemented.
- *Albania in 2011Q1 and 2011Q2.* Based on stress-testing findings, the Bank of Albania requested banks to recognize their non-performing loans and

set aside the appropriate provision coverage (Bank of Albania, 2011, p. 10). As a result, LLPs increased by more than 27 % in the first half of 2011 in comparison to the end of 2010 (Bank of Albania, 2011, p. 79).
- *Bosnia and Herzegovina in 2011Q4.* At the end of 2011, due to the application of the accounting standards IAS/IFRS in the banking sector of the Federation of Bosnia and Herzegovina, loans were reclassified and, consequently, the amount of LLPs increased considerably (Central Bank of Bosnia and Herzegovina, 2011, p. 168).
- *North Macedonia in 2016Q2.* The central bank obliged banks to transfer non-performing loans that were fully covered with provisions for more than two years from their balance sheets to their off-balance sheets (National Bank of the Republic of North Macedonia, 2016, p. 6).
- *Serbia in 2017Q3.* To further contribute to the reduction in NPL stock in the country, in August 2017 the National Bank of Serbia issued a regulation concerning the immediate write-off of those non-performing loans that were fully provisioned (Bauze, 2019). As a result, LLPs accelerated their decreasing trend.

LLPs enter ratios that form IMF FSI and, as such, provide insight into the vulnerability of a national financial system. Based on an analysis of outliers, it becomes clear that monetary authorities target the quality of banks' assets by specific measures in times of economic upswings and even more so in times of economic downturns. In times of need, monetary authorities apply, sooner or later, measures whose aim it is to attenuate the macro-financial instability. As monetary interventions are usual practice, I decided not to treat outlying observations in panels but to make estimations based on the data as they are. Authors of similar types of empirical research do not treat outliers in their panel data before VAR estimation either (Klein, 2013; Pool et al., 2015).

### 5.2.2 Method

In order to analyze the response of loan loss provisions to various macroeconomic shocks in the economies of Southeast Europe, I chose the structural vector auto-regression model. It is a relatively simple macroeconometric model that estimates the short-term linear interdependence of selected variables, in this study: LLPs, real GDP, and number of unemployed.

The reduced-form VAR(1)[44] model:

---

44 The VAR model of order 1 is presented for the sake of simplicity. All three variables in the VAR model are in their transformed forms.

$$\begin{bmatrix} LLP_t \\ GDP_t \\ Unemp_t \end{bmatrix} = \begin{bmatrix} a_{11} & a_{12} & a_{13} \\ a_{21} & a_{22} & a_{23} \\ a_{31} & a_{32} & a_{33} \end{bmatrix} \begin{bmatrix} LLP_{t-1} \\ GDP_{t-1} \\ Unemp_{t-1} \end{bmatrix} + \begin{bmatrix} u_{LLP,t} \\ u_{GDP,t} \\ u_{Unemp,t} \end{bmatrix} \qquad (13)$$

where:

| | |
|---|---|
| $LLP_t$ | Denotes LLPs as the first endogenous variable in the ordering of variables |
| $GDP_t$ | Real GDP as the second endogenous variable |
| $Unemp_t$ | Number of unemployed as the last endogenous variable |
| $a_{11}, a_{12}, \ldots, a_{33}$ | Coefficients of the endogenous variables |
| $LLP_{t-1}, GDP_{t-1}, Unemp_{t-1}$ | First lag values of the endogenous variables |
| $u_{LLP,t}, u_{GDP,t}, u_{Unemp,t}$ | Forecast error terms of the endogenous variables |

The equation (13) can be written in the form of a general linear model:

$$Y_t = A_1 Y_{t-1} + u_t \qquad (14)$$

where:

$Y_t$ is a $(1x3)$ vector of the contemporaneous values of endogenous variables
$A_1$ is a $(3x3)$ matrix of coefficients to be estimated; subscript 1 denotes the order of the VAR model
$Y_{t-1}$ is a $(1x3)$ vector of endogenous variables in time $t-1$ (i.e. the first lag values)
$u_t$ is a $(1x3)$ vector of contemporaneous forecast errors (reduced form residuals or shocks)

In any VAR model, it is assumed that *error terms* are *white noise processes* with mean zero and a non-singular variance-covariance matrix of forecast error terms (Lütkepohl, 2005):

$$E(u_t) = 0 \qquad (15)$$

$$E(u_t u_t') = \Sigma_u \qquad (16)$$

The *stability condition* of a VAR model assumes that a $Y_t$ process is stable if its reverse characteristic polynomial has no roots in and on the complex unit circle. Because stability implies stationarity, the stability condition is often called the stationarity condition (Lütkepohl, 2005).

A reduced-form VAR model has a variance-covariance matrix of error terms $\Sigma_u$ that shows only instantaneous *correlations* between forecast error terms, i.e. a shock in one variable is accompanied by a shock to another variable:

$$\Sigma_u = \begin{bmatrix} \sigma^2_{LLP} & \sigma_{LLP,GDP} & \sigma_{LLP,Unemp} \\ \sigma_{GDP,LLP} & \sigma^2_{GDP} & \sigma_{GDP,Unemp} \\ \sigma_{Unemp,LLP} & \sigma_{Unemp,GDP} & \sigma^2_{Unemp} \end{bmatrix} \quad (17)$$

where:

$\sigma^2_{LLP}, \sigma^2_{GDP}, \sigma^2_{Unemp}$     as diagonal elements denote variances of variables

$\sigma_{LLP,GDP}, \sigma_{LLP,Unemp}, \ldots, \sigma_{Unemp,GDP}$     as off-diagonal elements denote co-variances

In structural VAR modeling the aim is to reveal *causalities*, i.e. that a shock in one variable provokes the response of another variable. This is the identification problem that is resolved by imposing restrictions on a reduced-form VAR model. Structural VAR is a linear transformation of a reduced-form VAR of order $p$:

$$Y_t = A_1 Y_{t-1} + \ldots + A_p Y_{t-p} + u_t \quad (18)$$

that is pre-multiplied by matrix $\mathbf{A}$:

$$\mathbf{A} Y_t = A_1^* Y_{t-1} + \ldots + A_p^* Y_{t-p} + \varepsilon_t \quad (19)$$

where:

$\mathbf{A}$     Denotes a lower triangular matrix with identifying restrictions and unities as diagonals

$A_j^* := \mathbf{A} A_j \ (j=1,\ldots,p)$     is a matrix of structural coefficients as a linear transformation of reduced-form coefficients

$\varepsilon_t := \mathbf{A}u_t$  is a vector of structural shocks as a linear transformation of reduced form residuals

The *ordering* of variables in a SVAR model matters because a shock in variables of a higher order contemporaneously affects variables of a lower order; otherwise the effect comes with a lag. That is why identifying restrictions are imposed based on theoretical grounds. The number of required identifying restrictions is calculated by $\dfrac{K(K-1)}{2}$, where K is the number of variables in the VAR model (Lütkepohl, 2005). In a VAR model with three endogenous variables, for example, three identifying restrictions need to be imposed to obtain a unique solution.

In this study, the SVAR model (presented in order 1 for simplicity), after imposing restrictions, is as follows:

$$AY_t = A_1^* Y_{t-1} + \varepsilon_t \qquad (20)$$

or

$$\begin{bmatrix} 1 & 0 & 0 \\ a_{21} & 1 & 0 \\ a_{31} & a_{32} & 1 \end{bmatrix} \begin{bmatrix} LLP_t \\ GDP_t \\ Unemp_t \end{bmatrix} = \begin{bmatrix} a_{11}^* & a_{12}^* & a_{13}^* \\ a_{21}^* & a_{22}^* & a_{23}^* \\ a_{31}^* & a_{32}^* & a_{33}^* \end{bmatrix} \begin{bmatrix} LLP_{t-1} \\ GDP_{t-1} \\ Unemp_{t-1} \end{bmatrix} + \begin{bmatrix} \varepsilon_{LLP,t} \\ \varepsilon_{GDP,t} \\ \varepsilon_{Unemp,t} \end{bmatrix} \qquad (21)$$

where:

$A$  is a lower triangular $(3x3)$ matrix with 3 identifying restrictions in the upper triangule

$A_1^*$  is a $(3x3)$ matrix of coefficients to be estimated; subscript 1 denotes the lag order of the model

$\varepsilon_t$  is a $(1x3)$ vector of structural shocks, also white noise processes

By identifying restrictions, the number of shocks and associated responses are just-identified. The variance-covariance matrix of structural residuals $\Sigma_\varepsilon = A\Sigma_u A'$ contains uncorrelated error terms, also called orthogonal errors. A stable VAR(p) has a *Wold moving average (MA)* representation:

$$Y_t = \Theta_0 \varepsilon_t + \Theta_1 \varepsilon_{t-1} + \Theta_2 \varepsilon_{t-2} + \ldots \qquad (22)$$

The elements of the $\Theta$ matrices are the responses to structural or orthogonal $\varepsilon$ shocks (Lütkepohl, 2005, p. 359). In this study, the analysis of impulse response functions is performed on a panel level as well as on an individual country level. In general, the panel SVAR model examines how countries respond to composite shocks that include both idiosyncratic and common effects (Pedroni, 2013). Idiosyncratic effects are unique to each country, while common effects are shared across countries. Therefore, an approach that involves examining individual country impulse response functions alongside panel response functions not only enhances our understanding with finer granularity but also reveals the underlying heterogeneities that stem from diverse economic contexts.

The Akaike information criterion (AIC) is used to determine the optimal lag length for each individual SVAR model, with preference given to the model with the lowest AIC value. Although the information presented for individual SVAR models is succinct and includes only the chosen lag length, Table 50 offers a more comprehensive overview for panel SVAR models. This table provides additional insights into the selection process of the optimal lag length using the same criteria.

Two specific cases should be mentioned in the creation of the optimal SVAR model at the level of individual countries. First, a dummy variable had to be used in the Slovenian SVAR model to attenuate the effect of introducing the new IFRS 9 standard, which is why it takes the value of 1 in 2018Q1 and is otherwise zero. Second, in the case of Romania, as previously mentioned, one of the three variables is stationary (Table 31), but since the SVAR model based on mixed stationary and non-stationary data cannot pass diagnostic checks, I constructed the Romanian SVAR model on an arbitrarily chosen lag.

All individual SVAR models successfully passed diagnostic checks for stability, absence of residual autocorrelation at the chosen lag, and absence of heteroscedasticity. Detailed reports on the results of the diagnostic checks are provided in tables for each individual SVAR model. More precisely, the report on the SVAR model for Croatia is in Table 24, with Cyprus in Table 27, Greece in Table 30, Romania in Table 33, and Slovenia in Table 36; Albania is then in Table 39, Bosnia and Herzegovina in Table 42, North Macedonia in Table 45, and Serbia in Table 48.

Regarding the panel SVAR models created at the level of the SEE EU region and the Western Balkans region, both successfully passed the stability test for panels as no root lies outside the unit circle (Figure 27). Additionally, as a type of robustness check, I report on the results of a Granger causality test conducted at panel level (Table 51), in order to determine the presence of dynamics between the three endogenous variables in my SVAR models and to understand the direction of causality between them. The Granger causality test indicates, namely, the direction of causality between a pair of variables, if such causality exists: If "variable x Granger-causes variable y", it means that the historical values of x contain statistically significant information to predict variable y better than information in the historical values of variable y alone (Granger, 1969). As reported in Table 51, at the level of statistical significance of 5 %, the dynamic between the selected variables does exist and it is such that unemployment has predictive power for LLPs in both regions, while real GDP has predictive power for LLPs in the group of SEE EU member states.

After conducting diagnostic checks to ensure the successful validation of all individual and panel SVAR models, estimation and forecasting were carried out. EViews was employed for OLS regression in estimating all SVAR models. In EViews, impulses or shocks are defined as positive due to simulation requirements. However, for the purpose of my empirical study, it is necessary to compare the response functions of LLPs not only to positive unemployment shocks but also to negative GDP shocks across various countries and between the two observed regions. Fortunately, there is a solution to addressing this limitation. Given the linearity of the SVAR model, interpreting a negative shock can be resolved by envisioning it as a mirror-like reflection of a positive shock. Each shock is simulated at the level of one standard deviation, and the future horizon extends to 10 quarters ahead.

## 5.3 Results

The research aim is to examine possible macro-financial asymmetries between the observed countries and regions. For that purpose, first, forecasts of transmission of macroeconomic shocks were simulated on an individual level to observe impulse response functions across countries. Impulses and responses from the SVAR model for Croatia are presented in Figure 10, with Cyprus in Figure 12, Greece in Figure 14, for Romania in Figure 16 and Slovenia in the Figure 18. Second, forecasts are performed on a panel level for two regions, the SEE EU region and the Western Balkans region. Impulses and responses from the panel SVAR model for the SEE EU are presented in Figure 28, and for the Western Balkans in Figure 29.

Each of the figures with the impulses and responses of the constructed SVAR models consists of three graphs and one table. The first graph represents the Δ ln GDP response function to the positive Δ ln GDP shock; that is, it gives an indication of the magnitude and persistence of the GDP shock and should be interpreted as if in a mirror. The second graph represents the Δ ln unemployment response function to the positive Δ ln unemployment shock; that is, it gives an indication of the magnitude and persistence of the unemployment shock. The third graph represents the Δ LLP response functions to the GDP shock and the unemployment shock,[45] while the adjacent table provides the exact values of the Δ LLP response functions to the two shocks for each of the 10 quarters ahead. To reiterate, negative values of Δ LLP responses to GDP shock should be read as positive and, conversely, positive values should be read as negative. It should also be kept in mind that the LLP variable as a share in total loans is a stock variable, and that its first difference (Δ LLP) shows the change in this stock variable.

In addition, I conducted robustness checks by altering the order of macroeconomic variables, placing variable Δ ln unemployment as the second variable and variable Δ ln GDP as the third. These robustness checks resulted in largely similar outcomes for both the individual and panel SVAR models.

The results were interpreted by comparing outcomes from the individual SVAR models, followed by the results from the two panel SVAR models. A comparative analysis was also performed, contrasting my empirical study with findings from similar studies.

### 5.3.1 Within regions

When interpreting the forecasting results of individual SVAR models, it is worth starting with a comparison of the size and persistence of the shocks. Among the **SEE EU countries**, the greatest magnitude of the negative GDP shock is in Greece (equal to a decrease by 1.66 %), followed by Croatia (1.28 %), Cyprus (1.19 %), Romania (0.97 %), and Slovenia (0.85 %). A visual inspection of the relevant graphs shows that although the effect of the negative GDP shock decreases over time, it is forecast to last the longest in Greece and Cyprus and the shortest in Romania. The largest magnitude of the unemployment shock is in Cyprus (an increase of 9.49 % in the number of unemployed), followed by Croatia (7.25 %), Slovenia (6.49 %), Greece (4.9 %), and Romania (1.51 %). A visual inspection of the relevant graphs shows that although the effect of the unemployment shock

---

45 The decision to present both response functions of Δ LLP on a single graph has a dual purpose. Primarily, it facilitates enhanced comparability regarding the size and duration of the Δ LLP responses to the two macroeconomic shocks. Additionally, this presentation approach serves the secondary objective of conserving valuable space.

diminishes over time, it is again forecast to last the longest in Greece and Cyprus and the shortest in Romania. The size and persistence of the macroeconomic shocks simulated in the SVAR models based on historical data reveal the strong negative impact of the GFC and the sovereign debt crisis on Cyprus and Greece, on the one hand, and the positive impact of implemented stabilization measures in Romania, on the other.

When it comes to the forecast responses of LLPs[46] to the negative GDP shock, it should be pointed out that they record a positive change (increase) in all countries. In Greece and Cyprus, the effects of the transmission of the negative GDP shock to LLPs are the largest, and the persistence is the longest. In Cyprus, the positive change in LLP has two peaks, in the second quarter (0.002) and in the third quarter ahead (0.002), after which there is a very long and slow return to equilibrium. Similarly, in Greece, positive changes in LLP have two peaks, in the second quarter (0.001) and the fifth quarter ahead (0.001), after which there is an even longer and slower return to equilibrium. In Romania the peak of positive change in LLP (0.001) is in the second quarter ahead, after which the shock transmission effect subsides very quickly and changes in LLPs return to equilibrium. In Slovenia, the peak of positive change in LLP (0.001) is reached in the third quarter ahead, after which the equilibrium is quickly restored. In Croatia, there are two peaks of positive changes in LLP, in the second (0.0006) and fourth (0.0006) quarters ahead; they are smallest compared to the other countries, although the size of the GDP shock is not the smallest, on the contrary.

When it comes to forecast responses of LLP to the unemployment shock, it should be pointed out that they record a positive change (increase) in all countries except in Romania. In Greece, positive changes in LLP have two peaks, in the second quarter (0.0018) and the fifth quarter ahead (0.0015), after which there is a long and slow return to equilibrium. In Slovenia, the peak of the positive change in LLP is reached in the second quarter ahead (0.002), after which equilibrium is reached very quickly. When it comes to Cyprus, the peak positive change in LLP is reached in the fourth quarter ahead (0.0008), after which equilibrium is reached very slowly. In Croatia, the positive change in LLP already has its peak in the second quarter ahead (0.0004), and soon after that equilibrium is reached. Only in Romania, for the reasons mentioned earlier, after the simulated unemployment shock, are there small negative changes in LLPs, reaching a peak in the second quarter ahead (0.0002), and equilibrium is restored immediately.

---

46  As a reminder, these are LLPs as a share of total loans (a stock variable).

In this stress test of the SEE EU banking sector, it can be observed that the effects of the transmission of the negative GDP shock to credit risk are somewhat more pronounced than the effects of the transmission of the positive unemployment shock, although the magnitude of the latter is somewhat greater. In addition, based on a comparative analysis of individual SVAR models in the SEE EU, the findings suggest that the Greek and Cypriot banking sectors are the most vulnerable. Indeed, the creation of the individual SVAR models is based on historical data for endogenous variables, but even when supplementing the analysis with NPL ratio data and, in particular, NPL coverage ratio data (Figure 3), the same assertion can be reached, namely that the share of NPLs in total loans in Greece and Cyprus is high compared to other countries, and their coverage by LLPs is quite low, which suggests a lower absorption power for future potential loan losses. On the other hand, the Croatian, Slovenian, and Romanian banking sectors demonstrate somewhat greater resilience, especially when the findings from macro-econometric stress tests are supplemented with an analysis of their NPL ratios and NPL coverage ratios. In these banking sectors, namely, the share of NPLs in total loans is relatively low, and the NPL coverage with LLPs is solid, which favorably affects the ability to absorb new loan losses. Robustness checks of the response of LLPs to both macroeconomic shocks provide similar results.

In the **Western Balkans**, the greatest magnitude of the simulated negative GDP shock is in North Macedonia (equal to a decrease by 2.15 %), followed by Albania (1.96 %), Bosnia and Herzegovina (1.66 %), and Serbia (1.06 %). A visual inspection of the relevant graphs shows that the effect of the negative GDP shock dissipates very quickly in all economies. Similarly, the largest magnitude of the unemployment shock is in North Macedonia (an increase of 5.66 % in the number of unemployed), followed by Albania (5.49 %), Serbia (5.24 %), and Bosnia and Herzegovina (1.71 %). Interpreting the findings of the persistence of macroeconomic shocks is more demanding in the region of the Western Balkans because in the Albanian and Macedonian SVAR models, their response functions behave unusually in the second quarter ahead. Nevertheless, a visual inspection of the relevant graphs shows that the effect of the positive unemployment shock diminishes slowly over time, and that it lasts the longest in Albania.

When it comes to the forecast responses of LLP to the negative GDP shock, it should first be pointed out that they record a positive change (increase) in Bosnia and Herzegovina and Serbia. In Bosnia and Herzegovina, the positive change in LLP reaches its peak in the second quarter ahead (0.0017), and equilibrium is reached in the sixth quarter ahead. Similarly, in Serbia, the positive change in LLP reaches its peak in the second quarter ahead (0.0008), and equilibrium is

reached in a few quarters ahead. However, in Albania, and especially in North Macedonia, the LLP response functions to the GDP shock look unusual.
When it comes to forecast responses of LLP to the unemployment shock, they record a positive change (increase) in all countries. When it comes to Albania, the peak positive change in LLP is reached in the second quarter ahead (0.0011), after which the return to equilibrium is very slow. In North Macedonia, the positive change in LLP also reaches its peak in the second quarter ahead (0.001), after which equilibrium is swiftly attained. In Bosnia and Herzegovina, the positive change in LLP reaches its peak in the second quarter ahead (0.0009), while equilibrium is reached in the fifth quarter ahead. Similarly, in Serbia the positive change in LLP reaches its peak in the second quarter ahead (0.00059), while equilibrium is reached in the seventh quarter ahead.

A likely explanation of the specific Albanian and North Macedonian models can be found in their historical data, based on which the impulse response functions are estimated. As Figures 32 and 33 show, the business cycle in Albania and North Macedonia experienced only a mild economic slowdown, unlike all other observed countries that experienced a recession (or even a double dip one). North Macedonian professors Nenovski and Smilkovski (2012) explained that the Macedonian banking sector remained stable, well-capitalized, and without higher levels of non-performing loans during the GFC because it was poorly integrated in global financial markets. The crisis did not spill over into North Macedonia through financial channels in 2007/2008 but in 2009 through its main trading partners (Greece, Germany, Italy, etc.). However, due to the fact that at the beginning of 2010, there was an increase in the prices on the world stock markets of those metals that North Macedonia predominantly exports, the economy soon recovered (Nenovski & Smilkovski, 2012). Indeed, according to the research by Filipovski et al. (2018) on the synchronization of the business cycle of a small open economy, such as North Macedonia's, with the economy of the EU member states, it has been determined that there is an asymmetric adjustment, namely, the adjustment of the North Macedonian business cycle to the positive foreign economic shock was relatively more pronounced than the adjustment to the negative economic shock.

Additionally, the North Macedonian banking sector was unique for its level of NPL coverage with provisions. During the observed period, LLPs covered more than 100 % of NPL (Figure 4), which means that part of performing ("healthy") loans were also covered with provisions. This is a unique feature among the observed banking sectors, which indicates the higher absorption power of potential future loan losses in North Macedonia and, therefore, a greater likelihood of better resilience to potential shocks.

Through research on the transmission of external shocks (more precisely, the 1998 Russian financial crisis and the 2001 Turkish banking crisis) to the selected Southeast European financial markets, Fry and Sojli (2005) found that the Albanian market remained intact, unlike the others. The Albanian credit market is isolated and less developed compared to other Southeast European financial markets and these characteristics acted as a natural barrier to external shocks. Indeed, because of these same characteristics, the financial channel was not a channel for the transmission of the GFC to the Albanian economy (Sojli, 2009). In addition, the local elections in June 2009 also encouraged the Albanian authorities to make additional efforts to preserve the resilience of their economy (Sojli, 2009).

Considering that the individual SVAR models are based on historical macro-financial data, it is not surprising that they reveal more unusual findings for Albania and North Macedonia. In this stress test of the Western Balkans banking sectors, generally, it can be observed that the effects of the transmission of the positive unemployment shock to credit risk are somewhat more pronounced than the effects of the transmission of the negative GDP shock, and the magnitude of the former is also somewhat greater. Robustness checks of the response of LLPs to both macroeconomic shocks yield similar results.

### 5.3.2 Between regions

The next research interest is to perform macro stress tests at regional level, i.e. at the level of the SEE EU countries and the Western Balkans. First, the magnitude of the simulated negative GDP shock is higher in the Western Balkans (1.75 %) than in the SEE EU (1.32 %), as can be seen in Figures 28a and 29a. The effects of a negative GDP shock are, however, more persistent in the SEE EU panel because it takes much longer for the system to return to equilibrium. Second, the magnitude of the simulated positive unemployment shock is greater in the SEE EU than in the Western Balkans, but the shock is less persistent.

After the simulated negative GDP shock, the SEE EU panel SVAR model forecasts positive changes in the stock of LLPs as a share of total loans, peaking in the third quarter (0.001388) and then slowly diminishing. In contrast, after a simulated negative GDP shock, changes in the stock of LLPs mostly oscillate around zero in the Western Balkans.

After the simulated unemployment shock, the SEE EU panel SVAR model forecasts positive changes in the stock of LLPs as a share of total loans, peaking in the second quarter (0.000816) and then starting to slowly revert to equilibrium. In the Western Balkans, after the simulated unemployment shock, the SVAR

The effect of macroeconomic shocks 125

model also forecasts positive changes in the stock of LLPs as a share of total loans, peaking in the fourth quarter (0.001457) and then starting to return to equilibrium at an even slower pace.

In short, the macro stress tests forecast, first, that the effects of the transmission of the GDP shock to positive changes in the stock of LLPs as a share of total loans are greater in the SEE EU region (in this region the size of the GDP shock is smaller but it is more persistent than in the Western Balkans). Second, the forecasts indicate that the effects of the transmission of the unemployment shock to positive changes in the stock of LLPs as a share of total loans are greater in the Western Balkans (in this region the size of the unemployment shock is smaller but it is more persistent than in the SEE EU). Robustness checks based on the swapped order of variables give similar results.

Comparing my study with similar empirical ones, I can only provide a general assessment because the constructed VAR models represent dynamic systems of different endogenous variables in terms of their type, measurement units, and frequency. For example, in CESEE banking sectors, it was also found that the negative GDP shock leads to a cumulative increase in NPLs and that the unemployment shock has a significant impact on the increase in Δ NPLs (Klein, 2013). In the banking sectors of OECD countries, the output gap shock has also been found to make positive changes on LLPs as a share of total assets (Pool et al., 2015).

In the next step, by implementing a jackknife-type procedure like the one in the study by Hristov and Roth (2022), two countries are excluded from the panel SVAR model in order to determine whether this has a significant impact on the findings. First, the SEE EU panel was corrected by exempting data for Greece and Cyprus (Figure 28b). The relevant graphs show that the magnitudes of the GDP shock and the unemployment shock have not changed; neither has the persistence of the unemployment shock. What has changed compared to the original macro stress test (Figure 28a) is that the persistence of the GDP shock is significantly lower, and, as a result, the panel SVAR model now forecasts a quicker reversion to equilibrium of the Δ LLP response to the macroeconomic shocks.

Similarly, the Western Balkans panel is recreated without the data for Albania and North Macedonia (Figure 29b). Now the changes are more numerous in comparison to the original macro stress test because the new SVAR model outputs lower magnitudes for both macroeconomic shocks and shorter persistence in comparison with the original macro stress test (Figure 29a). As a result, the Δ LLP impulse response functions behave as expected, according to the economic literature, i.e. Δ LLP is positive after a negative GDP shock and a positive unemployment shock. It is noticeable that the Δ LLP quickly returns to equilibrium after reaching a peak in the second quarter.

The application of the jackknife-type procedure highlighted the heterogeneity of both panels, and in particular the Western Balkans panel. Macro stress tests on individual SVAR models are, therefore, very valuable, as are the robustness checks that were performed not only in the form of swapping the order of variables Δ ln GDP and Δ ln unemployment in the SVAR models, but also in the form of a Granger causality test. The findings remain unchanged in that the observed banking sectors are located in specific macroeconomic environments and at different levels of vulnerability.

Table 21. Variables in the SVAR model

| Variable | Source of data | Level data |
|---|---|---|
| Loan loss provisions (LLP) | IMF FSI (2021) & IMF Ecofin FSI (IMF. Dissemination Standards Bulletin Board, 2021), for Serbia only | LLPs are provided as a stock variable. Their share in total loans was computed. |
| Real GDP | IMF IFS (2021a) | In the cases of Albania, Bosnia and Herzegovina, and North Macedonia seasonally unadjusted real GDP data are adjusted using X13 ARIMA. The natural logarithm is then computed on data provided in millions of local currencies. |
| Number of unemployed persons | ILO (ILOSTAT, 2021) & IMF IFS (2021b), for Bosnia and Herzegovina only | In the cases of Croatia, Cyprus, Greece, Serbia, and Slovenia seasonally unadjusted data are adjusted using X13 ARIMA. In the case of Serbia, biannual data (reported during 2008–2013) are converted to quarter frequency using the Chow-Lin interpolation method. The natural logarithm is then computed on data provided in thousands. |

The effect of macroeconomic shocks 127

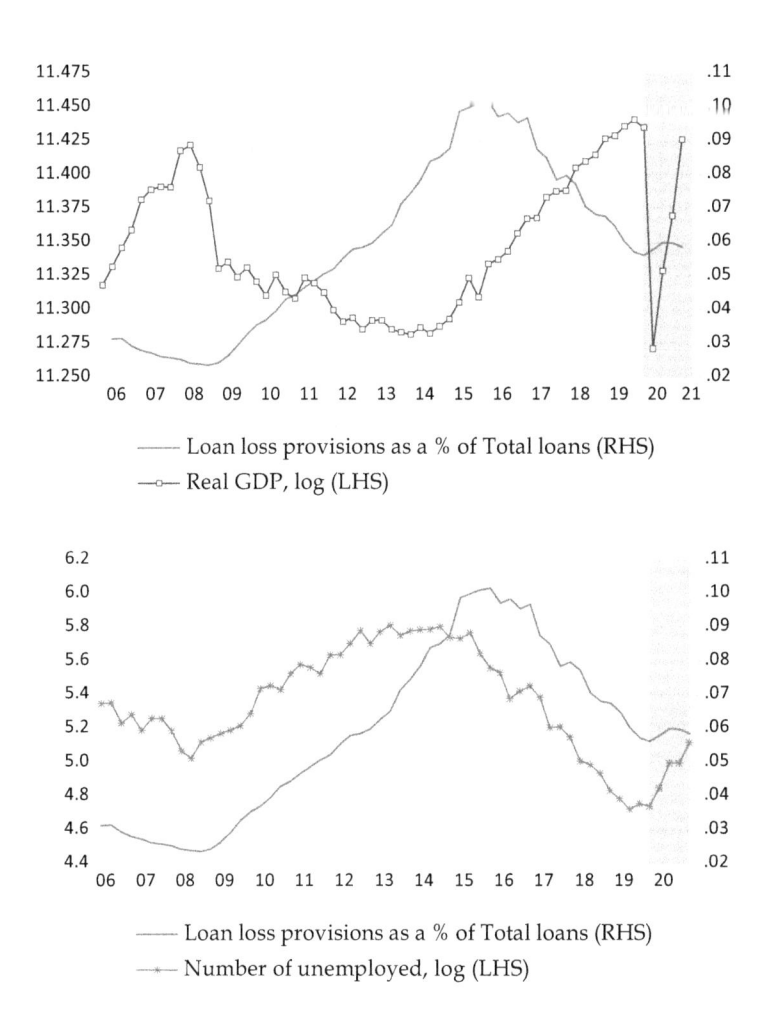

—— Loan loss provisions as a % of Total loans (RHS)
—□— Real GDP, log (LHS)

—— Loan loss provisions as a % of Total loans (RHS)
—✶— Number of unemployed, log (LHS)

Figure 9. Croatian Time series

**Table 22.** Croatia: Unit root tests (2006Q2-2020Q1) (quarterly data)

| Variable | T-statistic | Critical value (1 %) | Critical value (5 %) | Critical value (10 %) | Result |
|---|---|---|---|---|---|
| LLP | -0.261 | -2.609 | -1.947 | -1.612 | Non-stationary |
| GDP | 1.224 | -2.606 | -1.946 | -1.613 | Non-stationary |
| Unemployment | -0.633 | -2.609 | -1.947 | -1.612 | Non-stationary |
| Δ LLP | -2.339 | -2.609 | -1.947 | -1.612 | Stationary |
| Δ ln GDP | -2.443 | -2.611 | -1.947 | -1.612 | Stationary |
| Δ ln Unempl. | -2.547 | -2.609 | -1.947 | -1.612 | Stationary |

Note: The ADF unit root test was performed; deterministic component: none; maximum lags is 4 due to quarterly data frequency. The table reports on level and on transformed variables. Δ LLP = the first difference of LLP to total loans; Δ ln GDP = the log-difference of real GDP and Δ ln Unempl. = the log-difference of the number of unemployed.

**Table 23.** Croatia: Summary statistics (2006Q2-2020Q1)

| Variable | Obs. | Mean | Median | Max | Min | St.dev. |
|---|---|---|---|---|---|---|
| Δ LLP | 55 | 0.0004 | 0.0011 | 0.0109 | -0.0093 | 0.0033 |
| Δ ln GDP | 56 | 0.0020 | 0.0043 | 0.0268 | -0.0500 | 0.0128 |
| Δ ln Unempl. | 56 | -0.0088 | 0.0013 | 0.1491 | -0.1811 | 0.0725 |

Note: The table reports only on stationary (transformed) variables used in the SVAR model.

**Table 24.** Croatia: Diagnostic checks of the SVAR (2) model (2006Q2-2020Q1)

| Test | Criteria | Result |
|---|---|---|
| Stability test | No root lies outside the unit circle | Stability condition satisfied |
| VAR residual serial correlation LM test | p-value = 0.3817 | No serial correlation at lag 2 |
| VAR residual heteroskedasticity test | p-value = 0.7083 | No heteroscedasticity |

Note: The lag length of 2 was selected using the AIC.

The effect of macroeconomic shocks 129

Baseline model

Positive GDP shock

Positive Unemployment shock

Response functions of loan loss provisions

| Quarter | GDP shock | Unemp. shock |
|---|---|---|
| 1 | 0.000000 | 0.000000 |
| 2 | -0.000661 | 0.000461 |
| 3 | -0.000533 | 0.000348 |
| 4 | -0.000683 | 5.95E-05 |
| 5 | -0.000496 | 0.000121 |
| 6 | -0.000413 | 6.07E-05 |
| 7 | -0.000325 | 5.32E-05 |
| 8 | -0.000256 | 4.27E-05 |
| 9 | -0.000203 | 3.27E-05 |
| 10 | -0.000160 | 2.62E-05 |

─○─ Response to GDP shock   ─●─ Response to Unemp. shock

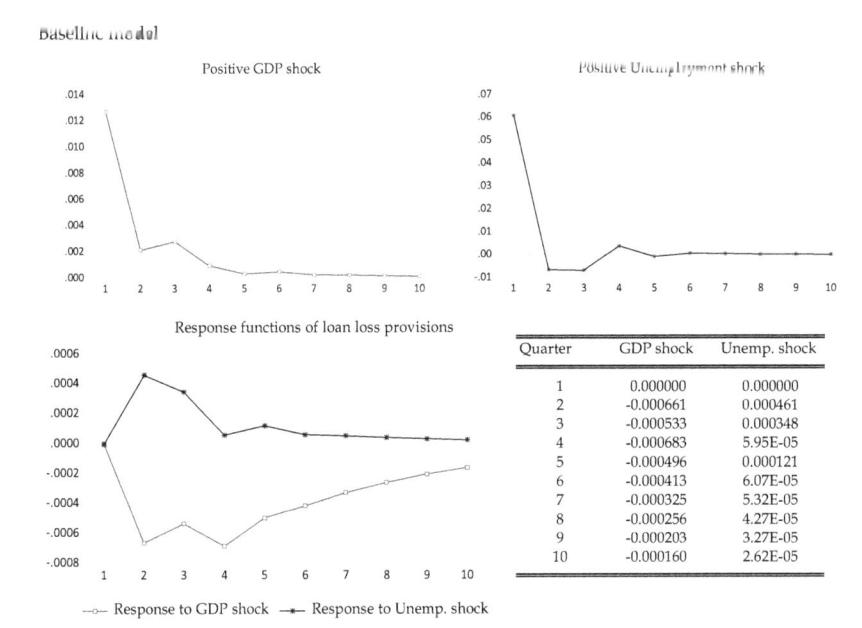

Robustness check

Response functions of loan loss provisions - Robustness check

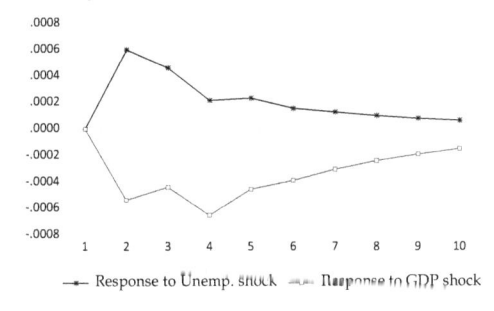

| Quarter | Unemp. shock | GDP shock |
|---|---|---|
| 1 | 0.000000 | 0.000000 |
| 2 | 0.000601 | -0.000536 |
| 3 | 0.000462 | -0.000438 |
| 4 | 0.000216 | -0.000651 |
| 5 | 0.000233 | -0.000455 |
| 6 | 0.000155 | -0.000388 |
| 7 | 0.000127 | -0.000304 |
| 8 | 0.000101 | -0.000239 |
| 9 | 7.87E-05 | -0.000189 |
| 10 | 6.25E-05 | -0.000150 |

─●─ Response to Unemp. shock   ─○─ Response to GDP shock

**Figure 10.** Croatia: Impulses and responses of Δ LLP

Note: All shocks are equal to one standard deviation. Due to the linear character of the SVAR model, a negative GDP shock should be treated as a mirror positive GDP shock. The robustness check is performed based on changing the order of the variables, so that the first is Δ LLP, the second is Δ ln unemployment and the third is Δ ln GDP.

130     The effect of macroeconomic shocks

—— Loan loss provisions as a % of Total loans (RHS)
—□— Real GDP, log (LHS)

—— Loan loss provisions as a % of Total loans (RHS)
—*— Number of unemployed, log (LHS)

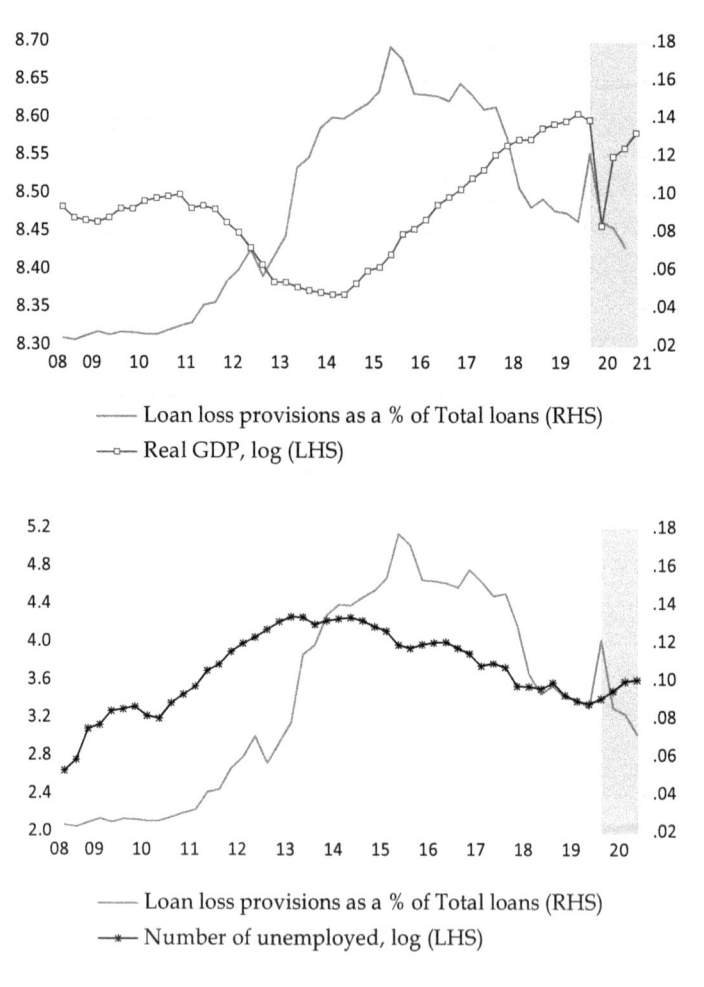

**Figure 11.** Cyprus: Time series

Table 25. Cyprus: Unit root tests (2008Q4-2020Q1) (quarterly data)

| Variable | T-statistic | Critical value (1 %) | Critical value (5 %) | Critical value (10 %) | Result |
|---|---|---|---|---|---|
| LLP | -1.313 | -3.588 | -2.929 | -2.603 | Non-stationary |
| GDP | -0.939 | -3.581 | -2.926 | -2.601 | Non-stationary |
| Unemployment | -1.650 | -3.581 | -2.926 | -2.601 | Non-stationary |
| Δ LLP | -4.467 | -3.588 | -2.929 | -2.603 | Stationary |
| Δ ln GDP | -5.695 | -3.581 | -2.926 | -2.601 | Stationary |
| Δ ln Unempl. | -2.973 | -3.581 | -2.926 | -2.601 | Stationary |

Note: The ADF unit root test was performed; deterministic component: intercept; maximum lags is 4 due to quarterly data frequency. The table reports on level and on transformed variables. Δ LLP = the first difference of LLP to total loans; Δ ln GDP = the log-difference of real GDP and Δ ln Unempl. = the log-difference of the number of unemployed.

Table 26. Cyprus: Summary statistics (2008Q4-2020Q1)

| Variable | Obs. | Mean | Median | Max | Min | St.dev. |
|---|---|---|---|---|---|---|
| Δ LLP | 44 | 0.0014 | 0.0014 | 0.0356 | -0.0257 | 0.0103 |
| Δ ln GDP | 45 | 0.0025 | 0.0036 | 0.0273 | -0.0226 | 0.0119 |
| Δ ln Unempl. | 45 | 0.0153 | 0.0178 | 0.3272 | -0.1963 | 0.0949 |

Note: The table reports only on stationary (transformed) variables used in the SVAR model.

Table 27. Cyprus: Diagnostic checks of the SVAR (2) model (2008Q4-2020Q1)

| Test | Criteria | Result |
|---|---|---|
| Stability test | No root lies outside the unit circle | Stability condition satisfied |
| VAR residual serial correlation LM test | p-value = 0.7207 | No serial correlation at lag 2 |
| VAR residual heteroskedasticity test | p-value = 0.4339 | No heteroscedasticity |

Note: The lag length of 2 was selected using the AIC.

## Baseline model

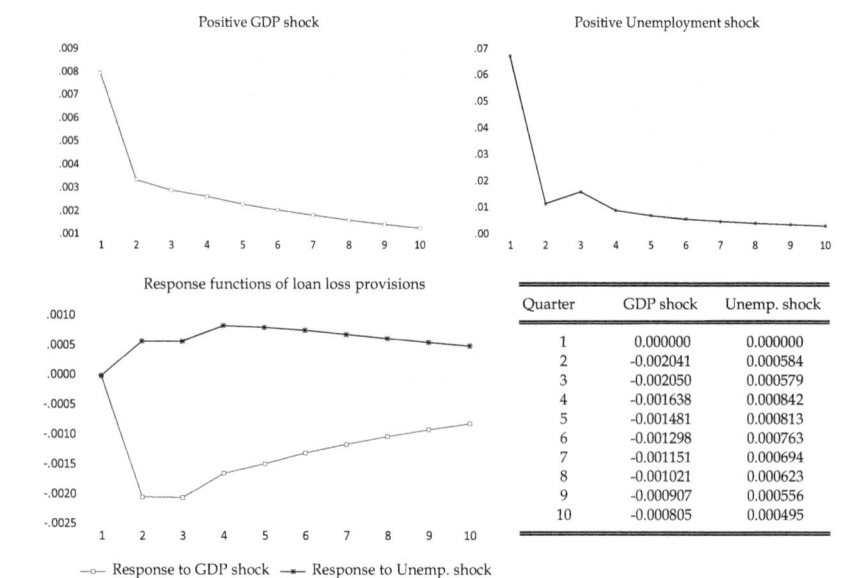

### Positive GDP shock

### Positive Unemployment shock

### Response functions of loan loss provisions

| Quarter | GDP shock | Unemp. shock |
|---|---|---|
| 1 | 0.000000 | 0.000000 |
| 2 | -0.002041 | 0.000584 |
| 3 | -0.002050 | 0.000579 |
| 4 | -0.001638 | 0.000842 |
| 5 | -0.001481 | 0.000813 |
| 6 | -0.001298 | 0.000763 |
| 7 | -0.001151 | 0.000694 |
| 8 | -0.001021 | 0.000623 |
| 9 | -0.000907 | 0.000556 |
| 10 | -0.000805 | 0.000495 |

—○— Response to GDP shock   —•— Response to Unemp. shock

## Robustness check

### Response functions of loan loss provisions - Robustness check

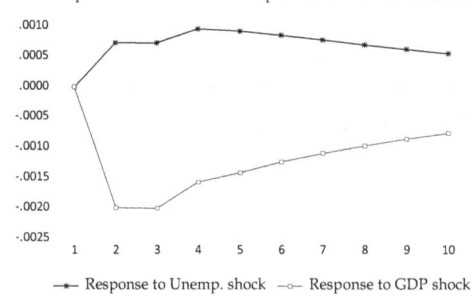

| Quarter | Unemp. Shock | GDP shock |
|---|---|---|
| 1 | 0.000000 | 0.000000 |
| 2 | 0.000728 | -0.001994 |
| 3 | 0.000724 | -0.002004 |
| 4 | 0.000956 | -0.001574 |
| 5 | 0.000916 | -0.001420 |
| 6 | 0.000853 | -0.001240 |
| 7 | 0.000774 | -0.001099 |
| 8 | 0.000694 | -0.000974 |
| 9 | 0.000619 | -0.000865 |
| 10 | 0.000551 | -0.000768 |

—•— Response to Unemp. shock   —○— Response to GDP shock

**Figure 12.** Cyprus: Impulses and responses of Δ LLP

Note: All shocks are equal to one standard deviation. Due to the linear character of the SVAR model, a negative GDP shock should be treated as a mirror positive GDP shock. The robustness check is performed based on changing the order of the variables, so that the first is Δ LLP, the second is Δ ln unemployment and the third is Δ ln GDP.

The effect of macroeconomic shocks 133

―― Loan loss provisions as a % of Total loans(RHS)
―□― Real GDP, log (LHS)

―― Loan loss provisions as a % of Total loans (RHS)
―*― Number of unemployed, log (LHS)

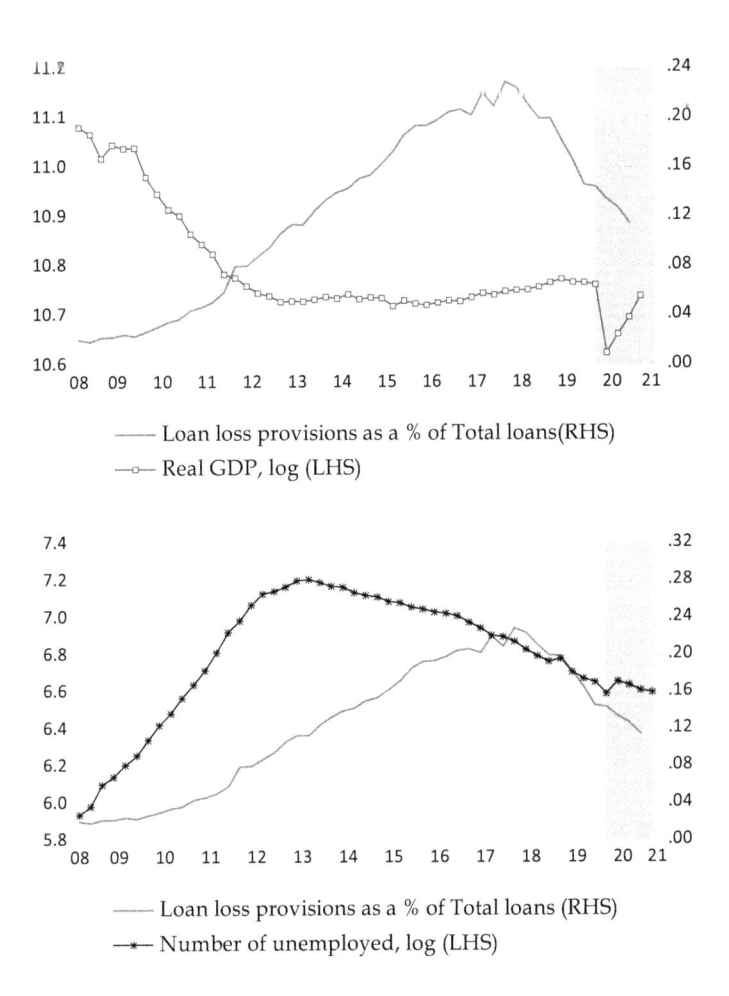

Figure 13 Greece: Time series

**Table 28.** Greece: Unit root tests (2008Q3-2020Q1) (quarterly data)

| Variable | Test statistic | Critical value (1 %) | Critical value (5 %) | Critical value (10 %) | Result |
|---|---|---|---|---|---|
| LLP | 1.745 | -4.170 | -3.510 | -3.185 | Non-stationary |
| GDP | -1.187 | -4.165 | -3.508 | -3.184 | Non-stationary |
| Unemployment | -0.392 | -4.165 | -3.508 | -3.184 | Non-stationary |
| Δ LLP | -5.660 | -4.175 | -3.513 | -3.186 | Stationary |
| Δ ln GDP | -6.780 | -4.170 | -3.510 | -3.185 | Stationary |
| Δ ln Unempl. | -5.032 | -4.170 | -3.510 | -3.185 | Stationary |

Note: The Phillips-Perron unit root test was performed; deterministic component: trend and intercept. The table reports on level and on transformed variables. Δ LLP = the first difference of LLP to total loans; Δ ln GDP = the log-difference of real GDP and Δ ln Unempl. = the log-difference of the number of unemployed.

**Table 29.** Greece: Summary statistics (2008Q3-2020Q1)

| Variable | Obs. | Mean | Median | Max | Min | St.dev. |
|---|---|---|---|---|---|---|
| Δ LLP | 46 | 0.0026 | 0.0034 | 0.0209 | -0.0202 | 0.0088 |
| Δ ln GDP | 47 | -0.0068 | -0.0028 | 0.0273 | -0.0595 | 0.0166 |
| Δ ln Unempl. | 47 | 0.0140 | -0.0062 | 0.1175 | -0.0713 | 0.0490 |

Note: The table reports only on stationary (transformed) variables used in the SVAR model.

**Table 30.** Greece: Diagnostic checks of the SVAR (3) model (2008Q3-2020Q1)

| Test | Criteria | Result |
|---|---|---|
| Stability test | No root lies outside the unit circle | Stability condition satisfied |
| VAR residual serial correlation LM test | p-value = 0.1834 | No serial correlation at lag 3 |
| VAR residual heteroskedasticity test | p-value = 0.1619 | No heteroscedasticity |

Note: The lag length of 3 was selected using the AIC.

The effect of macroeconomic shocks 135

Baseline model

Positive GDP shock

Positive Unemployment shock

Response functions of loan loss provisions

| Quarter | GDP shock | Unemp. shock |
|---|---|---|
| 1 | 0.000000 | 0.000000 |
| 2 | -0.001566 | 0.001833 |
| 3 | -0.001075 | 0.000421 |
| 4 | -0.000639 | 0.000531 |
| 5 | -0.001377 | 0.001471 |
| 6 | -0.000628 | 0.000655 |
| 7 | -0.001027 | 0.000874 |
| 8 | -0.000986 | 0.001026 |
| 9 | -0.000944 | 0.000827 |
| 10 | -0.000939 | 0.000895 |

─○─ Response to GDP shock ─●─ Response to Unemp. shock

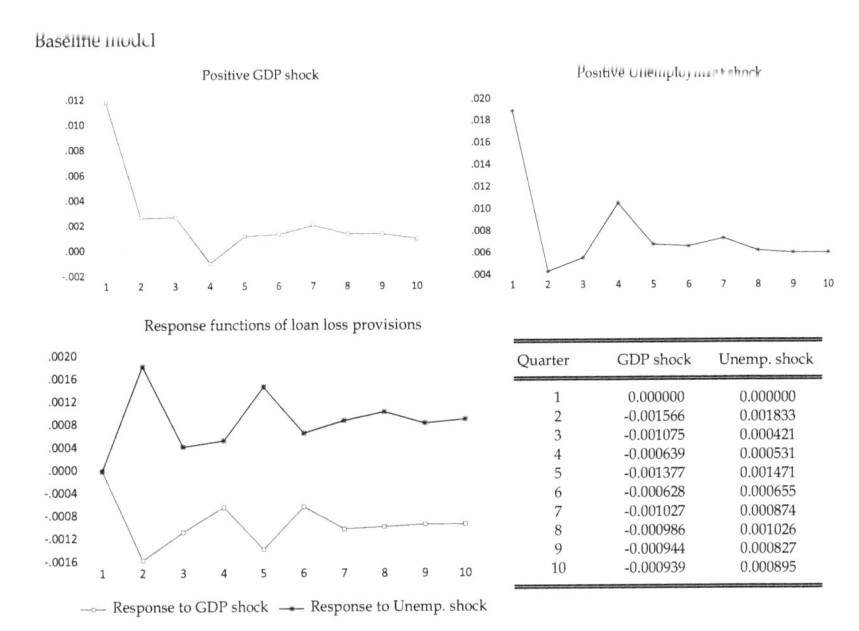

Robustness check

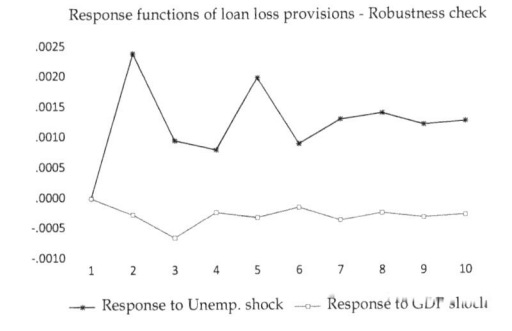

Response functions of loan loss provisions - Robustness check

| Quarter | Unemp. Shock | GDP shock |
|---|---|---|
| 1 | 0.000000 | 0.000000 |
| 2 | 0.002395 | -0.000269 |
| 3 | 0.000951 | -0.000655 |
| 4 | 0.000798 | -0.000231 |
| 5 | 0.001990 | -0.000316 |
| 6 | 0.000895 | -0.000153 |
| 7 | 0.001299 | -0.000360 |
| 8 | 0.001402 | -0.000241 |
| 9 | 0.001214 | -0.000318 |
| 10 | 0.001268 | -0.000276 |

─●─ Response to Unemp. shock ─○─ Response to GDP shock

**Figure 14.** Greece: Impulses and responses of Δ LLP

Note: All shocks are equal to one standard deviation. Due to the linear character of the SVAR model, a negative GDP shock should be treated as a mirror positive GDP shock. The robustness check is performed based on changing the order of the variables, so that the first is Δ LLP, the second is Δ ln unemployment and the third is Δ ln GDP.

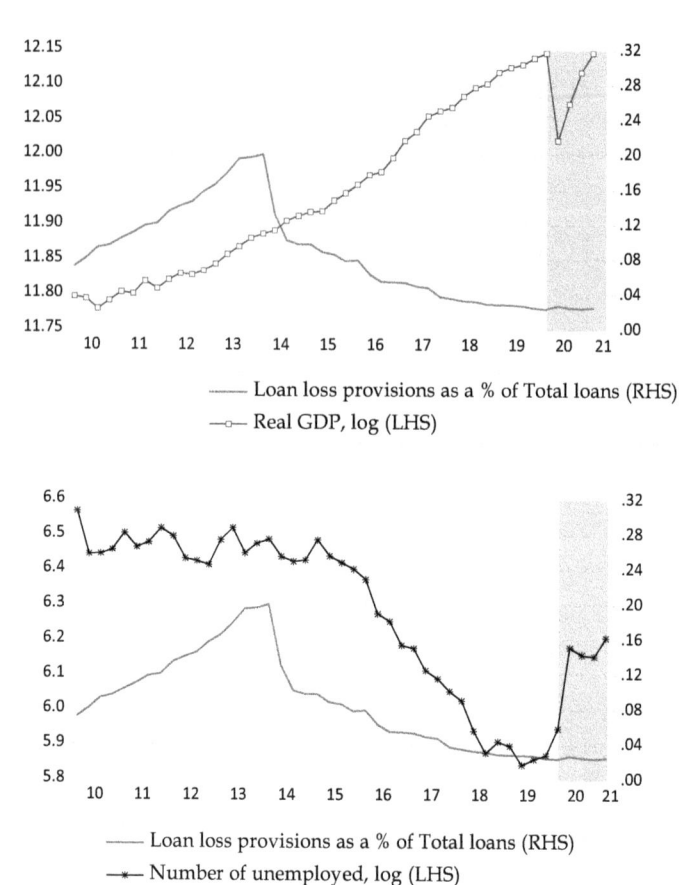

**Figure 15.** Romania: Time series

Table 31. Romania: Unit root tests (2010Q1-2020Q1) (quarterly data)

| Variable | Test statistic | Critical value (1 %) | Critical value (5 %) | Critical value (10 %) | Result |
|---|---|---|---|---|---|
| LLP | -2.244 | -4.205 | -3.526 | -3.194 | Non-stationary |
| GDP | -3.900 | -4.198 | -3.523 | -3.192 | Stationary |
| Unemployment | -1.684 | -4.198 | -3.523 | -3.192 | Non-stationary |
| Δ LLP | -4.122 | -4.211 | -3.529 | -3.196 | Stationary |
| Δ ln GDP | -6.171 | -4.198 | -3.523 | -3.192 | Stationary |
| Δ ln Unempl. | -5.541 | -4.198 | -3.523 | -3.192 | Stationary |

Note: The Phillips-Perron unit root test was performed; deterministic component: trend and intercept. The table reports on level and on transformed variables. Δ LLP = the first difference of LLP to total loans; Δ ln GDP = the log-difference of real GDP and Δ ln Unempl. = the log-difference of the number of unemployed.
As the SVAR model based on mixed I(0) and I(1) data could not pass diagnostic checks, I created the SVAR model based on I(1) data and 1 lag length due to the shortness of the time series.

Table 32. Romania: Summary statistics (2010Q1-2020Q1)

| Variable | Obs. | Mean | Median | Max | Min | St.dev. |
|---|---|---|---|---|---|---|
| Δ LLP | 40 | -0.0012 | -0.0004 | 0.0157 | -0.0688 | 0.0138 |
| Δ ln GDP | 41 | 0.0078 | 0.0091 | 0.0246 | -0.0287 | 0.0097 |
| Δ ln Unempl. | 41 | -0.0158 | -0.0182 | 0.0760 | -0.1235 | 0.0451 |

Note: The table reports only on stationary (transformed) variables used in the SVAR model.

Table 33. Romania: Diagnostic checks of the SVAR (1) model (2010Q1-2020Q1)

| Test | Criteria | Result |
|---|---|---|
| Stability test | No root lies outside the unit circle | Stability condition satisfied |
| VAR residual serial correlation LM test | p-value = 0.1763 | No serial correlation at lag 1 |
| VAR residual heteroskedasticity test | p-value = 0.3739 | No heteroscedasticity |

Note: The lag length of 1 was selected arbitrarily.

## Baseline model

### Positive GDP shock

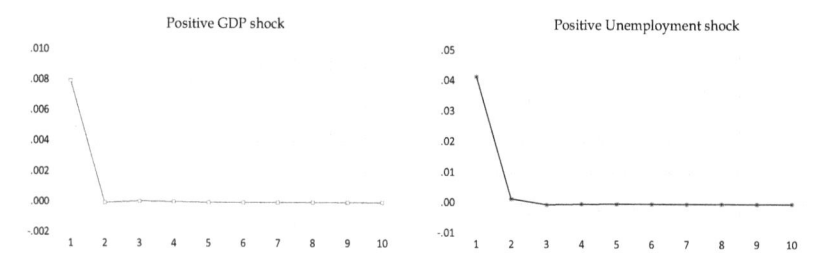

### Positive Unemployment shock

### Response functions of loan loss provisions

| Quarter | GDP shock | Unemp. shock |
|---|---|---|
| 1 | 0.000000 | 0.000000 |
| 2 | -0.001499 | -0.000216 |
| 3 | -0.000554 | -0.000169 |
| 4 | -0.000234 | -7.31E-05 |
| 5 | -0.000102 | -3.14E-05 |
| 6 | -4.43E-05 | -1.37E-05 |
| 7 | -1.93E-05 | -5.94E-06 |
| 8 | -8.38E-06 | -2.58E-06 |
| 9 | -3.64E-06 | -1.12E-06 |
| 10 | -1.58E-06 | -4.88E-07 |

—◦— Response to GDP shock  —•— Response to Unemp. shock

## Robustness check

### Response functions of loan loss provisions - Robustness check

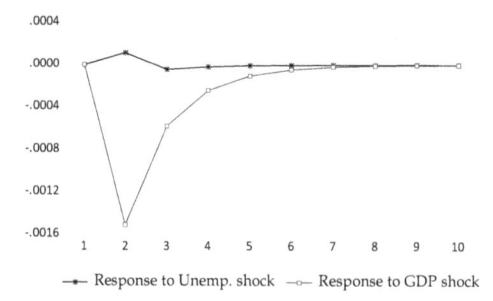

| Quarter | Unemp. Shock | GDP shock |
|---|---|---|
| 1 | 0.000000 | 0.000000 |
| 2 | 0.000115 | -0.001510 |
| 3 | -4.43E-05 | -0.000578 |
| 4 | -2.05E-05 | -0.000244 |
| 5 | -8.53E-06 | -0.000106 |
| 6 | -3.70E-06 | -4.63E-05 |
| 7 | -1.61E-06 | -2.01E-05 |
| 8 | -7.00E-07 | -8.74E-06 |
| 9 | -3.04E-07 | -3.80E-06 |
| 10 | -1.32E-07 | -1.65E-06 |

—•— Response to Unemp. shock  —◦— Response to GDP shock

**Figure 16.** Romania: Impulses and responses of Δ LLP

Note: All shocks are equal to one standard deviation. Due to the linear character of the SVAR model, a negative GDP shock should be treated as a mirror positive GDP shock. The robustness check is performed based on changing the order of the variables, so that the first is Δ LLP, the second is Δ ln unemployment and the third is Δ ln GDP.

The effect of macroeconomic shocks 139

—— Loan loss provisions as a % of Total loans (RHS)
—□— Real GDP, log (LHS)

—— Loan loss provisions as a % of Total loans (RHS)
—*— Number of unemployed, log (LHS)

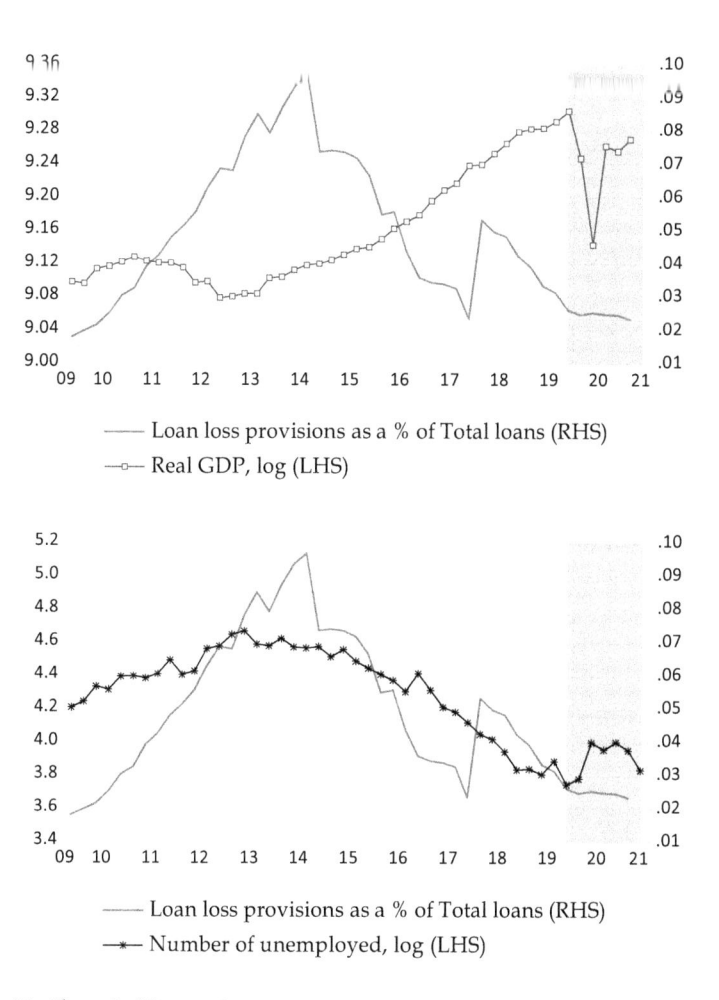

**Figure 17** Slovenia: Time series

140     The effect of macroeconomic shocks

Table 34. Slovenia: Unit root tests (2009Q4-2019Q4) (quarterly data)

| Variable | Test statistic | Critical value (1 %) | Critical value (5 %) | Critical value (10 %) | Result |
|---|---|---|---|---|---|
| LLP | -1.511 | -3.605 | -2.936 | -2.606 | Non-stationary |
| GDP | 1.878 | -3.600 | -2.935 | -2.605 | Non-stationary |
| Unemployment | -0.047 | -3.600 | -2.935 | -2.605 | Non-stationary |
| Δ LLP | -6.037 | -3.610 | -2.938 | -2.607 | Stationary |
| Δ ln GDP | -5.047 | -3.605 | -2.936 | -2.606 | Stationary |
| Δ ln Unempl. | -6.260 | -3.605 | -2.936 | -2.606 | Stationary |

Note: The Phillips-Perron unit root test was performed; deterministic component: intercept. The table reports on level and on transformed variables. Δ LLP = the first difference of LLP to total loans; Δ ln GDP = the log-difference of real GDP and Δ ln Unempl. = the log-difference of the number of unemployed.

Table 35. Slovenia: Summary statistics (2009Q4-2019Q4)

| Variable | Obs. | Mean | Median | Max | Min | St.dev. |
|---|---|---|---|---|---|---|
| Δ LLP | 40 | 0.0002 | -0.00003 | 0.0298 | -0.0231 | 0.0081 |
| Δ ln GDP | 41 | 0.0050 | 0.0056 | 0.0218 | -0.0199 | 0.0085 |
| Δ ln Unempl. | 41 | -0.0112 | -0.0127 | 0.1345 | -0.1404 | 0.0649 |

Note: The table reports only on stationary (transformed) variables used in the SVAR model.

Table 36. Slovenia: Diagnostic checks of the SVAR (1) model (2009Q4-2019Q4)

| Test | Criteria | Result |
|---|---|---|
| Stability test | No root lies outside the unit circle | Stability condition satisfied |
| VAR residual serial correlation LM test | p-value = 0.4972 | No serial correlation at lag 1 |
| VAR residual heteroskedasticity test | p-value = 0.1632 | No heteroscedasticity |

Note: The lag length of 1 was selected using the AIC. The SVAR (1) model is created with one exogenous variable, which is a dummy variable that is equal to 1 for 2018Q1 otherwise it is 0. In 2018Q1, a large growth of LLP is registered due to the beginning of the application of IFRS 9, and the use of the dummy variable aims to reduce the effect outlier on estimation.

The effect of macroeconomic shocks 141

Baseline model

Positive GDP shock

Positive Unemployment shock

Response functions of loan loss provisions

| Quarter | GDP shock | Unemp. shock |
|---|---|---|
| 1 | 0.000000 | 0.000000 |
| 2 | -0.001077 | 0.001918 |
| 3 | -0.001499 | -2.62E-05 |
| 4 | -0.000373 | 0.000261 |
| 5 | -0.000268 | 4.50E-05 |
| 6 | -9.91E-05 | 4.27E-05 |
| 7 | -5.38E-05 | 1.39E-05 |
| 8 | -2.31E-05 | 8.21E-06 |
| 9 | -1.14E-05 | 3.36E-06 |
| 10 | -5.16E-06 | 1.71E-06 |

—○— Response to GDP shock   —*— Response to Unemp. shock

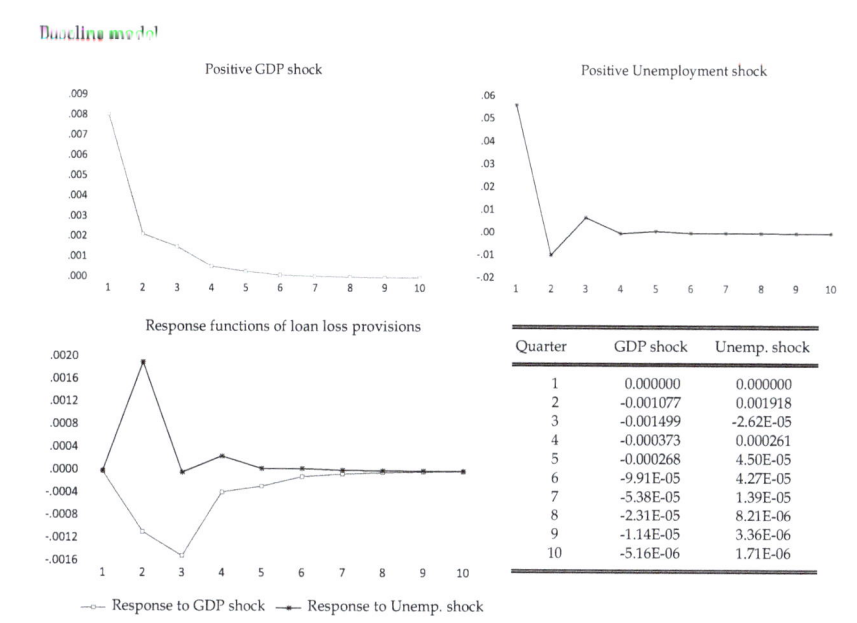

Robustness check

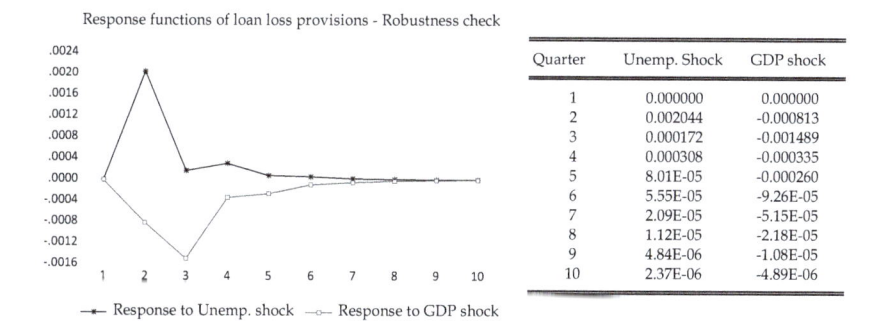

Response functions of loan loss provisions - Robustness check

| Quarter | Unemp. Shock | GDP shock |
|---|---|---|
| 1 | 0.000000 | 0.000000 |
| 2 | 0.002044 | -0.000813 |
| 3 | 0.000172 | -0.001489 |
| 4 | 0.000308 | -0.000335 |
| 5 | 8.01E-05 | -0.000260 |
| 6 | 5.55E-05 | -9.26E-05 |
| 7 | 2.09E-05 | -5.15E-05 |
| 8 | 1.12E-05 | -2.18E-05 |
| 9 | 4.84E-06 | -1.08E-05 |
| 10 | 2.37E-06 | -4.89E-06 |

—*— Response to Unemp. shock   —○— Response to GDP shock

**Figure 18.** Slovenia: Impulses and responses of $\Delta$ LLP

Note: All shocks are equal to one standard deviation. Due to the linear character of the SVAR model, a negative GDP shock should be treated as a mirror positive GDP shock. The robustness check is performed based on changing the order of the variables, so that the first is $\Delta$ LLP, the second is $\Delta$ ln unemployment and the third is $\Delta$ ln GDP (the same dummy variable is used in the model).

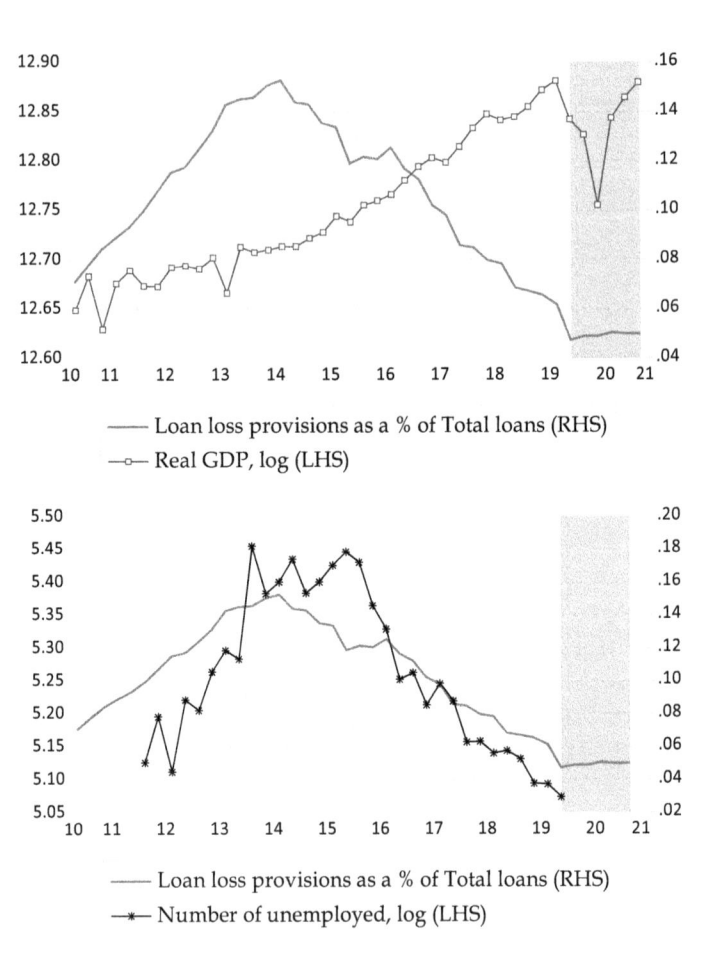

**Figure 19.** Albania: Time series

Table 37. Albania: Unit root tests (2010Q4-2019Q4) (quarterly data)

| Variable | Test statistic | Critical value (1 %) | Critical value (5 %) | Critical value (10 %) | Result |
|---|---|---|---|---|---|
| LLP | -0.582 | -3.626 | -2.945 | -2.611 | Non-stationary |
| GDP | -0.379 | -3.621 | -2.943 | -2.610 | Non-stationary |
| Unemployment | -1.192 | -3.661 | -2.960 | -2.619 | Non-stationary |
| Δ LLP | -3.321 | -3.632 | -2.948 | -2.612 | Stationary |
| Δ ln GDP | -12.521 | -3.626 | -2.945 | -2.611 | Stationary |
| Δ ln Unempl. | -7.191 | -3.670 | -2.963 | -2.621 | Stationary |

Note: The Phillips-Perron unit root test was performed; deterministic component: intercept. The table reports on level and on transformed variables. Δ LLP = the first difference of LLP to total loans; Δ ln GDP = the log-difference of real GDP and Δ ln Unempl. = the log-difference of the number of unemployed.

Table 38. Albania: Summary statistics (2010Q4-2019Q4)

| Variable | Obs. | Mean | Median | Max | Min | St.dev. |
|---|---|---|---|---|---|---|
| Δ LLP | 36 | -0.0006 | -0.0009 | 0.0110 | -0.0148 | 0.0068 |
| Δ ln GDP | 37 | 0.0050 | 0.0063 | 0.0467 | -0.0535 | 0.0196 |
| Δ ln Unempl. | 31 | -0.0017 | -0.0123 | 0.1710 | -0.0833 | 0.0549 |

Note: The table reports only on stationary (transformed) variables used in the SVAR model.

Table 39. Albania: Diagnostic checks of the SVAR (2) model (2010Q4-2019Q4)

| Test | Criteria | Result |
|---|---|---|
| Stability test | No root lies outside the unit circle | Stability condition satisfied |
| VAR residual serial correlation LM test | p-value = 0.1966 | No serial correlation at lag 2 |
| VAR residual heteroskedasticity test | p-value = 0.7845 | No heteroscedasticity |

Note: The lag length of 2 was selected using the AIC.

144        The effect of macroeconomic shocks

Baseline model

Positive GDP shock

[Chart showing values from .015 to -.015 over quarters 1-10]

Positive Unemployment shock

[Chart showing values from .04 to -.01 over quarters 1-10]

Response functions of loan loss provisions

[Chart showing values from .0020 to -.0004 over quarters 1-10]

—o— Response to GDP shock   —•— Response to Unemp. shock

| Quarter | GDP shock | Unemp. shock |
|---------|-----------|--------------|
| 1 | 0.000000 | 0.000000 |
| 2 | 0.000651 | 0.001121 |
| 3 | 0.000862 | 0.001654 |
| 4 | -1.86E-05 | 0.000461 |
| 5 | -4.50E-05 | 0.001283 |
| 6 | 0.000884 | 0.000615 |
| 7 | -0.000365 | 0.000864 |
| 8 | 0.000574 | 0.000661 |
| 9 | 4.64E-05 | 0.000687 |
| 10 | 0.000201 | 0.000542 |

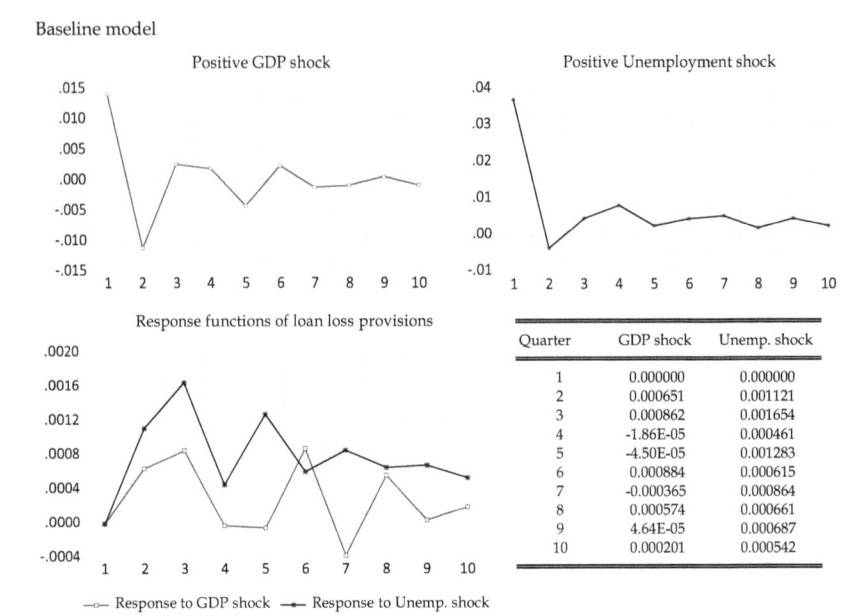

Robustness check

Response functions of loan loss provisions - Robustness check

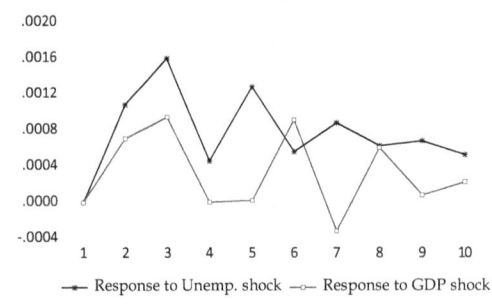

[Chart showing values from .0020 to -.0004 over quarters 1-10]

—•— Response to Unemp. shock   —o— Response to GDP shock

| Quarter | Unemp shock | GDP shock |
|---------|-------------|-----------|
| 1 | 0.000000 | 0.000000 |
| 2 | 0.001084 | 0.000710 |
| 3 | 0.001605 | 0.000951 |
| 4 | 0.000462 | 6.39E-06 |
| 5 | 0.001283 | 2.46E-05 |
| 6 | 0.000566 | 0.000916 |
| 7 | 0.000883 | -0.000317 |
| 8 | 0.000629 | 0.000609 |
| 9 | 0.000683 | 8.36E-05 |
| 10 | 0.000530 | 0.000230 |

**Figure 20.** Albania: Impulses and responses of Δ LLP

Note: All shocks are equal to one standard deviation. Due to the linear character of the SVAR model, a negative GDP shock should be treated as a mirror positive GDP shock. The robustness check is performed based on changing the order of the variables, so that the first is Δ LLP, the second is Δ ln unemployment and the third is Δ ln GDP.

The effect of macroeconomic shocks 145

—— Loan loss provisions as a % of Total loans (RHS)
—□— Real GDP, log (LHS)

—— Loan loss provisions as a % of Total loans (RHS)
—*— Number of unemployed, log (LHS)

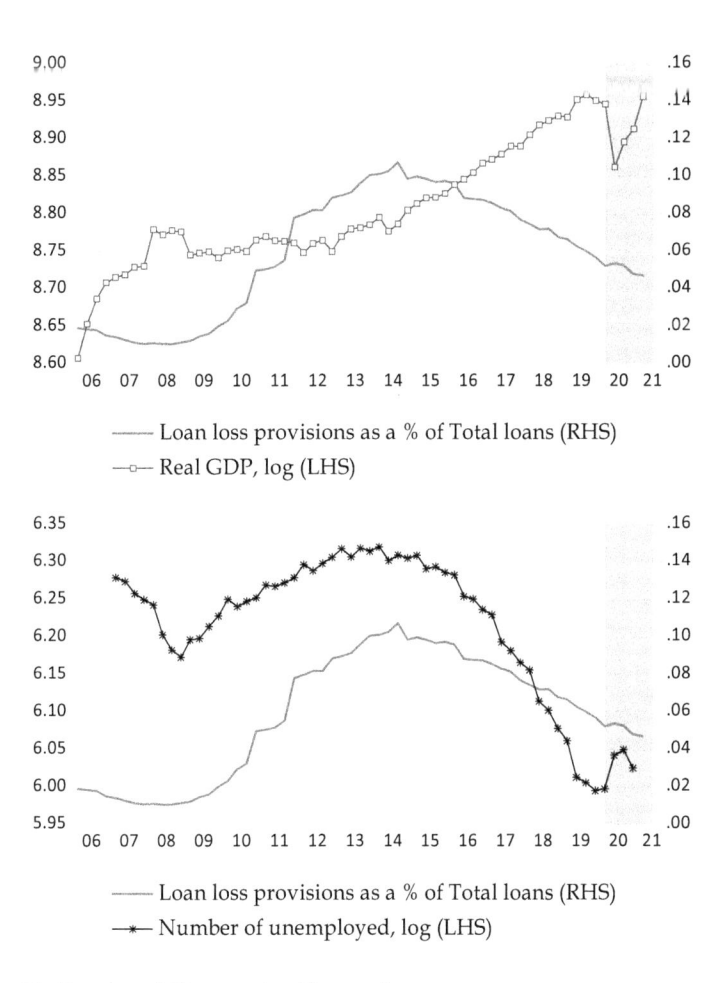

**Figure 21.** Bosnia and Herzegovina: Time series

**Table 40.** Bosnia and Herzegovina: Unit root tests (2007Q1-2020Q2) (quarterly data)

| Variable | Test statistic | Critical value (1 %) | Critical value (5 %) | Critical value (10 %) | Result |
|---|---|---|---|---|---|
| LLP | -1.404 | -3.557 | -2.916 | -2.596 | Non-stationary |
| GDP | -1.318 | -3.557 | -2.916 | -2.596 | Non-stationary |
| Unemployment | -0.089 | -3.560 | -2.917 | -2.596 | Non-stationary |
| Δ LLP | -5.622 | -3.560 | -2.917 | -2.596 | Stationary |
| Δ ln GDP | -5.086 | -3.560 | -2.917 | -2.596 | Stationary |
| Δ ln Unempl. | -4.427 | -3.562 | -2.918 | -2.597 | Stationary |

Note: The Phillips-Perron unit root test was performed; deterministic component: intercept. The table reports on level and on transformed variables. Δ LLP = the first difference of LLP to total loans; Δ ln GDP = the log-difference of real GDP and Δ ln Unempl. = the log-difference of the number of unemployed.

**Table 41.** Bosnia and Herzegovina: Summary statistics (2007Q1-2020Q2)

| Variable | Obs. | Mean | Median | Max | Min | St.dev. |
|---|---|---|---|---|---|---|
| Δ LLP | 54 | 0.0007 | 0.0003 | 0.0225 | -0.0087 | 0.0048 |
| Δ ln GDP | 54 | 0.0028 | 0.0051 | 0.0491 | -0.0843 | 0.0166 |
| Δ ln Unempl. | 53 | -0.0044 | -0.0050 | 0.0445 | -0.0485 | 0.0171 |

Note: The table reports only on stationary (transformed) variables used in the SVAR model.

**Table 42.** Bosnia and Herzegovina: Diagnostic checks of the SVAR (1) model (2007Q1-2020Q2)

| Test | Criteria | Result |
|---|---|---|
| Stability test | No root lies outside the unit circle | Stability condition satisfied |
| VAR residual serial correlation LM test | p-value = 0.1200 | No serial correlation at lag 1 |
| VAR residual heteroskedasticity test | p-value = 0.9531 | No heteroscedasticity |

Note: The lag length of 1 was selected using the AIC.

The effect of macroeconomic shocks 147

Baseline model

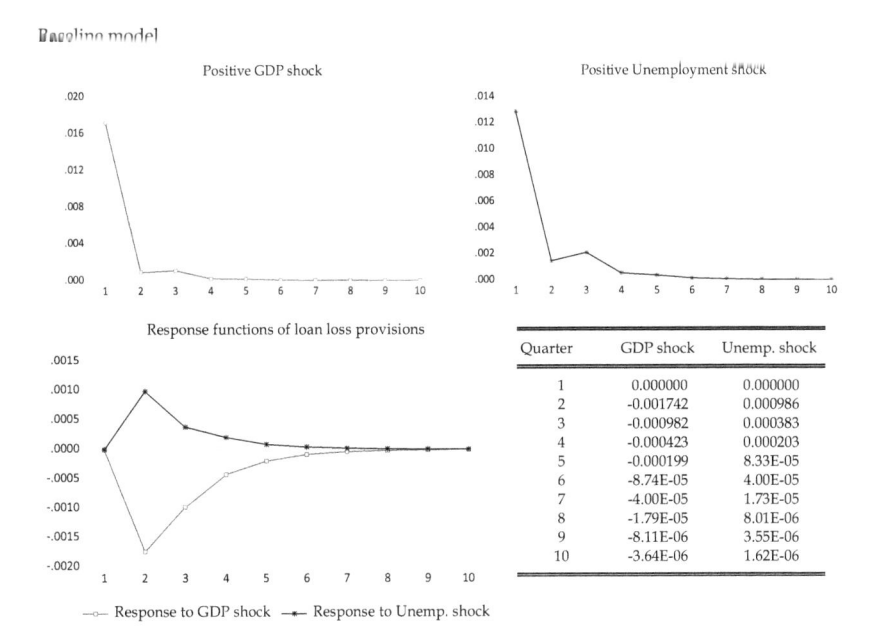

Positive GDP shock

Positive Unemployment shock

Response functions of loan loss provisions

| Quarter | GDP shock | Unemp. shock |
|---|---|---|
| 1 | 0.000000 | 0.000000 |
| 2 | -0.001742 | 0.000986 |
| 3 | -0.000982 | 0.000383 |
| 4 | -0.000423 | 0.000203 |
| 5 | -0.000199 | 8.33E-05 |
| 6 | -8.74E-05 | 4.00E-05 |
| 7 | -4.00E-05 | 1.73E-05 |
| 8 | -1.79E-05 | 8.01E-06 |
| 9 | -8.11E-06 | 3.55E-06 |
| 10 | -3.64E-06 | 1.62E-06 |

—o— Response to GDP shock  —•— Response to Unemp. shock

Robustness check

Response functions of loan loss provisions - Robustness check

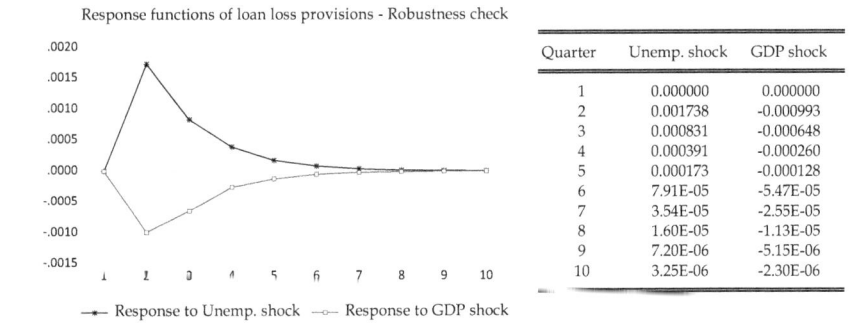

| Quarter | Unemp. shock | GDP shock |
|---|---|---|
| 1 | 0.000000 | 0.000000 |
| 2 | 0.001738 | -0.000993 |
| 3 | 0.000831 | -0.000648 |
| 4 | 0.000391 | -0.000260 |
| 5 | 0.000173 | -0.000128 |
| 6 | 7.91E-05 | -5.47E-05 |
| 7 | 3.54E-05 | -2.55E-05 |
| 8 | 1.60E-05 | -1.13E-05 |
| 9 | 7.20E-06 | -5.15E-06 |
| 10 | 3.25E-06 | -2.30E-06 |

—•— Response to Unemp. shock  —o— Response to GDP shock

**Figure 22.** Bosnia and Herzegovina: Impulses and responses of $\Delta$ LLP

Note: All shocks are equal to one standard deviation. Due to the linear character of the SVAR model, a negative GDP shock should be treated as a mirror positive GDP shock. The robustness check is performed based on changing the order of the variables, so that the first is $\Delta$ LLP, the second is $\Delta$ ln unemployment and the third is $\Delta$ ln GDP.

148  The effect of macroeconomic shocks

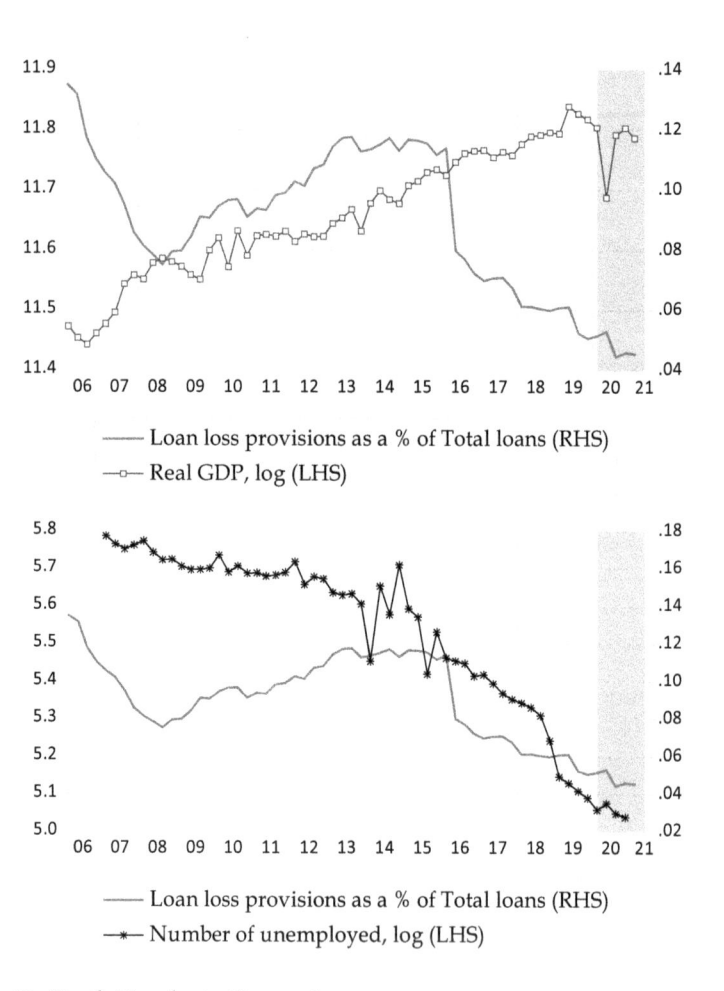

**Figure 23.** North Macedonia: Time series

The effect of macroeconomic shocks 149

Table 43. North Macedonia: Unit root tests (2007Q1-2020Q1) (quarterly data)

| Variable | T-statistic | Critical value (1 %) | Critical value (5 %) | Critical value (10 %) | Result |
|---|---|---|---|---|---|
| LLP | -0.975 | -3.560 | -2.917 | -2.596 | Non-stationary |
| GDP | -1.316 | -3.560 | -2.917 | -2.596 | Non-stationary |
| Unemployment | 1.671 | -3.574 | -2.923 | -2.599 | Non-stationary |
| Δ LLP | -3.669 | -3.565 | -2.919 | -2.597 | Stationary |
| Δ ln GDP | -6.753 | -3.565 | -2.919 | -2.597 | Stationary |
| Δ ln Unempl. | -12.688 | -3.565 | -2.919 | -2.597 | Stationary |

Note: The ADF unit root test was performed; deterministic component: intercept; maximum lags is 4 due to quarterly data frequency. The table reports on level and on transformed variables. Δ LLP = the first difference of LLP to total loans; Δ ln GDP = the log-difference of real GDP and Δ ln Unempl. = the log-difference of the number of unemployed.

Table 44. North Macedonia: Summary statistics (2007Q1-2020Q1)

| Variable | Obs. | Mean | Median | Max | Min | St.dev. |
|---|---|---|---|---|---|---|
| Δ LLP | 53 | -0.0011 | 0.00005 | 0.0067 | -0.0340 | 0.0059 |
| Δ ln GDP | 54 | 0.0064 | 0.0047 | 0.0599 | -0.0477 | 0.0215 |
| Δ ln Unempl. | 52 | -0.0140 | -0.0146 | 0.1993 | -0.1521 | 0.0566 |

Note: The table reports only on stationary (transformed) variables used in the SVAR model.

Table 45. North Macedonia: Diagnostic checks of the SVAR (1) model (2007Q1-2020Q1)

| Test | Criteria | Result |
|---|---|---|
| Stability test | No root lies outside the unit circle | Stability condition satisfied |
| VAR residual serial correlation LM test | p-value = 0.2394 | No serial correlation at lag 1 |
| VAR residual heteroskedasticity test | p-value = 0.6593 | No heteroscedasticity |

Note: The lag length of 1 was selected using the AIC.

## Baseline model

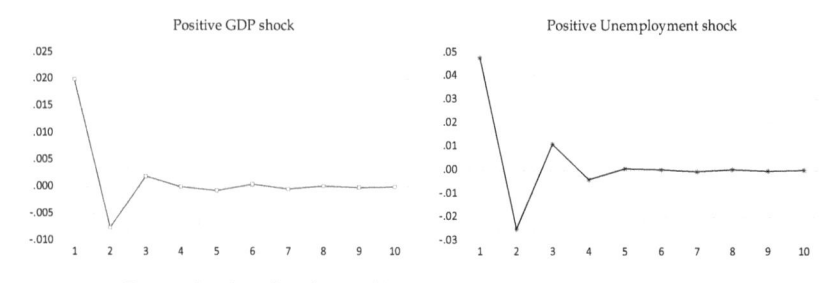

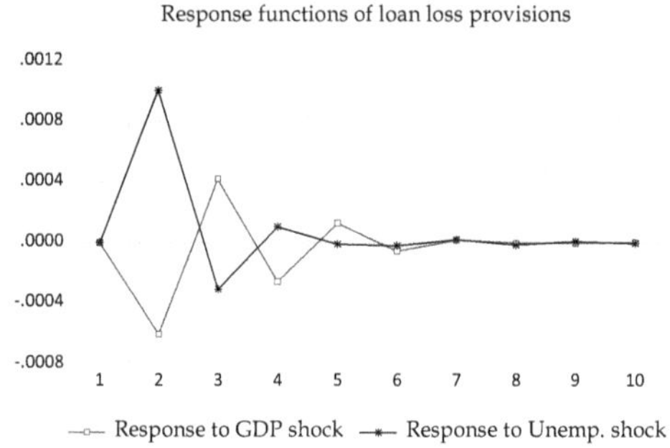

**Positive GDP shock**

**Positive Unemployment shock**

**Response functions of loan loss provisions**

| Quarter | GDP shock | Unemp. shock |
|---|---|---|
| 1 | 0.000000 | 0.000000 |
| 2 | -0.000606 | 0.001006 |
| 3 | 0.000421 | -0.000308 |
| 4 | -0.000256 | 0.000106 |
| 5 | 0.000129 | -9.20E-06 |
| 6 | -5.47E-05 | -1.78E-05 |
| 7 | 1.77E-05 | 1.94E-05 |
| 8 | -2.37E-06 | -1.36E-05 |
| 9 | -2.41E-06 | 7.70E-06 |
| 10 | 2.89E-06 | -3.71E-06 |

—○— Response to GDP shock   —•— Response to Unemp. shock

## Robustness check

Response functions of loan loss provisions - Robustness check

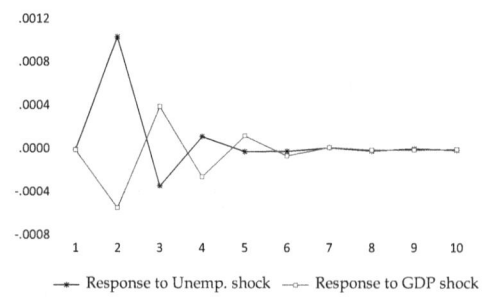

| Quarter | Unemp. shock | GDP shock |
|---|---|---|
| 1 | 0.000000 | 0.000000 |
| 2 | 0.001044 | -0.000538 |
| 3 | -0.000335 | 0.000399 |
| 4 | 0.000123 | -0.000249 |
| 5 | -1.77E-05 | 0.000128 |
| 6 | -1.41E-05 | -5.58E-05 |
| 7 | 1.81E-05 | 1.90E-05 |
| 8 | -1.34E-05 | -3.27E-06 |
| 9 | 7.85E-06 | -1.89E-06 |
| 10 | -3.89E-06 | 2.64E-06 |

—•— Response to Unemp. shock   —○— Response to GDP shock

**Figure 24.** North Macedonia: Impulses and responses of Δ LLP

Note: All shocks are equal to one standard deviation. Due to the linear character of the SVAR model, a negative GDP shock should be treated as a mirror positive GDP shock. The robustness check is performed based on changing the order of the variables, so that the first is Δ LLP, the second is Δ ln unemployment and the third is Δ ln GDP.

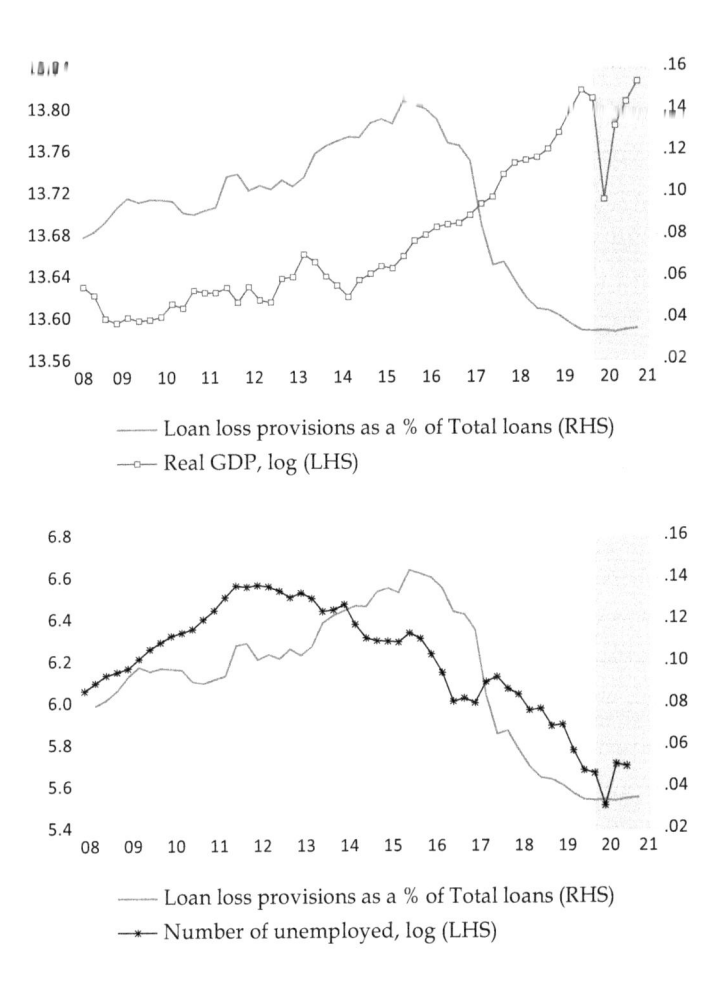

**Figure 25.** Serbia: Time series

**Table 46.** Serbia: Unit root tests (2008Q3-2020Q1) (quarterly data)

| Variable | Test statistic | Critical value (1 %) | Critical value (5 %) | Critical value (10 %) | Result |
|---|---|---|---|---|---|
| LLP | -0.419 | -3.581 | -2.926 | -2.601 | Non-stationary |
| GDP | 2.173 | -3.577 | -2.925 | -2.600 | Non-stationary |
| Unemployment | -0.237 | -3.577 | -2.925 | -2.600 | Non-stationary |
| Δ LLP | -4.147 | -3.584 | -2.928 | -2.602 | Stationary |
| Δ ln GDP | -5.672 | -3.581 | -2.926 | -2.601 | Stationary |
| Δ ln Unempl. | -4.417 | -3.581 | -2.926 | -2.601 | Stationary |

Note: The Phillips-Perron unit root test was performed; deterministic component: intercept. The table reports on level and on transformed variables. Δ LLP = the first difference of LLP to total loans; Δ ln GDP = the log-difference of real GDP and Δ ln Unempl. = the log-difference of the number of unemployed.

**Table 47.** Serbia: Summary statistics (2008Q3-2020Q1)

| Variable | Obs. | Mean | Median | Max | Min | St.dev. |
|---|---|---|---|---|---|---|
| Δ LLP | 46 | -0.0009 | -0.0004 | 0.0146 | -0.0311 | 0.0074 |
| Δ ln GDP | 47 | 0.0037 | 0.0027 | 0.0224 | -0.0219 | 0.0106 |
| Δ ln Unempl. | 47 | -0.0084 | 0.0069 | 0.1003 | -0.1386 | 0.0524 |

Note: The table reports only on stationary (transformed) variables used in the SVAR model.

**Table 48.** Serbia: Diagnostic checks of the SVAR (1) model (2008Q3-2020Q1)

| Test | Criteria | Result |
|---|---|---|
| Stability test | No root lies outside the unit circle | Stability condition satisfied |
| VAR residual serial correlation LM test | p-value = 0.8340 | No serial correlation at lag 1 |
| VAR residual heteroskedasticity test | p-value = 0.8638 | No heteroscedasticity |

Note: The lag length of 1 was selected using the AIC.

The effect of macroeconomic shocks 153

Baseline model

Positive GDP shock

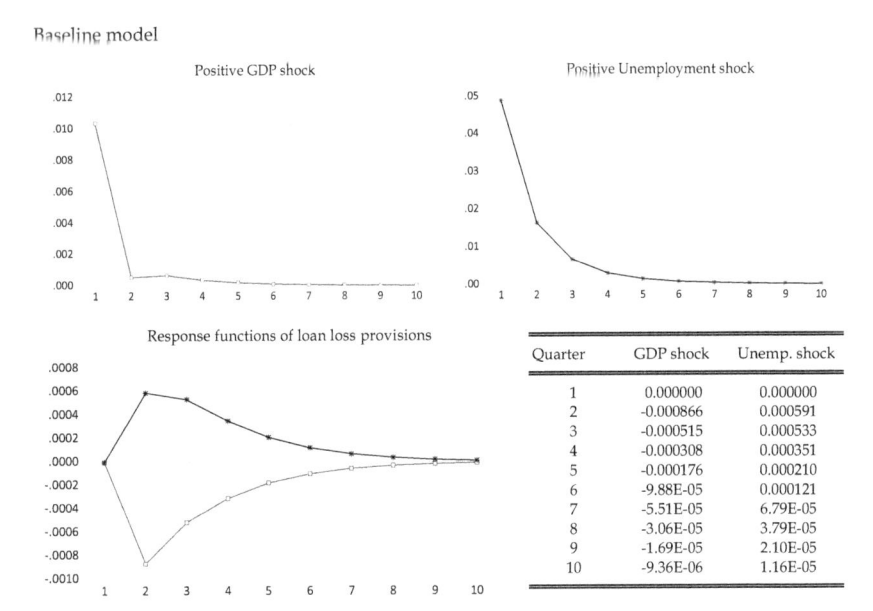

Positive Unemployment shock

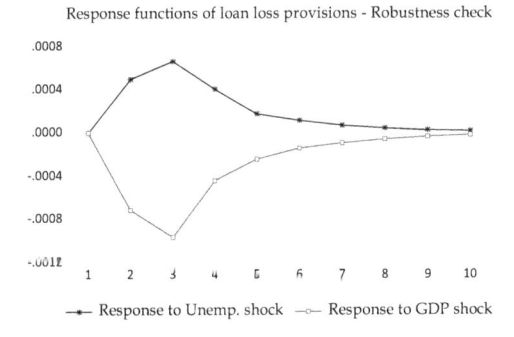

Response functions of loan loss provisions

| Quarter | GDP shock | Unemp. shock |
|---|---|---|
| 1 | 0.000000 | 0.000000 |
| 2 | -0.000866 | 0.000591 |
| 3 | -0.000515 | 0.000533 |
| 4 | -0.000308 | 0.000351 |
| 5 | -0.000176 | 0.000210 |
| 6 | -9.88E-05 | 0.000121 |
| 7 | -5.51E-05 | 6.79E-05 |
| 8 | -3.06E-05 | 3.79E-05 |
| 9 | -1.69E-05 | 2.10E-05 |
| 10 | -9.36E-06 | 1.16E-05 |

—○— Response to GDP shock  —●— Response to Unemp. shock

Robustness check

Response functions of loan loss provisions - Robustness check

| Quarter | Unemp. shock | GDP shock |
|---|---|---|
| 1 | 0.000000 | 0.000000 |
| 2 | 0.000496 | -0.000714 |
| 3 | 0.000662 | -0.000965 |
| 4 | 0.000405 | -0.000440 |
| 5 | 0.000176 | -0.000241 |
| 6 | 0.000115 | -0.000143 |
| 7 | 6.92E-05 | -9.27E-05 |
| 8 | 4.42E-05 | -5.66E-05 |
| 9 | 2.60E-05 | -3.39E-05 |
| 10 | 1.57E-05 | -2.05E-05 |

—●— Response to Unemp. shock  —○— Response to GDP shock

**Figure 26.** Serbia: Impulses and responses of Δ LLP

Note: All shocks are equal to one standard deviation. Due to the linear character of the SVAR model, a negative GDP shock should be treated as a mirror positive GDP shock. The robustness check is performed based on changing the order of the variables, so that the first is Δ LLP, the second is Δ ln unemployment and the third is Δ ln GDP.

**Table 49.** Descriptive statistics for the panels

| | Variable | Obs | Mean | Std. dev. | Min | Max | Median |
|---|---|---|---|---|---|---|---|
| SEE EU Panel | Δ LLP | 225 | 0.0007 | 0.0092 | -0.0688 | 0.0356 | 0.0012 |
| | Δ ln GDP | 230 | 0.0019 | 0.0132 | -0.0595 | 0.0273 | 0.0043 |
| | Δ ln Unempl. | 230 | -0.0011 | 0.0688 | -0.1963 | 0.3272 | -0.0065 |
| Western Balkans Panel | Δ LLP | 189 | -0.0004 | 0.0062 | -0.0340 | 0.0225 | -0.0002 |
| | Δ ln GDP | 191 | 0.0045 | 0.0175 | -0.0843 | 0.0599 | 0.0050 |
| | Δ ln Unempl. | 183 | -0.0077 | 0.0468 | -0.1521 | 0.1993 | -0.0068 |

**Table 50.** Optimal panel SVAR model selection

| | Lag | AIC | Optimal model selection |
|---|---|---|---|
| SEE EU Panel | 0 | -15.23834 | SVAR(2) |
| | 1 | -15.68499 | |
| | 2 | -15.77046* | |
| Western Balkans Panel | 0 | -16.08249 | SVAR(4) |
| | 1 | -16.32106 | |
| | 2 | -16.45682 | |
| | 3 | -16.46365 | |
| | 4 | -16.47440* | |

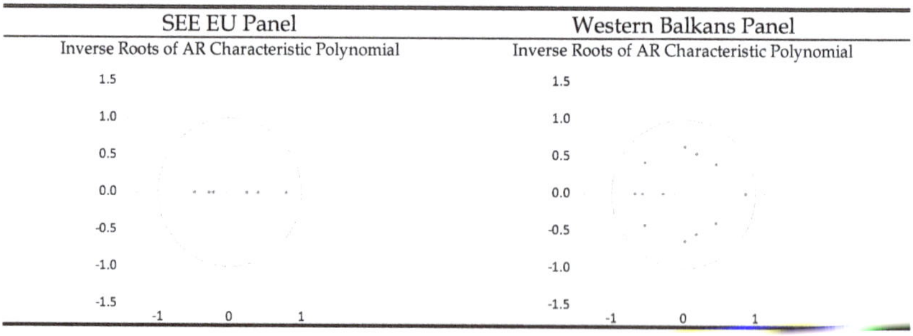
SEE EU Panel
Inverse Roots of AR Characteristic Polynomial
1.5
1.0
0.5
0.0
-0.5
-1.0
-1.5
-1
0
1
Western Balkans Panel
Inverse Roots of AR Characteristic Polynomial
1.5
1.0
0.5
0.0
-0.5
-1.0
-1.5
-1
0
1

**Figure 27.** Stability test for the panels

No root lies outside the unit circle. Both SVAR models satisfy the stability condition.

Table 51. Granger causality tests for the panels

|  | Causality | Granger test F-stat | p-value |
|---|---|---|---|
| SEE EU Panel | GDP does not Granger cause LLP | 5.83568 | 0.0034 |
|  | LLP does not Granger cause GDP | 1.17508 | 0.3108 |
|  | Unemployment does not Granger cause LLP | 5.21874 | 0.0061 |
|  | LLP does not Granger cause Unemployment | 1.17741 | 0.3101 |
| Western Balkans Panel | GDP does not Granger cause LLP | 0.24167 | 0.9144 |
|  | LLP does not Granger cause GDP | 2.23670 | 0.0673 |
|  | Unemployment does not Granger cause LLP | 3.39625 | 0.0107 |
|  | LLP does not Granger cause Unemployment | 1.27958 | 0.2803 |

Note: Variables are transformed ($\Delta$ LLP, $\Delta$ ln GDP, and $\Delta$ ln Unempl.). Null hypothesis: Variable x does not Granger cause variable y.

**Figure 28.** Panel SVAR SEE EU: Impulses and responses of Δ LLP

a) Croatia, Cyprus, Greece, Romania and Slovenia

Baseline model

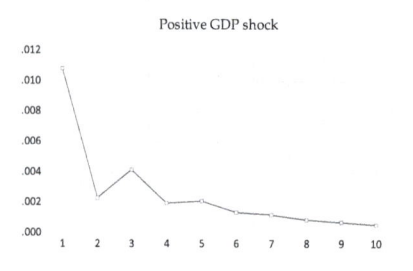

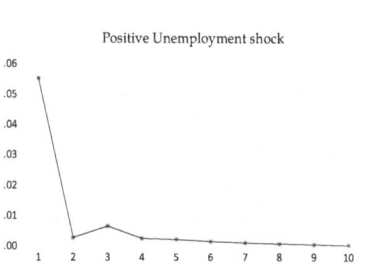

Positive GDP shock

Positive Unemployment shock

Response functions of loan loss provisions

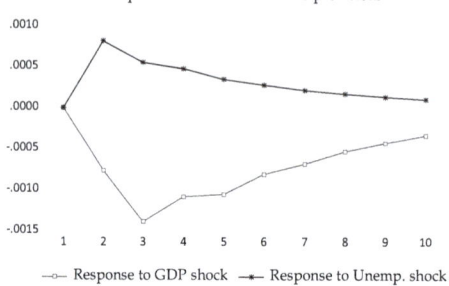

| Quarter | GDP shock | Unemp. shock |
|---|---|---|
| 1 | 0.000000 | 0.000000 |
| 2 | -0.000769 | 0.000816 |
| 3 | -0.001388 | 0.000553 |
| 4 | -0.001086 | 0.000474 |
| 5 | -0.001059 | 0.000347 |
| 6 | -0.000814 | 0.000277 |
| 7 | -0.000688 | 0.000213 |
| 8 | -0.000535 | 0.000169 |
| 9 | -0.000433 | 0.000132 |
| 10 | -0.000340 | 0.000105 |

—o— Response to GDP shock  —•— Response to Unemp. shock

Robustness check

Response functions of loan loss provisions - Robustness check

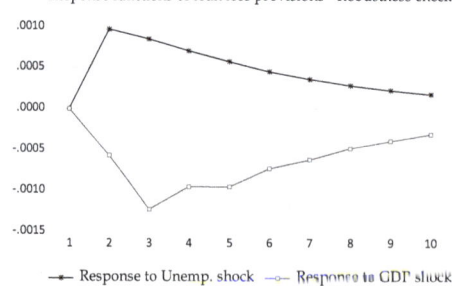

| Quarter | Unemp. shock | GDP shock |
|---|---|---|
| 1 | 0.000000 | 0.000000 |
| 2 | 0.000967 | -0.000567 |
| 3 | 0.000849 | -0.001229 |
| 4 | 0.000705 | -0.000953 |
| 5 | 0.000574 | -0.000955 |
| 6 | 0.000452 | -0.000731 |
| 7 | 0.000361 | -0.000623 |
| 8 | 0.000284 | -0.000484 |
| 9 | 0.000226 | -0.000393 |
| 10 | 0.000178 | -0.000308 |

—•— Response to Unemp. shock  —o— Response to GDP shock

# The effect of macroeconomic shocks

**Figure 20. Continued**

b) Croatia, Romania and Slovenia

Baseline model after the jackknife-type procedure

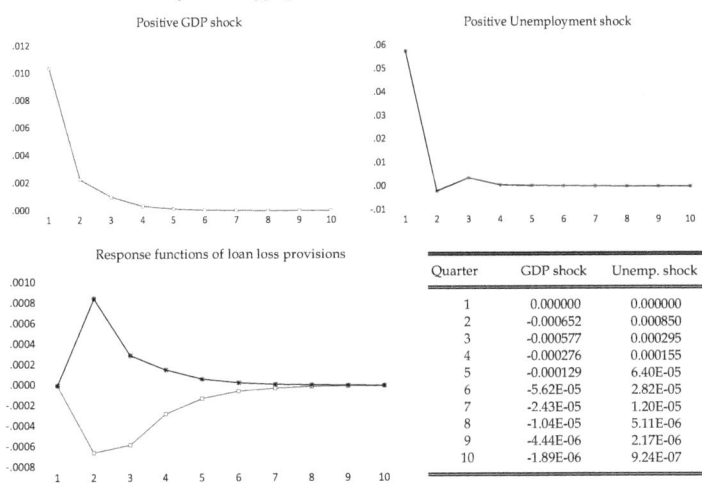

*Positive GDP shock*

*Positive Unemployment shock*

*Response functions of loan loss provisions*

| Quarter | GDP shock | Unemp. shock |
|---|---|---|
| 1 | 0.000000 | 0.000000 |
| 2 | -0.000652 | 0.000850 |
| 3 | -0.000577 | 0.000295 |
| 4 | -0.000276 | 0.000155 |
| 5 | -0.000129 | 6.40E-05 |
| 6 | -5.62E-05 | 2.82E-05 |
| 7 | -2.43E-05 | 1.20E-05 |
| 8 | -1.04E-05 | 5.11E-06 |
| 9 | -4.44E-06 | 2.17E-06 |
| 10 | -1.89E-06 | 9.24E-07 |

—○— Response to GDP shock —●— Response to Unemp. shock

Robustness check

*Response functions of loan loss provisions - Robustness check*

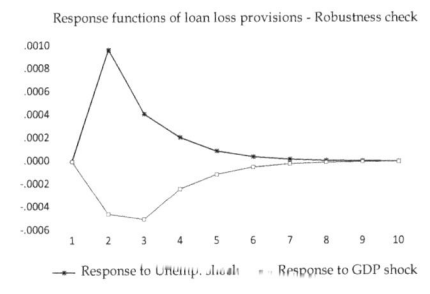

| Quarter | Unemp. shock | GDP shock |
|---|---|---|
| 1 | 0.000000 | 0.000000 |
| 2 | 0.000969 | -0.000457 |
| 3 | 0.000411 | -0.000501 |
| 4 | 0.000210 | -0.000237 |
| 5 | 8.99E-05 | -0.000112 |
| 6 | 3.95E-05 | -4.90E-05 |
| 7 | 1.68E-05 | -2.13E-05 |
| 8 | 7.20E-06 | -9.08E-06 |
| 9 | 3.06E-06 | -3.88E-06 |
| 10 | 1.30E-06 | -1.65E-06 |

—●— Response to Unemp. shock —○— Response to GDP shock

Croatia, Cyprus, Greece, Romania and Slovenia

Note: All shocks are equal to one standard deviation. Due to the linear character of the SVAR model, a negative GDP shock should be treated as a mirror positive GDP shock. The robustness check is performed based on changing the order of the variables, so that the first is Δ LLP, the second is Δ ln unemployment and the third is Δ ln GDP.

158 The effect of macroeconomic shocks

**Figure 29.** Panel SVAR, Western Balkans: Impulses and responses of Δ LLP

a) Albania, Bosnia and Herzegovina, North Macedonia and Serbia
Baseline model

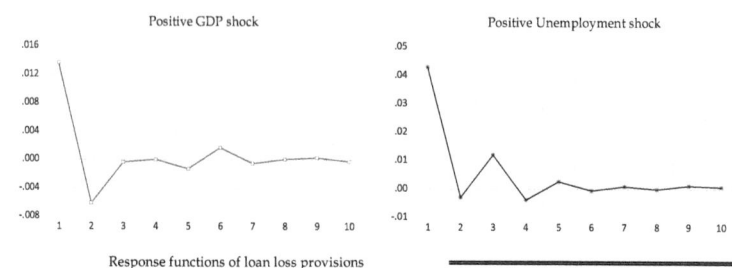

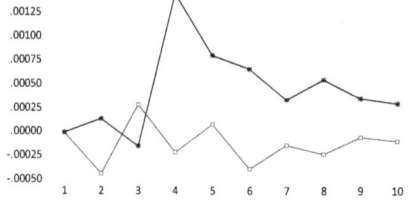

| Quarter | GDP shock | Unemp. shock |
|---|---|---|
| 1 | 0.000000 | 0.000000 |
| 2 | -0.000427 | 0.000145 |
| 3 | 0.000295 | -0.000142 |
| 4 | -0.000206 | 0.001457 |
| 5 | 8.75E-05 | 0.000809 |
| 6 | -0.000380 | 0.000666 |
| 7 | -0.000130 | 0.000344 |
| 8 | -0.000225 | 0.000556 |
| 9 | -4.70E-05 | 0.000358 |
| 10 | -8.89E-05 | 0.000304 |

Robustness check

| Quarter | Unemp. shock | GDP shock |
|---|---|---|
| 1 | 0.000000 | 0.000000 |
| 2 | 0.000239 | -0.000494 |
| 3 | -0.000167 | 0.000248 |
| 4 | 0.001482 | -1.66E-05 |
| 5 | 0.000754 | 0.000245 |
| 6 | 0.000706 | -0.000333 |
| 7 | 0.000366 | -0.000137 |
| 8 | 0.000593 | -0.000181 |
| 9 | 0.000360 | -2.49E-05 |
| 10 | 0.000298 | -4.70E-05 |

Figure 29. Continued

b) Bosnia and Herzegovina and Serbia

Baseline model after the jackknife-type procedure

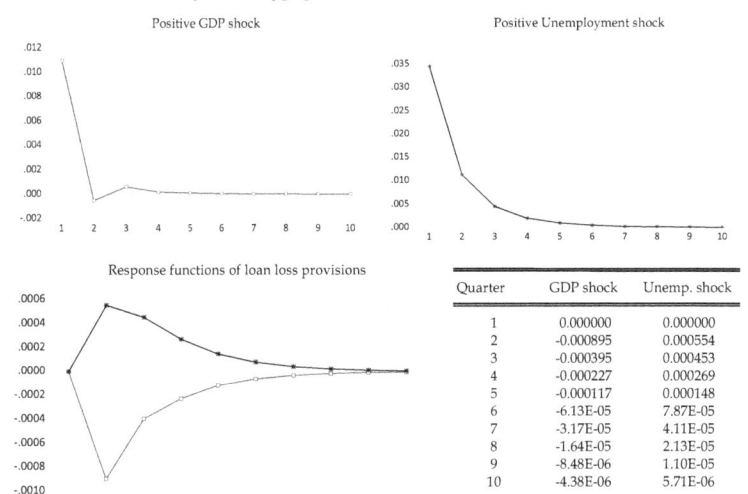

Positive GDP shock

Positive Unemployment shock

Response functions of loan loss provisions

| Quarter | GDP shock | Unemp. shock |
|---|---|---|
| 1 | 0.000000 | 0.000000 |
| 2 | -0.000895 | 0.000554 |
| 3 | -0.000395 | 0.000453 |
| 4 | -0.000227 | 0.000269 |
| 5 | -0.000117 | 0.000148 |
| 6 | -6.13E-05 | 7.87E-05 |
| 7 | -3.17E-05 | 4.11E-05 |
| 8 | -1.64E-05 | 2.13E-05 |
| 9 | -8.48E-06 | 1.10E-05 |
| 10 | -4.38E-06 | 5.71E-06 |

—○— Response to GDP shock   —●— Response to Unemp. shock

Robustness check

Response functions of loan loss provisions - Robustness check

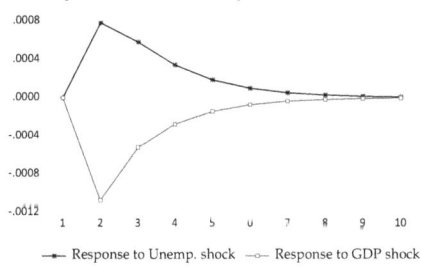

| Quarter | Unemp. shock | GDP shock |
|---|---|---|
| 1 | 0.000000 | 0.000000 |
| 2 | 0.000781 | -0.001071 |
| 3 | 0.000580 | -0.000520 |
| 4 | 0.000341 | -0.000277 |
| 5 | 0.000185 | -0.000143 |
| 6 | 9.70E-05 | -7.32E-05 |
| 7 | 5.01E-05 | -3.74E-05 |
| 8 | 2.57E-05 | -1.91E-05 |
| 9 | 1.31E-05 | -9.73E-06 |
| 10 | 6.69E-06 | -4.96E-06 |

—●— Response to Unemp. shock   —○— Response to GDP shock

Albania, Bosnia and Herzegovina, North Macedonia and Serbia

Note: All shocks are equal to one standard deviation. Due to the linear character of the SVAR model, a negative GDP shock should be treated as a mirror positive GDP shock. The robustness check is performed based on changing the order of the variables, so that the first is Δ LLP, the second is Δ ln unemployment and the third is Δ ln GDP.

**Figure 30.** Detected outliers in the SEE EU Panel

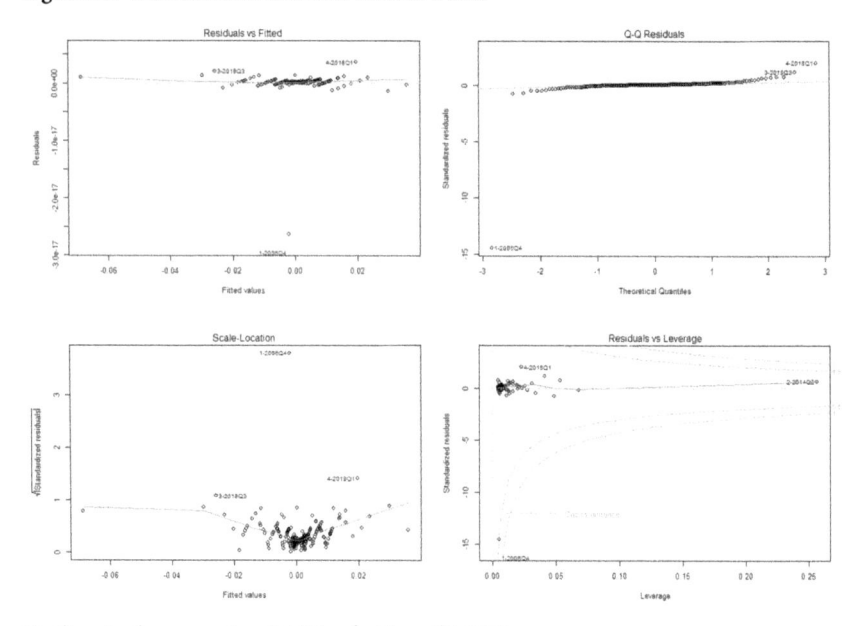

Outliers in the regression Δ LLP ~ first lag of Δ LLP

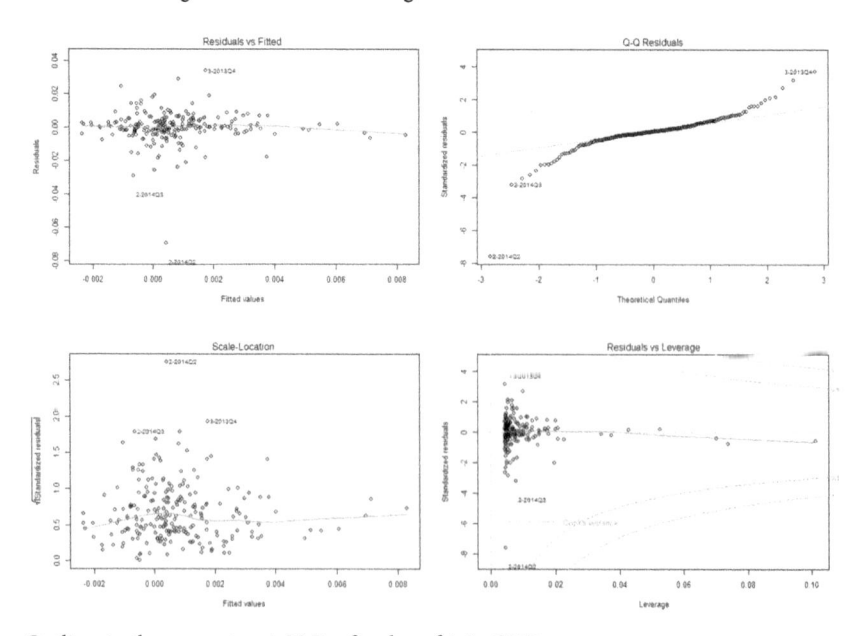

Outliers in the regression Δ LLP ~ first lag of Δ ln GDP

The effect of macroeconomic shocks 161

Figure 30. Continued

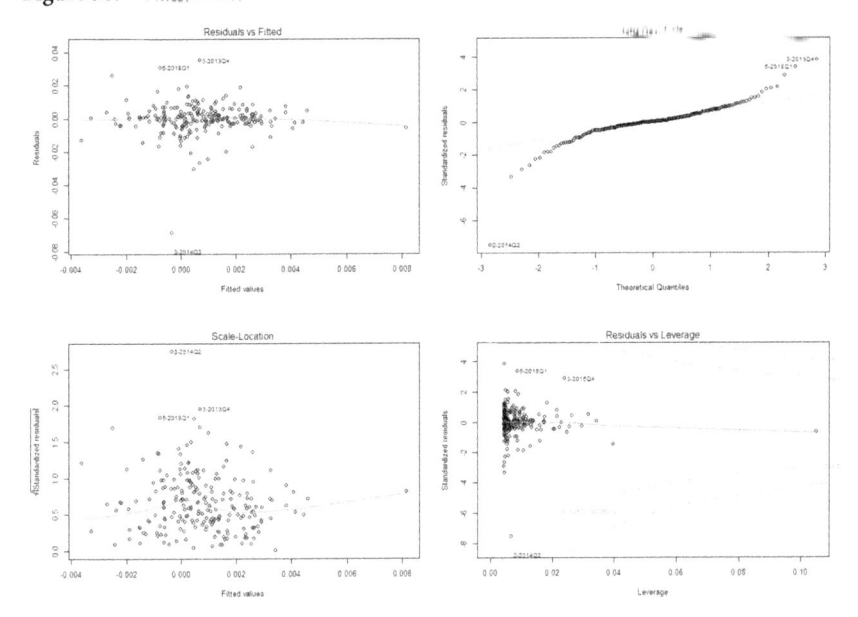

Outliers in the regression Δ LLP ~ first lag of Δ ln Unemployment
Note: Identified outliers are: Romania in 2014Q2 and 2014Q3 (identifiers: 2-2014Q2 and 2-2014Q3), Cyprus in 2013Q4 and 2015Q4 (identifiers: 3-2013Q4 & 3-2015Q4), Croatia in 2006H2 (identifiers: 1-2006Q3 and 1-2006Q4), and Slovenia in 2018Q1 (identifier: 5-2018Q1).

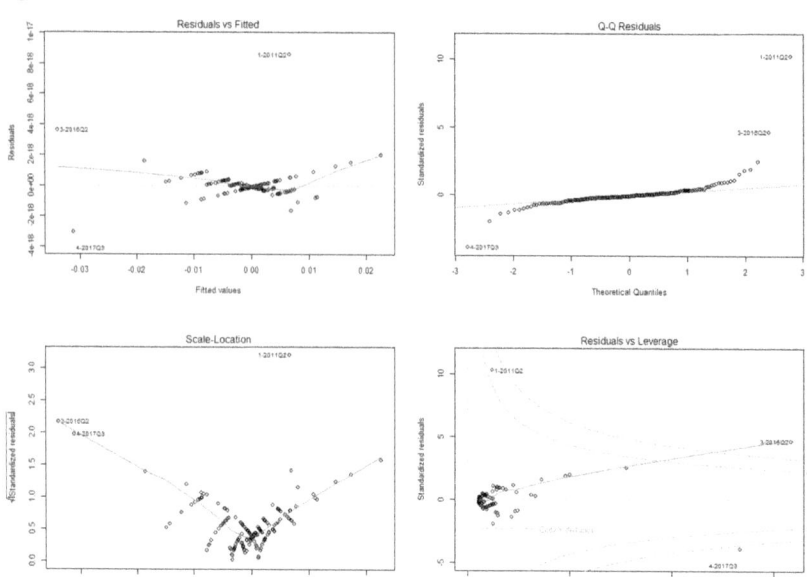

**Figure 31.** Detected outliers in the Western Balkans Panel

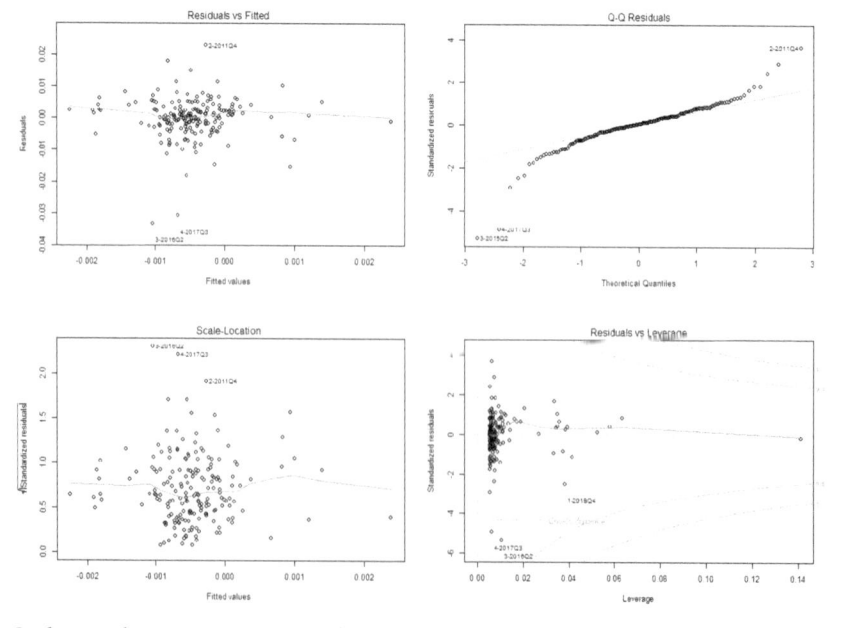

Outliers in the regression Δ LLP ~ first lag of Δ LLP

Outliers in the regression Δ LLP ~ first lag of Δ ln GDP

The effect of macroeconomic shocks 163

**Figure 31.** Continued

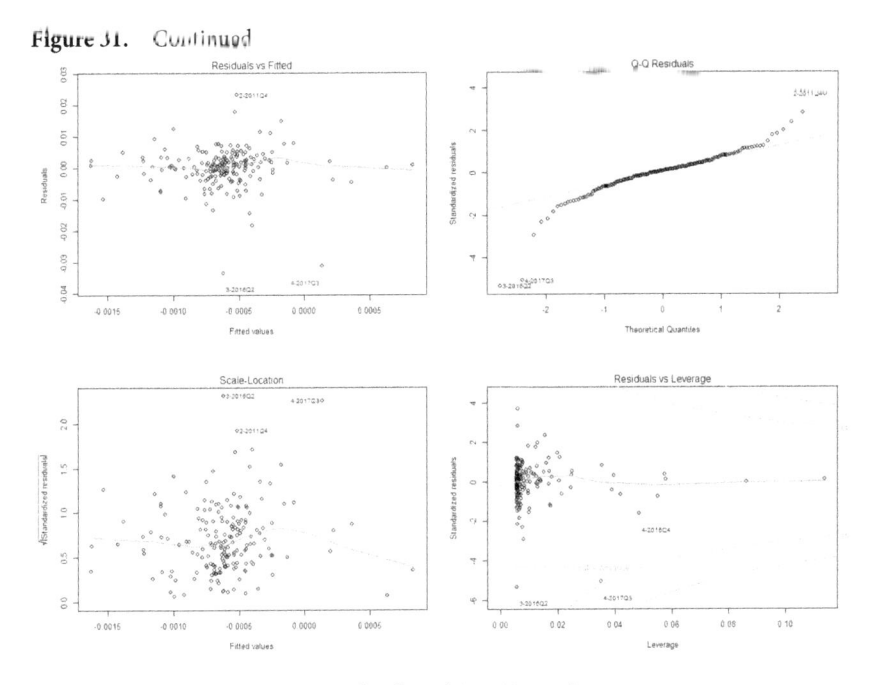

Outliers in the regression Δ LLP ~ first lag of Δ In Unemployment

Note: Identified outliers are: Albania in 2011Q1 and 2011Q2 (identifiers: 1-2011Q1 and 1-2011Q2), Bosnia and Herzegovina in 2011Q4 (identifier: 2-2011Q4), North Macedonia in 2016Q2 (identifier: 3-2016Q2), and Serbia in 2017Q3 (identifier: 4-2017Q3).

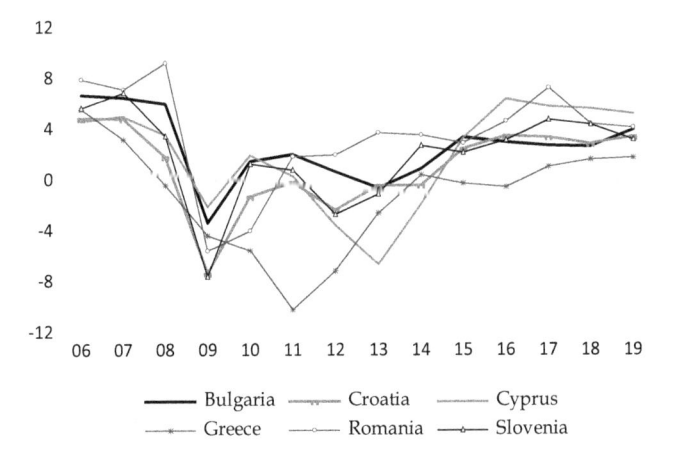

**Figure 32.** Annual growth rate of real GDP in EU members in Southeast Europe
Source: World Development Indicators database (2022).

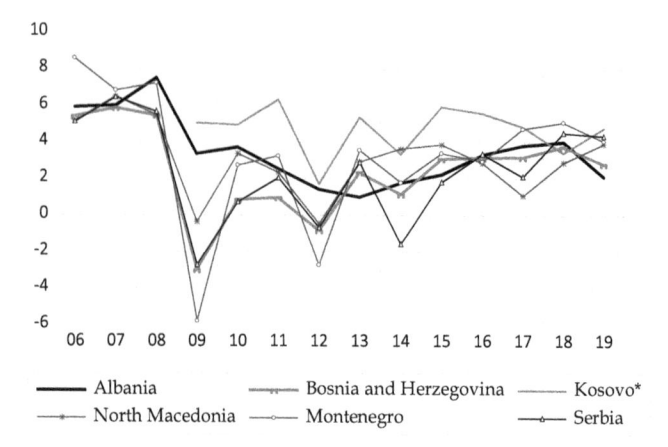

**Figure 33.** Annual growth rate of real GDP in Western Balkans
Source: World Development Indicators database (2022).

# 6. Conclusions

**In the first part of my research**, several questions are examined empirically: first, whether commercial banks in Southeast Europe use loan loss provisions to manage their earnings and capital as well as to signal their financial strength; second, whether loan loss provisions in Southeast Europe are pro-cyclical; third, whether there are differences in provisioning practices between banks located in the Western Balkans and those located in other SEE countries which are members of the EU; finally, whether there are differences in provisioning between domestic and foreign owned banks. For this purpose, I constructed: (i) a panel of all commercial banks in the SEE EU region as well as in the Western Balkans region that contain datasets in the period from 2010 to 2017 and (ii) a panel of selected commercial banks for the same two regions excluding those banks that had gone through consolidation requested by the monetary authorities. The reason for creating the panels of selected commercial banks is that I wanted to further investigate the decision making on loan loss provisions under the influence of market and macroeconomic conditions, i.e. by removing the influence of state interventions.

Regarding the tested hypotheses, my empirical study has the following findings:

(i) Capital management hypothesis

My study finds that in the SEE EU region, the group of all commercial banks tends to manage regulatory capital using LLPs; also, the same group of all commercial banks has, on average, lower capitalization than the group of selected banks. In the Western Balkans region, in contrast, the group of selected commercial banks tends to manage regulatory capital using LLPs; also, the same group of selected commercial banks has, on average, lower capitalization than the group of all commercial banks.

This finding first suggests that commercial banks with lower capitalization are more inclined to manage regulatory capital using LLPs. During bank supervision, more attention should, therefore, be devoted to commercial banks with a lower level of regulatory capital.

In addition, this finding indicates the strong influence of consolidated banks, given that, as soon as they are removed from the panels concerned, completely new results are obtained regarding the capital management hypothesis in the SEE EU in comparison to the Western Balkans. Some international banks had solvency problems in their home markets (e.g. some banks in Greece and Cyprus) in the observed period and were forced to divest or downsize their subsidiaries in non-core markets during the consolidation process. On the other hand, the question arises as to how the credit market in the Western Balkans will develop in the future, bearing in mind that the mentioned subsidiaries were otherwise solvent and contributed to overall financial stability. This is a question that the authorities in the Western Balkans should address, considering the importance of a functioning banking sector for the real economy.

Even the less robust finding about the greater tendency of domestic banks in the group of all commercial banks in the SEE EU to practice capital management using LLPs supports the given interpretation. In addition, the less robust finding of a greater tendency of domestic banks in the group of all banks in the Western Balkans to practice capital management points to the need to keep monitoring the level of regulatory capital in domestic banks in that region.

(ii) Income smoothing hypothesis

My study provides a robust finding that the group of selected banks in the SEE EU tend to use LLPs in order to reduce income volatility. Additionally, there are also weakly robust findings on income smoothing practices in all other observed panels, i.e. the group of all commercial banks in the SEE EU and in the Western Balkans as well as the group of selected banks in the Western Balkans.

The study finds evidence that commercial banks with lower profitability are more inclined to reduce the volatility of their income by using LLPs. This suggests that the motives for income smoothing by using LLPs in individual banks need to be investigated more closely. There is a difference whether discretionary decisions on the level of LLPs are motivated by the expectation of changes in the quality of the loan portfolio, by the avoidance of paying taxes, or by the desired level of bonuses, etc. Understanding motives is also important because in the group of selected banks, i.e. those functioning according to market principles without major government intervention, income smoothing stands out as the dominant discretionary component of LLPs.

(iii) Signaling hypothesis

My study provides a weakly robust finding on the greater tendency of domestic banks in the SEE EU to signal their strength to withhold larger LLPs by increasing income from fees and commissions, even more so in the group of all commercial banks than in the group of selected banks in the SEE EU. My study also finds that less strong banks are more likely to signal their strength, which suggests the need for a better supervision of commercial banks that engage in such practices.

(iv) Pro-cyclicality hypothesis

The character of LLPs can be asserted both against credit cyclicality and business cyclicality. My study finds that banks in the SEE EU tend to provision more during credit contraction and that this is somewhat more pronounced in the group of all commercial banks than in the group of selected banks. At the same time, the descriptive statistics indicate that, on average, the group of all commercial banks is less inclined to new lending. This suggests that banks that are less inclined to new lending tend to provision more during credit contraction, i.e. to provision less during credit expansion. My study additionally finds that the group of selected banks in the SEE EU tends to provision more during economic recession. As economic theory characterizes such behavior as undesirable procyclical or backward-looking provisioning, it is important to ensure the inverse behavior of banks. In other words, there is a need to strengthen supervisory control and to ensure counter-cyclical, far-sighted provisioning practices.

When it comes to the Western Balkans region, my study finds that the group of selected banks tends to have higher provisioning when GDP per capita growth rates fall (indicating a decline in living standards) and that this tendency is more pronounced in domestic banks. Otherwise, no other pro-cyclicality of LLPs was established. Additional analyses are necessary to understand whether this finding is related to a higher share of household loans compared to corporate loans, whether it is related to the fact that the GFC caused a greater economic recession in the SEE EU than in the Western Balkans, or whether there is another explanation.

Due to the COVID-19 pandemic crisis in 2020, the widespread adoption of the new IFRS 9 approach to the estimation of LLPs has, in fact, been delayed. But even if it had not been, it has not yet been reliably established that the new approach will ensure the expected and desired counter-cyclical effect. That is why national supervisory control needs to be particularly active and vigilant due to the challenges of the current crises.

(v) Additional findings

My study establishes that the most persistent LLPs are in the group of all commercial banks in the Western Balkans, although, on average, the risk profile of these banks is solid, even better than in SEE EU banks. However, bearing in mind that some international banks are leaving the Western Balkans, it is prudent for LLPs to remain persistent and for the NPL coverage ratio to remain high.

Given that motives for discretionary management judgment have to be better understood, my outlier analysis to some extent indicates possible motives for reducing (or increasing) LLPs. My simple analysis of outliers suggests the need for closer follow-up of provisioning practices after a change of bank ownership and/or bank management. However, more in-depth empirical research aimed at revealing the motives for management judgement related to the LLPs would be an interesting direction for future research.

In the **second part of my research**, I examined empirically how macroeconomic shocks affect LLPs as well as whether there are differences between individual (national) banking sectors, or differences between the Western Balkans and SEE EU. Simulated macroeconomic shocks refer to a negative GDP shock and a positive unemployment shock, and they are equal to one standard deviation. The research question was analyzed first using the SVAR model at the level of individual countries and then using the panel SVAR model at the two regional levels. The interpretation of the research findings was supplemented by taking the analysis of outliers into account as well as analyses of the NPL coverage ratio and the NPL ratio.

Individual macro stress tests among the SEE EU countries provide evidence of the greater vulnerability of the Greek and Cypriot banking sectors, measured by the size and persistence of responses, that is, changes in the stock of LLPs as a share of total loans ($\Delta$ LLP) to a negative GDP shock ($\Delta$ ln GDP) and to a positive unemployment shock ($\Delta$ ln number of unemployed). It should be mentioned that the magnitude of the negative GDP shock was the largest in the Greek model, with the magnitude of the positive unemployment shock largest in the Cypriot model. Compared to the Croatian, Romanian, and Slovenian models, the two macroeconomic shocks in the Greek and Cypriot models also lasted the longest.

It is true that the analysis of individual SVAR models is based on historical data, which, in the case of Greece and Cyprus, captured both the GFC and the sovereign debt crisis, but when a comparative analysis of NPL ratios and NPL coverage ratios is added, the Greek and Cypriot banking sectors stand out again as those that have the least capacity to absorb potential new loan losses.

Individual macro stress tests in the Western Balkans show unorthodoxy in reference to the prevailing economic literature as credit risk (measured by the change in the stock of LLPs as a share of total loans) in the Albanian, and especially the North Macedonian, model does not increase after a negative GDP shock. This resilience is particularly interesting because the size of the negative GDP shock is the largest in the Albanian and North Macedonian models. These two banking sectors do not have such resilience when it comes to the transmission of a positive unemployment shock to credit risk, which actually grows the most in the Albanian and North Macedonian models. At the same time, the unemployment shock is the most persistent in the Albanian model.

Albania and North Macedonia did not experience severe economic recession in the observed period, unlike other countries, which is why their SVAR models are not founded on the entire business cycle. Nevertheless, the very high level of NPL coverage by LLPs in North Macedonia (more than 100 %) indeed indicates a greater ability to absorb possible future loan losses.

The panel SVAR model estimates can be considered macro stress tests for the SEE EU region and the Western Balkans region. Evidence was found that the banking sectors in the SEE EU region are more vulnerable to a negative GDP shock, with the banking sectors in the Western Balkans region more vulnerable to a positive unemployment shock. In the SEE EU region, the size of the GDP shock is smaller, but its persistence is greater, while in the Western Balkans, the size of the unemployment shock is smaller but more persistent, which indicates a greater importance of persistence in relation to the size of the macroeconomic shock.

The application of the jackknife-type procedure, whereby banking sectors that were too vulnerable (Greece and Cyprus in the SEE EU model) or too resilient (Albania and North Macedonia in the Western Balkans model) were removed from their regional models, provided evidence of faster dissipation to equilibrium by the change in stock of LLP as a share of total loans after an increase caused by macroeconomic shocks. Therefore, the observed individual banking sectors are heterogeneous, or rather specific in terms of pre-existing vulnerabilities that have the potential to augment the effects of potentially new macroeconomic shocks to a greater or lesser extent.

Certainly, the fact that the banking sectors in the Western Balkans have shown greater resilience because credit risk is less responsive to a negative GDP shock should be taken with a grain of salt as these banking sectors are mostly poorly integrated into global financial markets, and their macroeconomic environment is characterized by lower economic strength, lower living standards, and other fragilities. On the other hand, the analysis of outliers shows similarities between the observed credit markets: sooner or later, the authorities react to preserve financial stability, most often by implementing measures for banks to improve capitalization, improve their timely recognition of loan losses, and set aside an adequate level of provisions.

The results of my empirical research have implications for regulators and banking supervision. As my research includes estimations and forecasts at the level of the banking sector as a whole, and thus represents a stress test run in a top-down manner, it points to the potential vulnerabilities/resilience of the banking sectors in Southeast Europe. They suggest a more vigilant approach is needed to verify the application of prudential measures, in particular related to active NPL resolution and timely loan loss provisioning but always ensuring adequate bank capitalization, especially in those economies where the capacity to absorb potential new loan losses is lower. An even more vigilant approach is generally needed because the COVID-19 pandemic has occurred: its negative macroeconomic consequences, albeit somewhat mitigated by various state measures, may have delayed negative effects on the creditworthiness and solvency of businesses and households alike. Any possible new macroeconomic shocks could aggravate financial stability as banks tend to become more fragile during economic downturns.

Finally, these findings may be valuable not only to banking regulators and supervisors but also to potential investors interested in the economies of the observed SEE EU member states and the Western Balkans economies. Specifically, in anticipation of the inevitable further consolidation of banking groups in Southeast Europe, the research findings that illuminate the characteristics of the observed banking sectors indicate opportunities for new market entrants.

# Bibliography

Abad, J., & Suarez, J. (2020). IFRS 9 and COVID-19: Delay and Freeze the Transitional Arrangements Clock. In A. Bénassy-Quéré, & B. Weder di Mauro (Eds.), *Europe in the Time of Covid-19* (pp. 98–103). London: Center for Economic Policy Research.

Agénor, P.-R., & Zilberman, R. (2015). Loan Loss Provisioning Rules, Procyclicality, and Financial Volatility. *Journal of Banking and Finance, 61*, 301–315.

Aguinis, H., Gottfredson, R., & Joo, H. (2013). Best-Practice Recommendations for Defining, Identifying, and Handling Outliers. *Organizational Research Methods, 16*(2), 270–301.

Ahmed, A., Takeda, C., & Thomas, S. (1998). Bank Loan Loss Provisions: A Reexamination of Capital Management, Earnings Managment and Signaling Effects. *Journal of Accounting and Economics, 28*, 1–26.

Akerlof, G. (1970). The Market for "Lemons": Quality Uncertainty and the Market Mechanism. *The Quarterly Journal of Economics, 84*(3), 488–500.

Allen, F., & Gale, D. (2004). Competition and Financial Stability. *Journal of Money, Credit and Banking, 36*(3b), 453–480.

Almunia, J. (2020). *Lessons from Financial Assistance to Greece.* Luxembourg: European Stability Mechanism. Independent Valuation Report.

Anandarajan, A., Hasan, I., & Lozano-Vivas, A. (2005). Loan Loss Provision Decisions: An Empirical Analysis of the Spanish Depository Institutions. *Journal of International Accounting, Auditing and Taxation, 14*, 55–77.

Anandarajan, A., Hasan, I., & McCarthy, C. (2007). Use of Loan Loss Provisions for Capital, Earnings Management and Signalling by Australian Banks. *Accounting & Finance, 47*, 357–379.

Arellano, M., & Bond, S. (1991). Some Tests of Specification for Panel Data: Monte Carlo Evidence and an Application to Employment Equations. *The Review of Economic Studies, 58*(2), pp. 277–297.

Arpa, M., Giulini, I., Ittner, A., & Pauer, F. (2001). The Influence of Macroeconomic Developments on Austrian banks: Implications for Banking Supervision. In B. P. 1, *Marrying the Macro- and Microprudential Dimensions of Financial Stability* (pp. 91–116). Bank for International Settlements.

Asea, P., & Blomberg, B. (1997). *Lending Cycles.* National Bureau of Economic Research (NBER). Working Paper 5951.

Asteriou, D., & Hall, G. (2016). *Applied Econometrics* (3rd ed.). Palgrave, Macmillan Education.

Athanasoglou, P., Georgiou, E., & Staikouras, C. (2008). *Assessing Output and Productivity Growth in the Banking Industry.* Bank of Greece, Working Paper 92.

Babouček, I., & Jančar, M. (2005). *A VAR Analysis of the Effects of Macroeconomic Shocks to the Quality of the Aggregate Loan Portfolio of the Czech Banking Sector.* Czech National Bank, Working Paper Series 1.

Baltagi, B. (2005). *Econometric Analysis of Panel Data* (3rd ed.). John Wiley & Sons Ltd, England.

Bandyopadhyay, A. (2016). *Managing Portfolio Credit Risk in Banks.* Cambridge University Press.

Bank of Albania. (2011). *Financial Stability Report 2011 H1.* Bank of Albania. Statistics Department. Retrieved 01 10, 2021, from https://www.bankofalbania.org/Publications/Periodic/Financial_Stability_Report/Financial_Stability_Report-2011_H1.html

Bank of Greece. (2012). *Report on the Recapitalization and Restructuring of the Greek Banking Sector.* Bank of Greece, Financial Stability Department.

Bank of Greece. (2015). *Results of the 2015 Comprehensive Assessment for Attica Bank.* Athens: Press Release, 31-Oct-2015.

Barisitz, S. (2005). Banking in Central and Eastern Europe Since the Turnof the Millenium – An Overview of Structural Modernization in Ten Countries. *Focus on European Economic Integration, 2*, 58–82.

Barisitz, S. (2008). *Banking in Central and Eastern Europe 1980–2006.* Routledge.

Basel Committee on Banking Supervision. (2016). *Prudential Treatment of Problem Assets – Definitions of Non-Performing Exposures and Forbearance.* Basel: Bank for International Settlements.

Basel Committee on Banking Supervision. (2021). *The Procyclicality of Loan Loss Provisions: A Literature Review.* Bank for International Settlements. Working Paper 39.

Bauze, K. (2019). *Non-Performing Loan Write-Offs: Practices in the CESEE Region.* World Bank Group.

Beaver, W., & Engel, E. (1996). Discretionary Behaviour with Respect to Allowances for Loan Losses and the Behaviour of Security Prices. *Journal of Accounting and Economics, 22*, pp. 177–206.

Beaver, W., Eger, C., Ryan, S., & Wolfson, M. (1989). Financial Reporting, Supplemental Disclosures, and Bank Share Prices. *Journal of Accounting Research, 27*(2), 157–178.

Bernanke, B., & Gertler, M. (1989). Agency Costs, Net Worth, and Business Fluctuations. *The American Economic Review, 79*(1), pp. 14-31

Bernanke, B., Gertler, M., & Gilchrist, S. (1996). The Financial Accelerator and the Flight to Quality. *The Review of Economics and Statistics, 78*(1), pp. 1-15.

Bernanke, B., Gertler, M., & Gilchrist, S. (1999). The Financial Accelerator in a Quantitative Business Cycle Framework. In J. Taylor, & M. Woodford (Eds.), *Handbook of Macroeconomics* (pp. 1341-1393). Elsevier.

Bholat, D., Lastra, R., Markose, S., Miglionico, A., & Sen, K. (2018). Non-Performing Loans at the Dawn of IFRS 9: Regulatory and Accounting Treatment of Asset Quality. *Journal of Banking Regulation, 19*(1), 33-54.

Bikker, J., & Metzemakers, P. (2005). Bank Provisioning Behaviour and Procyclicality. *Journal of International Financial Markets, Institutions and Money, 15*, 141-157.

Billings, M., & Capie, F. (2009). Transparency and Financial Reporting in Mid-20th Century British Banking. *Accounting Forum, 33*(1), 38-53.

Bischof, J., Laux, C., & Leuz, C. (2021). Accounting for Financial Stability: Bank Disclosure and Loss Recognition in the Financial Crisis. *Journal of Financial Economics, 141*, 1188-1217.

Bonin, J., & Košak, M. (2013). *Loan/Loss Provisioning in Emerging Europe: Precautionary or Pro-Cyclical?* Weslian Economics Working Papers 2013-010. Weslian University, Department of Economics.

Bonin, J., Hasan, I., & Wachtel, P. (2014). *Banking in Transition Countries.* Bank of Finland, BOFIT Institute for Economies in Transition, Discussion Papers 8/2014.

Borish, M., Long, M., & Noël, M. (1995). Banking Reform in Transition Economies. *IMF, Finance & Development*, 23-26.

Bornemann, S., Homölle, S., Hubensack, C., Kick, T., & Pfingsten, A. (2014). Visible Reserves in Banks – Determinants of Initial Creation, Usage and Contribution to Bank Stability. *Journal of Business Finance and Accounting, 41*(5-6), 507-544.

Bouvatier, V., & Lepetit, L. (2012a). Effects of Loan Loss Provisions on Growth in Bank Lending: Some International Comparisons. *International Economics, 132*, pp. 91-116.

Bouvatier, V., & Lepetit, L. (2012b). Provisioning Rules and Bank Lending: A Theoretical Model. *Journal of Financial Stability, 8*(1), 25-31.

Bouvatier, V., Lepetit, L., & Strobel, F. (2014). Bank Income Smoothing, Ownership Concentration and the Regulatory Environment. *Journal of Banking and Finance, 41*, pp. 253-270.

Brandao-Marques, L., Correa, R., & Sapriza, H. (2020). Government Support, Regulation, and Risk Taking in the Banking Sector. *Journal of Banking & Finance, 112.*

Brauneis, A., & Rausch, A. (2013). Simulationsbasierte Investitionsentscheidungen in österreichischen und deutschen KMUs – Handlungsspielräume unter Risikoaspekten. *Zeitschrift für KMU und Entrepreneurship, 61*(2), pp. 265–290.

Brunnermeier, M. (2009). Deciphering the Liquidity and Credit Crunch 2007–2008. *Journal of Economic Perspectives, 23*(1), pp. 77–100.

Brunnermeier, M. (2023, March). Rethinking Monetary Policy in a Changing World. *Finance & Development, 60*(1), pp. 4–9.

Bushman, R., & Williams, C. (2012). Accounting Discretion, Loan Loss Provisioning, and Discipline of Banks' Risk-Taking. *Journal of Accounting and Economics, 54*(1), 1–18.

Business Review. (2014). *EEAF completes takeover of Nextebank Romania.* Retrieved 06 07, 2023, from https://business-review.eu/featured/eeaf-completes-takeover-of-nextebank-romania-61788

Calvo, G., & Kumar, M. (1994). Money Demand, Bank Credit, and Economic Performance in Former Socialist Economies. *Staff Paper (International Monetary Fund), 41*(2), 314–349.

Camfferman, K., & Zeff, S. (2007). *Financial Reporting and Global Capital Markets. History of the International Accounting Standards Committee, 1973–2000.* Oxford University Press.

Capital bank. (2013). *Financial statements for the year ended at December 31, 2013.*

Čaušević, F. (2003). *Financial Liberalisation and Globalisation – Impact and Effects in South-East European Countries.* Centre for the Study of Global Governance.

Central Bank of Bosnia and Herzegovina. (2011). *4/2011 Bulletin.*

Chen, Y.-A., Sivec, V., & Volk, M. (2018). *Empirical Evidence on the Effectiveness of Capital Buffer Release.* Munich: MPRA Paper No. 84323.

Christiano, L., Motto, R., & Rostagno, M. (2014). Risk Shocks. *American Economic Review, 104*(1), 27–65.

Clerides, S. (2014). The Collapse of the Cypriot Banking System: A Bird's Eye View. *Cyprus Economic Policy Review, 8*(2), 3–35.

Cottarelli, C., Dell'Ariccia, G., & Vladkova-Hollar, I. (2003). *Early Birds, Late Risers, and Sleeping Beauties: Bank Credit Growth to the Private Sector in Central and Eastern Europe and the Balkans.* IMF Economic Department.

Credicom Consumer Finance Bank SA (2017). *2016 Annual Report.* Retrieved 12 10, 2020, from https://www.praxiabank.com/financial_data/financial_repo rts/en/2016_report.pdf

Crespo Cuaresma, J., Oberhofer, H., Smits, K., & Vincelette, A. (2012). *Drivers of Convergence in Eleven Eastern European Countries.* Policy Research Working Paper; No. 6185. World Bank, Washington, DC.

Cúrdia, V., & Woodford, M. (2010). Credit Spreads and Monetary Policy. *Journal of Money, Credit and Banking, 42*(s1), 3–35.

Dabrowski, M., & Myachenkova, Y. (2018). *The Western Balkans on the Road to the European Union.* Bruegel Policy Contribution, No. 2018/04.

De Bock, R., & Demyantes, A. (2012). *Bank Asset Quality in Emerging Markets: Determinants and Spillovers.* IMF Working Papers no. WP/12/71.

Dellas, H., & Tavlas, G. (2013). The Gold Standard, the Euro, and the Origins of the Greek Sovereign Debt Crisis. *Cato Journal, 33*(3), 491–520.

Deloitte. (2019). *CEE Banking Consolidation Perking Up.*

EBRD. (1995). *Transition Report 1995.* European Bank for Reconstruction and Development.

EBRD. (2016). *How We Assess Transition Qualities.* European Bank for Reconstruction and Development. Sector Transition Indicators 2016, Financial Sectors, Banking. Retrieved from https://www.ebrd.com/economic-research-and-data/transition-qualities-asses.html

ECB. (2017). *Guide for the Targeted Review of Internal Models.* European Central Bank. Retrieved from https://www.bankingsupervision.europa.eu/ecb/pub/pdf/trim_guide.en.pdf

ECB. (2020). *IFRS 9 in the Context of the Coronavirus (COVID-19) Pandemic.* Letter to all Significant Institutions. Retrieved from https://www.bankingsupe rvision.europa.eu/press/letterstobanks/shared/pdf/2020/ssm.2020_letter_ IFRS_9_in_the_context_of_the_coronavirus_COVID-19_pandemic.en.pdf

Eckel, N. (1901). *Income Smoothing Hypothesis Revisited. Abacus, 17*(1), 28–40.

Economist Intelligence. (2015). *Bank Recapitalization Gets Under Way.* London: Economist Intelligence Unit. Retrieved 04 16, 2015, from http://coun try.eiu.com/article.aspx?articleid=1193711503

Enria, A. (2017). *The EU Banking Sector – Risks and Recovery. A Single Market Perspective.* European Banking Authority.

Ernst and Young & Institute for International Finance. (2021). *11th Annual EY/IIF Global Bank Risk Management Survey. Resilient Banking: Capturing Opportunities and Managing Risks over the Long Term.* Retrieved 12 26, 2021, from https://eyfinancialservicesthoughtgallery.ie/wp-content/uploads/2021/08/ey-iif-global-bank-risk-survey-web.pdf

Euromoney. (2020). *Having Your Cake and Provisioning for It: How CECL and IFRS 9 are Fighting the Last War*. Retrieved 08 04, 2020, from https://www.euromoney.com/article/b1lfprys2w0lf9/having-your-cake-and-provisioning-for-it-how-cecl-and-ifrs-9-are-fighting-the-last-war

European Banking Authority. (2014). *Implementing Technical Standard on Supervisory Reporting (Forbearance and Non-Performing Exposures)*.

European Banking Authority. (2017). *Guidelines on Credit Institutions' Credit Risk Management Practices and Accounting for Expected Credit Losses*. EBA, Final Report EBA/GL/2017/06.

European Banking Authority. (2018). *Guidelines on Management of Non-Performing and Forborne Exposures*. Final Report, EBA/GL/2018/06.

European Commission. (2012). *State Aid: Commission Temporarily Approves Aid to Alpha Bank, EFG Eurobank, Piraeus Bank and National Bank of Greece; Opens In_Depth Investigations*. Press Release, 27-Jul-2012.

European Commission. (2015a). *State Aid: Commission Approves Amended Restructuring Plans for Alpha Bank and Eurobank*. Brussels: Press Release, 26-Nov-2015.

European Commission. (2015b). *State Aid: Commission Approves Aid for National Bank of Greece on the Basis of an Amended Restructuring Plan*. Brussels: Press Release, 4-Dec-2015.

European Commission. (2015c). *State Aid: Commission Approves Aid for Piraeus Bank on the Basis of an Amended Restructuring Plan*. Brussels: Press Release, 29-Nov-2015.

European Commission. (2019). *Implementing Measures for Regulation (EC) No 1606/2002 on International Accounting Standards*. Retrieved from Implementation by EU Countries: https://ec.europa.eu/info/law/internatio nal-accounting-standards-regulation-ec-no-1606-2002/implementation/imp lementation-eu-countries_en

European Commission. (2020). *Coronavirus Response: Tackling Non-Performing Loans (NPLs) to Enable Banks to Support EU Households and Businesses*. Brussels: Press Release, 16-Dec-2020.

European Court of Auditors. (2020). *Special Report. Control of State aid to Financial Institutions in the EU: In Need of a Fitness Check*.

European Securities Markets Authority. (2020). *ESMA Statement on Markets and Covid-19*. Retrieved 08 05, 2020, from https://www.esma.europa.eu/document/esma-statement-markets-and-covid-19

Eurostat. (2020). *Government Deficit/Surplus, Debt and Associated Data.* Retrieved 04 11, 2020, from https://appsso.eurostat.ec.europa.eu/nui/submit ViewTableAction.do

Fabris, N. (2009). Global Financial Crisis and Its Impact on Monetary Policy of Serbia. In M. Jakšić, & A. Praščević (Eds.), *Economic Policy of Serbia in 2009 and Challenges of the Global Economic Crisis: Proceedings from a Scientific and Professional Conference* (pp. 279–291). Economic Faculty, University of Belgrade.

Faia, E., & Monacelli, T. (2007). Optimal Interest Rate Rules, Asset Prices and Credit Frictions. *Journal of Economic Dynamics and Control, 31*(10), pp. 3228–3254.

Faria-e-Castro, M. (2020). *Fiscal Policy During a Pandemic.* Economic Research Federal Reserve Bank of St. Louis Working Paper 2020-006E.

Fiechter, J., Ötker-Robe, I., Ilyna, A., Hsu, M., Santos, A., & Surti, J. (2011). *Subsidiaries or Branches. Does One Size Fit All?* IMF, Monetary and Capital Markets Department.

Filipovski, V., Trpeski, P., & Bogoev, J. (2018). Business Cycle Synchronization of a Small Open EU-Candidate Country's Economy with the EU Economy. *Panoeconomicus, 65*(5), 609–631.

Financial Stability Forum. (2009). *Report of the Financial Stability Forum on Addressing Procyclicality in the Financial System.* FSF, 2-Apr-2009.

Fitch Ratings. (2013a). *The Evolving Dynamics of Support for Banks.*

Fitch Ratings. (2013b). *Fitch Outlines Approach for Addressing Support in Bank Ratings.*

Fonseca, A., & González, F. (2008). Cross-Country Determinants of Bank Income Smoothing by Managing Loan-Loss Provisions. *Journal of Banking and Finance, 32,* 217–228.

Freixas, X., & Rochet, J.-C. (2008). *Microeconomics of Banking (2nd Edition).* The MIT Press.

Fry, R., & Sojli, E. (2005). *Financial Crises Propagation to Albania: A Comparison of the Russian and Turkish Crises.* Paper presented at Evaluating the Effectiveness of Monetary Policy. Retrieved 12 11, 2021, from http://hdl.handle.net/1885/76547

Fudenberg, D., & Tirol, J. (1995). A Theory of Income and Dividend Smoothing Based on Incumbency Rents. *Journal of Political Economy, 103*(1), 75–93.

Gambera, M. (2000). *Simple Forecasts of Bank Loan Quality in the Business Cycle.* Federal Reserve Bank of Chicago. Emerging Issues Series.

Gardo, S. (2008). Croatia: Coping with Rapid Financial Deepening. *Focus on European Economic Integration Q1/08. Austrian National Bank*, pp. 61–81.

Gebhardt, G., & Novotny-Farkas, Z. (2011). Mandatory IFRS Adoption and Accounting Quality of European Banks. *Journal of Business Finance and Accounting, 38*(3), pp. 289–333.

Georghadji, C. (2017). *The Evolution of the Cyprus Banking System: A Reform Story and Its Challenges*. Keynote speech by the Governor of the Central Bank of Cyprus at the event organised by the Representation of the European Commission in Cyprus and the Central Bank of Cyprus on the "Achievements and Challenges of the Banking Sector in Cyprus".

Gertler, M., & Karadi, P. (2011). A Model of Unconventional Monetary Policy. *Journal of Monetary Economics, 58*(1), pp. 17–34.

Gilchrist, S., Ortiz, A., & Zakrajsek, E. (2009). *Credit Risk and the Macroeconomy: Evidence from an Estimated DSGE Model*. Washington, D.C.: Prepared for the Conference "Financial Markets and Monetary Policy" held at the Federal Reserve Board.

Glen, J., & Mondragón-Vélez, C. (2011). Business Cycle Effects on Commercial Bank Loan Portfolio Performance in Developing Economies. *Review of Development Finance, 1*, 150–165.

Gorenjska bank. (2013). *Annual Report*.

Gorton, G., & Winton, A. (2002). Bank Liquidity Provision and Capital Regulation in Transition Economies. In A. Meyendorff, & A. Thakor (Eds.), *Designing Financial Systems in Transition Economies. Strategies for Reform in Central and Eastern Europe* (pp. 129–146). The William Davidson Institute. The MIT Press.

Granger, C. (1969). Investigating Causal Relations by Econometric Models and Cross-spectral Methods. *Econometrica, 37*(3), 424–438.

Gregory, R., & Stuart, C. (2014). *The Global Economy and Its Economic Systems*. USA: Cengage Learning Company.

Guerrieri, V., Lorenzoni, G., Straub, L., & Werning, I. (2020). Macroeconomic Implications of COVID-19: Can Negative Supply Shocks Cause Demand Shortages?

Guttentag, J., & Herring, R. (1986). *Disaster Myopia in International Banking*. Princeton University; Essays in Internationl Finance.

Hansen, L. (1982). Large Sample Properties of Generalized Method of Moments Estimators. *Econometrica, 50*, 1029–1054.

Healy, P., & Palepu, K. (2001). Information Asymmetry, Corporate Disclosure, and the Capital Markets: A Review of the Empirical Disclosure Literature. *Journal of Accounting and Economics, 31*, 405–440.

Healy, P., & Wahlen, J. (1999). A Review of the Earnings Management Literature and Its Implications for Standard Setting. *Accounting Horizons, American Accounting Association, 13*(4), 365–383.

Hellmann, T., Murdock, K., & Stigliz, J. (2000). Liberalization, Moral Hazard in Banking, and Prudential Regulation: Are Capital Requirements Enough? *American Economic Review, 90*(1), 147–165.

Hoggarth, G., Logan, A., & Zicchino, L. (2005). Macro stress tests of UK banks. *BIS Papers No. 22. Investigating the relationship between the financial and real economy*, pp. 392–409.

Hristov, N., & Hülsewig, O. (2017). Unexpected Loan Losses and Bank Capital in an Estimated DSGE Model of the Euro Area. *Journal of Macroeconomics, 54*(part B), pp. 161–186.

Hristov, N., & Roth, M. (2022). Uncertainty Shocks and Systemic-risk Indicators. *Journal of International Money and Finance, 122*, 1–25.

Huizinga, H., & Laeven, L. (2019). The Procyclicality of Banking: Evidence from the Euro Area. *CentER Discussion Paper Series No. 2019–010, European Banking Center No. 2019–001.*

IFRS. (2020, 03 27). *Application of IFRS 9 in the Light of the Coronavirus Uncertainty*. Retrieved 08 05, 2020, from https://www.ifrs.org/news-and-events/2020/03/application-of-ifrs-9-in-the-light-of-the-coronavirus-uncertainty/

IFRS. (2021). *IFRS: Use Around the World*. Retrieved from Use of IFRS Standards by Jurisdictions: https://www.ifrs.org/use-around-the-world/use-of-ifrs-standards-by-jurisdiction/

ILOSTAT. (2021). *Statistics on Unemployment and Supplementary Measures of Labour Underutilization*. Retrieved 09 21, 2021, from https://ilostat.ilo.org/topics/unemployment-and-labour-underutilization/

IMF. (2015). *Bosnia and Herzegovina. Financial System Stability Assessment.* IMF Country Report No. 15/164.

IMF. (2019). *Financial Soundness Indicators Compilation Guide.* International Monetary Fund.

IMF European Department. (2013). *Financing Future Growth: The Evolving Role of Banking Systems in CESEE.* IMF, CESEE: Regional Economic Issues Apr/2013.

IMF European Department. (2016). *Cyprus: Ninth Review Under the Extended Arrangement Under the Extended Fund Facility and Request for Waiver of Applicability of Performance Criteria.*

IMF Financial Soundness Indicators. (2021). *FSIs and Underlying Series.* Retrieved 09 06, 2021, from https://data.imf.org/aspx?key=61404590

IMF Monetary and Capital Markets Department. (2017). *Bulgaria. Financial System Policy Assessment*. IMF.

IMF Policy Tracker. (2021). *Policy Responses to COVID-19*. Retrieved 01 31, 2021, from https://www.imf.org/en/Topics/imf-and-covid19/Policy-Responses-to-COVID-19.

IMF. Dissemination Standards Bulletin Board. (2021). *National Summary Data Pages/Serbia*. Retrieved 09 06, 2021, from https://dsbb.imf.org/nsdp, with a link to https://www.stat.gov.rs/en-US/nsdp-serbia

IMF. International Financial Statistics. (2021a). *Gross Domestic Product and Components Selected Indicators. Metadata by Country*. Retrieved 09 07, 2021, from https://data.imf.org/regular.aspx?key=61545852

IMF. International Financial Statistics. (2021b). *International Financial Statistics (IFS)*. Retrieved 09 21, 2021, from https://data.imf.org/?sk=4c514d48-b6ba-49ed-8ab9-52b0c1a0179b&sId=1390030341854

Jović, D. (2014). Loši krediti i kozmetičko računovodstvo/Bad Loans and Cosmetic Accounting. *Tranzicija/Transition, 16*(33), 30–46.

Judson, R., & Owen, L. (1999). Estimating Dynamic Panel Data Models: A Guide for Macroeconomists. *Economics Letters, 65*, pp. 9–15.

Kanagaretnam, K., Krishnan, G., & Lobo, G. (2009). Is the market valuation of banks' loan loss provision conditional on auditor reputation? *Journal of Banking & Finance, 33*, 1039–1047.

Kanagaretnam, K., Lobo, G., & Yang, D. (2004). Joint tests of signaling and income smoothing through bank loan loss provisions. *Contemporary Accounting Research, 21*(4), 843–884.

Keeton, W. (1999). Does Faster Loan Growth Lead to Higher Loan Losses? *Economic Review of Federal Reserve Bank of Kansas City*, 57–75.

Kim, M.-S., & Kross, W. (1998). The Impact of the 1989 Change in Bank Capital Standards on Loan Loss Provisions and Loan Write-Offs. *Journal of Accounting and Economics, 25*, 69–99.

Kiviet, J., & Bun, M. (2006). The Effects of Dynamic Feedbacks on LS and MM Estimator Accuracy in Panel Data Models. *Journal of Econometrics, 132*, 409–444.

Klein, N. (2013). *Non-Performing Loans in CESEE: Determinants and Impact on Macroeconomic Performance*. IMF Working Papers no. WP/13/72.

Knott, S., Richardson, P., Rismanchi, K., & Sen, K. (2014). *Understanding the Fair Value of Banks' Loans*. Bank of England, Financial Stability Paper No. 31.

Krznar, M. (2009). *Contagion Risk in the Croatian Banking System*. Working Papers W-20. Croatian National Bank.

Kulača, Đ., & Radočević, S. (2012). Innovation Capacity in SEE Region. In D. Sternad, & T. Döring (Eds.), *Handbook of Doing Business in South East Europe* (pp. 207–231). UK: Palgrave Macmillan.

Laeven, L., & Majnoni, G. (2003). Loan Loss Provisioning and Economic Slowdowns: Too Much, Too Late? *Journal of Financial Intermediation, 12*, pp. 178–197.

Lambert, R. (1984). Income Smoothing as Rational Equilibrium Behaviour. *Accounting Review, 59*, 604–618.

Leaven, L., & Majnoni, G. (2003). Loan Loss Provisioning and Economic Slowdowns: Too Much, Too Late? *Journal of Financial Intermediation, 12*, 178–197.

Leko, V., & Stojanović, A. (2006). Sector and Purpose Structure of Bank Loans. *Zbornik Ekonomskog fakulteta u Zagrebu*, 239–261.

Leland, H., & Pyle, D. (1977). Informational Assymetries, Financial Structure, and Financial Intermediation. *The Journal of Finance, 32*(2), pp. 371–387.

Leventis, S., Dimitropoulos, P., & Anandarajan, A. (2012). Signalling by Banks Using Loan Loss Provisions: The Case of the European Union. *Journal of Economic Studies, 39*, 604–618.

Lleshanaku, A., & Üç, M. (2014). *From the Perspective of Accounting Theory: Banks' Loan Loss Provisions and Tax Legislation in Albania.* Epoka Universtiy, Albania.

Lütkepohl, H. (2005). *New Introduction to Multiple Time Series Analysis.* Springer-Verlag Berlin, Heidelberg.

Maddala, G. (1992). *Introduction to Econometrics* (2nd ed.). Macmillan Publishing Company.

Makri, V., & Papadatos, K. (2014). How Accounting Information and Macroeconomic Environment Determine Credit Risk? Evidence from Greece. *International Journal of Economic Sciences and Applied Research, 7*(1), 129–143.

Männasoo, K., & Mayes, D. (2005). *Investigating the Early Signals of Banking Sector Vulnerabilities in Central and Eastern European Emerging Markets.* Tallinn: Eesti Pank, Working Papers no. 8.

Marcucci, J., & Quagliariello, M. (2008). *Is Bank Portfolio Riskiness Procyclical? Evidence from Italy Using a Vector Autoregression.* The University of York. Discussion Papers in Economics.

Marinković, S., & Radović, O. (2017). What Drives a Local Currency Away from Banking Markets? Some Southeast Europe Insights. In S. Goić, A. Karasavvoglou, & P. Polychronidou (Eds.), *Finance in Central and Southeastern Europe* (pp. 35–56). Springer.

Market Screener. (2013). *JSC VTB Bank acquired VRB Moscow Bank from Vietnam-Russia Joint Venture Bank*. Retrieved 06 07, 2023, from https://www.marketscreener.com/quote/stock/VTB-BANK-6499155/news/JSC-VTB-Bank-acquired-VRB-Moscow-Bank-from-Vietnam-Russia-Joint-Venture-Bank-38964896/

Merchant, K. (1990). The Effects of Financial Controls on Data Manipulation and Management Myopia. *Accounting, Organizations and Society, 15*(4), 297–313.

Mihaljek, D. (2010). The Spread of the Financial Crisis to Central and Eastern Europe: Evidence from the BIS Data. In R. Matousek (Ed.), *Money, Banking and Financial Markets in Central and Eastern Europe. 20 Years of Transition* (pp. 5–31). Palgrave Macmillan.

Mill, J. ([1848] 2009). *The Principles of Political Economy*. The Project Gutenberg EBook.

Montes-Negret, F., & Cloutier, E. (2016). *What Lessons from Romania's Early Success in NPL Reduction?* Vienna Institute.

Moyer, S. (1990). Capital Adequacy Ratio Regulations and Accounting Choices in Commercial Banks. *Journal of Accounting and Economics, 13*, 123–154.

MS Auditor's Report. (2016). *Izveštaj nezavisnog revizora o izvršenoj reviziji finansijskih izveštaja za 2015. godinu*. MS Auditor's Report for JUBMES bank. Retrieved 12 9, 2020, from https://altabanka.rs/o-alta-banci/finansijski-izvestaji/finansijski-izvestaji-u-2015-godini/

National Bank of the Republic of North Macedonia. (2016). *Извештај за ризиците во банкарскиот систем на Република Македонија во вториот квартал од 2016 година*. National Bank of the Republic of North Macedonia. Retrieved 10 01, 2021, from http://www.nbrm.mk/ns-newsarticle-izvieshtaj_za_rizitsitie_vo_bankarskiot_sistiem_na_riepublika_makiedonija_vo_vtoriot_kvartal_od_2016_ghodina.nspx

Neck, R. (2012). Macro-Economic Consequences of the Integration of the SEE Area Into the Eurozone. In D. Sternad, & T. Döring (Eds.), *Handbook of Doing Business in South East Europe* (pp. 189–206). Palgrave Macmillan.

Nenovski, T., & Smilkovski, I. (2012). Macedonian Economy Before and After the Global Financial and Economic Crisis. *Procedia - Social and Behavioral Sciences, 417*–427.

Nickell, S. (1981). Biases in Dynamic Models with Fixed Effects. *Econometrica, 49*(6), 1417–1426.

Nikolaidou, E., & Vogiazas, S. (2013). Credit Risk in the Romanian Banking System: Evidence from an ARDL Model. In A. Karasavvoglou, & P. Polychronidou (Eds.), *Balkan and Eastern European Countries s in the Midst of the Global Economic Crisis* (pp. 87–101). Springer.

NLB banka AD Beograd (2014). *Finansijski izveštaji za godinu koja se završila 31.12.2013. godine.* Retrieved 12 9, 2020, from https://www.nlb.rs/index.php?go=strana&ID=16821&jezik=lat&year=2013

NLB Montenegrobanka AD. (2013). *Finansijski izvještaj na dan 31.12.2012. i izvještaj nezavisnog revizora.* Retrieved 12 9, 2020, from https://www.nlb.me/me/nlb-banka/finansijski-izvjestaji?year=2012

Nomura Research Institute. (2020). *Putting the Economic Shock of the Coronavirus in Context. Overview Using a Macroeconomic Model.* Nomura Research institute.

Oehler-Şincai, I. (2013). *Financial Contagion Reloaded: The Case of Cyprus.* MPRA Paper from University Library of Munich, Germany.

Ozili, P., & Outa, E. (2017). Bank Loan Loss Provisions Research: A Review. *Borsa Istanbul Review, 17*(3), 144–163.

Ozili, P., & Outa, E. (2017). Bank Loan Loss Provisions Research: A Review. *Borsa Istanbul Review, 17*(3), 144–163.

Pain, D. (2003). *The Provisioning Experience of the Major UK Banks: A Small Panel Investigation.* London: Bank of England, Working Paper 177.

Pedroni, P. (2013). Structural Panel VARs. *Econometrics, 2*, 180–206.

Pérez, D., Salas, V., & Saurina, J. (2006). *Earnings and Capital Management in Alternative Loan Loss Regulatory Regimes.* Madrid: Banco de España.

Pool, S., de Haan, L., & Jacobs, J. (2015). Loan Loss Provisioning, Bank Credit and the Real Economy. *Journal of Macroeconomics, 45*, 124–136.

Popov, A., & Udell, G. (2012). Cross-Border Banking, Credit Access, and the Financial Crisis. *Journal of International Economics, 87*, 147–161.

Praxia bank. (2018). *Annual Financial Report for the Year Ended 31.12.2017.* Retrieved 12 10, 2020, from https://www.praxiabank.com/financial_data/financial_reports/en/2017_report.pdf

Quagliariello, M. (2006). *Bank's Riskiness Over the Business Cycle: A Panel Analysis on Italian Intermediaries.* Banca d'Italia.

Rajan, R. (1994). Why Bank Credit Policies Fluctuate: A Theory and Some Evidence. *The Quarterly Journal of Economics, 109*(2), pp. 399–441.

Restoy, F., & Zamil, R. (2018). *The Times They are A-Changin': Loan Valuations in the Age of Expected Loss Provisioning.* VoxEU, 06-Apr-2018.

Rezitis, A. (2010). Evaluating the State of Competition of the Greek Banking Industry. *Journal of International Financial Markets, Institutions & Money, 20*, 68–90.

Rigot, S., & Demaira, S. (2020). Outil de maîtrise de risqués ou accélérator de crise. *Revue Banque, 849*. Retrieved 11 19, 2020, from http://www.revue-banque.fr/risques-reglementations/article/ifrs-9-outil-maitrise-des-risques-accelerateur-cri

Ristić, Ž. (2006). Privatizacioni procesi u bankarstvu. *Panoeconomicus, 2*, 191–221.

Romania-Insider.com. (2013). *Polish Group Getin Holding Takes Over Romanian International Bank from American Owners*. Retrieved 12 10, 2020, from https://www.romania-insider.com/polish-group-getin-holding-takes-over-romanian-international-bank-from-american-owners

Roodman, D. (2009). How to Do xtabond2: An Introduction to Difference and System GMM in Stata. *The Stata Journal, 9*(1), pp. 86–136.

Rostowski, J. (Ed.). (1995). *Banking Reform in Central Europe and the Former Soviet Union*. Central European University Press.

Rozmahel, P., Kouba, L., Grochová, L., & Najman, N. (2013). *Integration of Central and Eastern European Countries: Increasing EU Heterogeneity?* European Commission, European Research Area, Working Paper no. 9.

Saurina, J. (2009). *Dynamic Provisioning: The Experience of Spain*. The World Bank. Crisis Response Note 7.

SEENews. (2014). *Interview – Romania's BCR cleans up balance sheet, eyes better results in 2015*. Retrieved 06 07, 2023, from https://seenews.com/news/interview-romanias-bcr-cleans-up-balance-sheet-eyes-better-results-in-2015-444934

SEENews. (2020). *TBI Bank EAD*. SEENews Business Intelligence for Southeast Europe. Retrieved 12 10, 2020, from https://seenews.com/companies/company_profile/tbi-bank-ead-8642

Šević, Ž. (2000). Banking Reform in South East European Transitional Economies: An Overview. *MOCT-MOST 3–4: Economic Policy in Transitional Economies*, 271–283.

Skala, D. (2021). Loan Loss Provisions and Income Smoothing – Do Shareholders Matter? *International Review of Financial Analysis, 78*.

Sojli, E. (2009). *Albania and the Global Crisis*. VoxEU.

Šoškić, D. (2015). Financial Intermediation in South East Europe: Obstacles and Opportunities. *Limesplus, XII*(1), 31–48.

Spendzharova, A. (2014). *Regulating Banks in Central and Eastern Europe. Through Crisis and Boom*. Palgrave Macmillan.

Stamegna, C. (2019). *Minimum Loss Coverage for Non-Performing Loans*. European Parliament. Briefing, 20-May-2019.

Stephanou, C. (2011). The Banking System in Cyprus: Time to Rethink the Business Model!? *Cyprus Economic Policy Review, 3*(2), 123–130.

Stojkov, A., & Zalduendo, J. (2011). *Europe as a Convergence Engine. Heterogeneity and Investment Opportunities in Emerging Europe.* The World Bank, Europe and Central Asia Region, Policy Research Working Paper 5837.

Tayler, W., & Zilberman, R. (2021). Optimal Loan Loss Provisions and Welfare. *Journal of Macroeconomics, 69*(C), 1–16.

The World Bank. World Development Indicators. (2019). *GDP growth (annual %).* Retrieved 08 21, 2019, from https://databank.worldbank.org/reports.aspx?source=World-Development-Indicators

The World Bank. World Development Indicators. (2021). *GDP per capita, PPP (constant 2017 international $).* Retrieved 06 29, 2021, from https://databank.worldbank.org/reports.aspx?source=World-Development-Indicators

The World Bank. World Development Indicators. (2022). *GDP growth (annual %).* Retrieved 02 24, 2022, from https://databank.worldbank.org/reports.aspx?source=World-Development-Indicators

Totîlca, A., & Bratu, R.-S. (2014). Actions to Reduce Unemployment in Romania. *Annals of University of Craiova – Economic Sciences Series, 1*(42), pp. 13–22.

Uvalić, M. (2003). Economic Transition in Southeast Europe. *Journal of Southeast European and Black Sea Studies, 3*(1), 63–80.

Wachtel, P. (2001). Growth and Finance: What Do We Know and How Do We Know It? *International Finance, 4*(3), 335–362.

Wahlen, J. (1994). The Nature of Information in Commercial Bank Loan Loss Disclosures. *The Accounting Review, 69*(3), pp. 455–478.

Wall, L., & Koch, T. (2000). *Bank Loan Loss Accounting: A Review of Theoretical and Empirical Evidence.* Federal Reserve Bank of Atlanta. Economic Review.

Windmeijer, F. (2005). A Finite Sample Correction for the Variance of Linear Efficient Two-Step GMM Estimators. *Journal of Econometrics, 126*, 25–51.

Wooldridge, J. (2002). *Econometric Analysis of Cross Section and Panel Data.* MIT Press.

Wooldridge, J. (2009). *Introductory Econometrics. A Modern Approach* (4th ed.). Cengage Learning.

World Bank. (2013). *Report No: ACS4924. Europe 2020 Romania: Evidence-based Policies for Productivity, Employment, and Skills Enhancement.*

## Schriftenreihe des Kärntner Instituts für Höhere Studien

Herausgegeben von Robert Holzmann und Reinhard Neck

Bisher erschienene Bände der Schriftenreihe

| | |
|---|---|
| Bd. 1–8: | Ludwig Boltzmann-Institut für ökonomische Analysen wirtschaftspolitischer Aktivitäten |
| Bd. 9–20: | Ludwig Boltzmann-Institut zur Analyse wirtschaftspolitischer Aktivitäten |
| Bd. 21: | Robert Holzmann-Institut zur Analyse wirtschaftspolitischer Aktivitäten |
| Bd. 22: | Schriftenreihe des Kärntner Instituts für Höhere Studien |
| Bd. 1–20 | im Manz Verlag Wien, ab Bd. 21 im Verlag Peter Lang, Frankfurt am Main et al. |
| Bd. 1: | Bernd Genser (Hrsg.): Abfertigungsregelungen im Spannungsfeld der Wirtschaftspolitik. Eine Interdisziplinäre Analyse, 1987. |
| Bd. 2: | Peter Findl, Robert Holzmann, Rainer Münz: Bevölkerung und Sozialstaat. Szenarien bis 2050, 1987. |
| Bd. 3: | Robert Holzmann (Hrsg.): Ökonomische Analyse der Sozialversicherung. Ergebnisse für Österreich, 1988. |
| Bd. 4: | Gerhard Clemenz, Georg Inderst: Ökonomische Analyse der Ladenöffnungszeiten, 1989. |
| Bd. 5: | Friedrich Schneider, Rainer Bartel: Gemeinwirtschaft versus Privatwirtschaft. Ein Effizienzvergleich, 1989. |
| Bd. 6: | Friedrich Schneider, Markus F. Hofreither (Hrsg.): Privatisierung und Deregulierung öffentlicher Unternehmen in westeuropäischen Ländern. Erste Erfahrungen und Analysen, 1990. |
| Bd. 7: | Rainer Bartel, Gerald Pruckner: Deficit Spending and Stabilization Behaviour in Austria. An Empirical Analysis of the Budget Balance in the Central and General Government Sector, 1992. |
| Bd. 8: | Günther Pöll, Friedrich Schneider: Einweg-Mehrweg-Verpackungsdiskussion. Ökonomische und abfallwirtschaftliche Beurteilung von Mehrweg-Quoten am Beispiel Fruchtsaft, 1992. |
| Bd. 9: | Reinhard Neck, Friedrich Schneider (Hrsg.): Österreich und Europa 1993. Herausforderungen der europäischen Integration für eine kleine offene Volkswirtschaft, 1993. |
| Bd. 10: | Robert Holzmann, Reinhard Neck (Hrsg.): Konjunktureffekte der österreichischen Budgetpolitik, 1993. |
| Bd. 11: | Manfried Gantner (Hrsg.): Budgetausgliederungen – Fluch(t) oder Segen? 1994. |
| Bd. 12: | Sohbet Karbuz: Macroeconomic Decision Support for Developing Countries. The Case of Turkey, 1995. |
| Bd. 13: | Wolfram Krendlesberger: Handelbare Belastungsrechte in der Umweltpolitik. Theorieorientierte Untersuchung mit Schwerpunkt Österreich, 1996. |
| Bd. 14: | Robert Holzmann, Reinhard Neck (Hrsg.): Ostöffnung: Wirtschaftliche Folgen für Österreich, 1996. |
| Bd. 15: | Reinhard Neck, Friedrich Schneider (Hrsg.): Politik und Wirtschaft in den neunziger Jahren. Empirische Untersuchungen zur Neuen Politischen Ökonomie, 1996. |
| Bd. 16: | Reinhard Neck, Robert Holzmann (Hrsg.): Was wird aus Euroland? Makroökonomische Herausforderungen und wirtschaftspolitische Antworten, 1999. |
| Bd. 17: | Reinhard Neck, Robert Holzmann, Friedrich Schneider (Hrsg.): Staatsschulden am Ende? Ursachen, Wirkungen und Zukunftsperspektiven, 2000. |
| Bd. 18: | Klaus Weyerstraß: SLOPOL. Ein makroökonomisches Modell für Slowenien, 2001. |
| Bd. 19: | Werner Neudeck: Das österreichische Gesundheitssystem. Eine ökonomische Analyse, 2002. |
| Bd. 20: | Gottfried Haber: Simulation und optimale Kontrolle der österreichischen Wirtschaft, 2002. |
| Bd. 21: | Reinhard Neck, Robert Holzmann (Hrsg.): Nachhaltigkeit der Staatsverschuldung, 2017 |
| Bd. 22: | Ksenija Popović: Loan Loss Provisions in Alternative Banking Landscapes. 2024. |

www.peterlang.com